MW01628921

MOMENTO

This word does not exist, but it exists for me...

MOMENTO

A BOOK OF MOMENTS

---

by George S. Zimbel

black dog publishing
london uk

For Elaine

I often think in pairs. I see pairs. Sometimes I see them in my mind's eye, remembering an image I may have made long ago and matching it with one I made yesterday. Sometimes the pairing is obvious, sometimes not obvious to anyone but me. I can't explain it.

'Momento' is a word I made up; it is neither 'memento' nor 'moment' (as in the decisive one). Sometimes it happens instantly, and sometimes you have to wait for it. It comes in its own sweet time.

All of the 'momentos' in this book have come from a long time photographing. This is, in a sense, my life's work. I am presenting it to you with delight and hope you are delighted in turn.

George S. Zimbel, Montreal, 2015

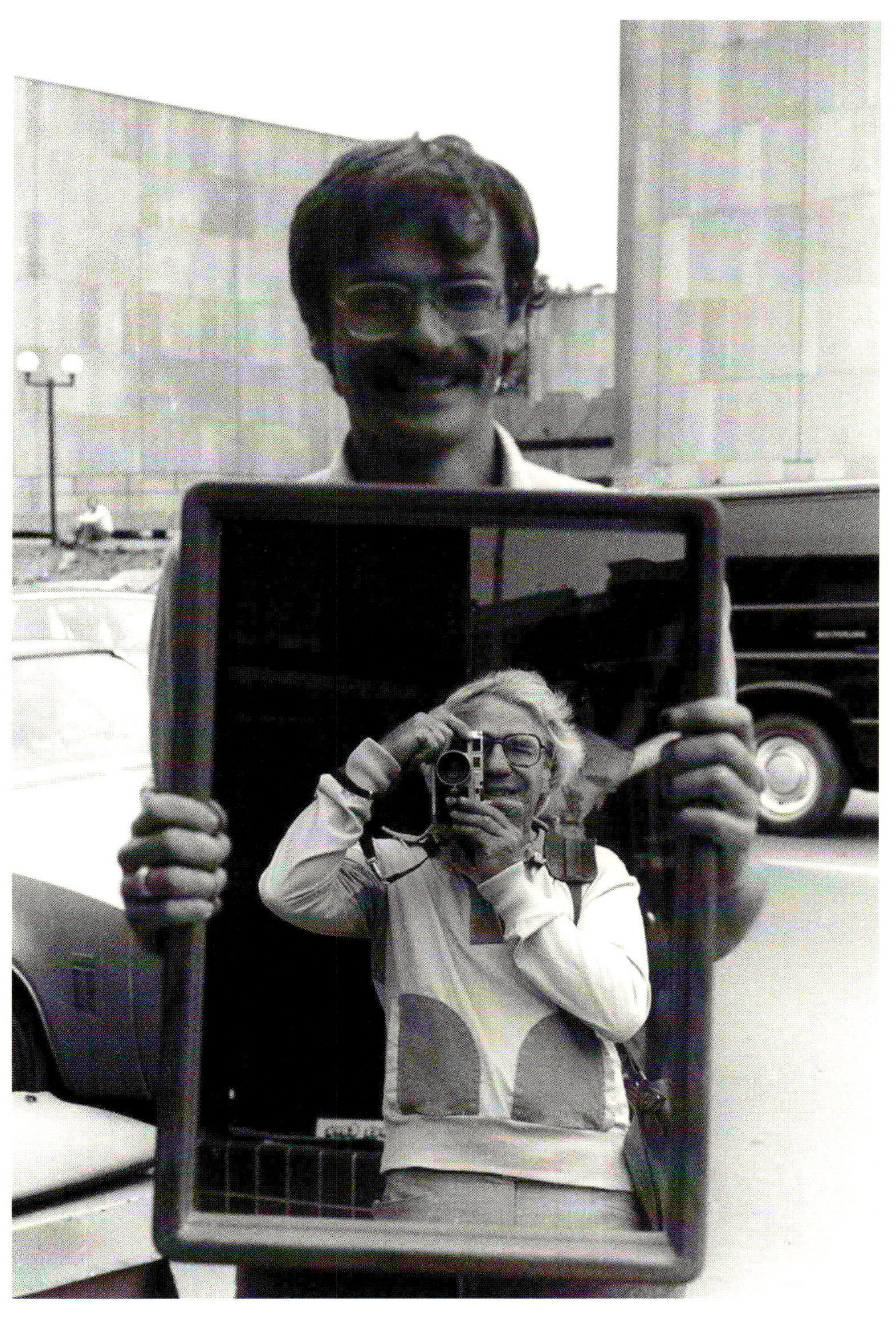

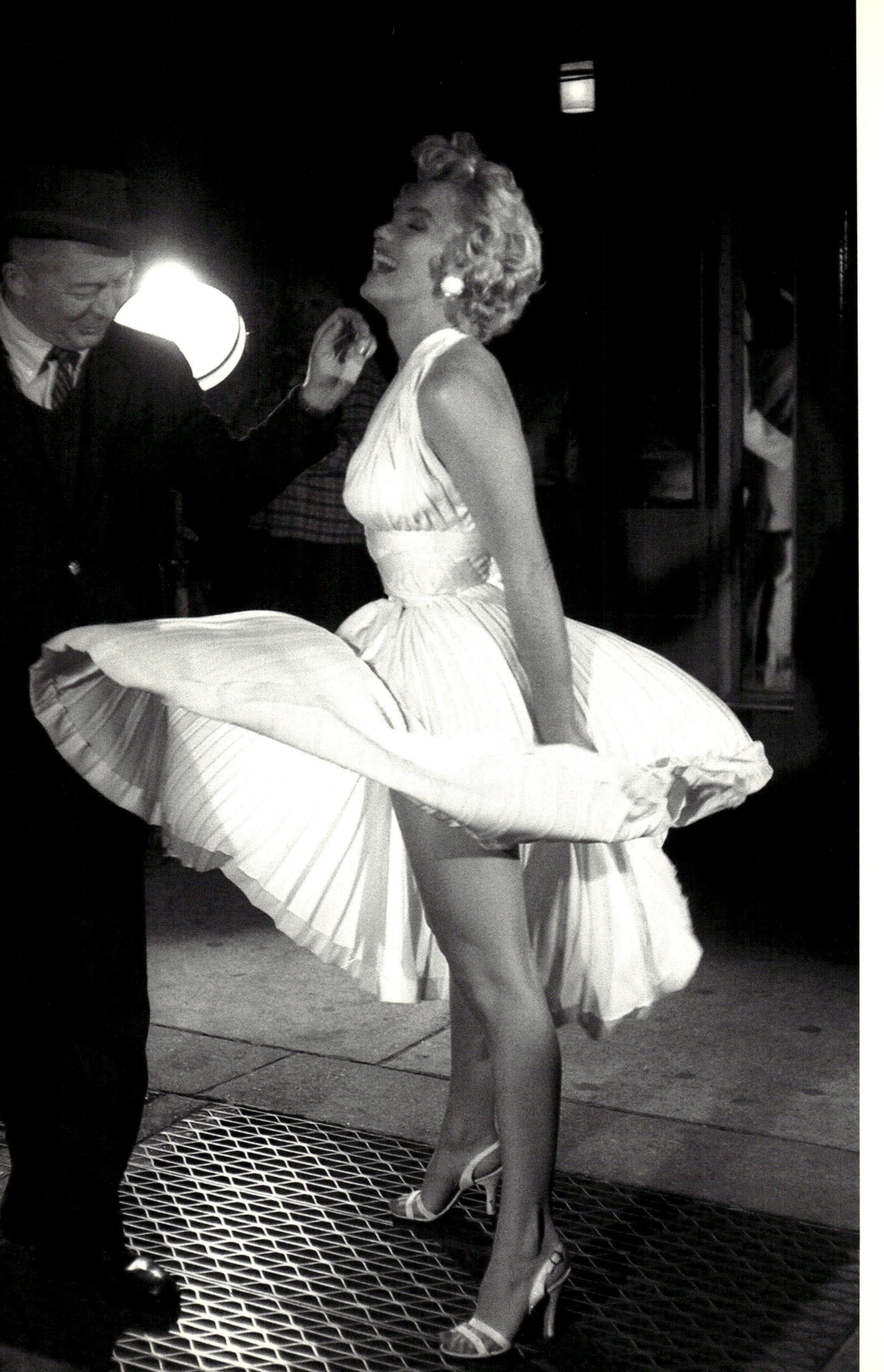

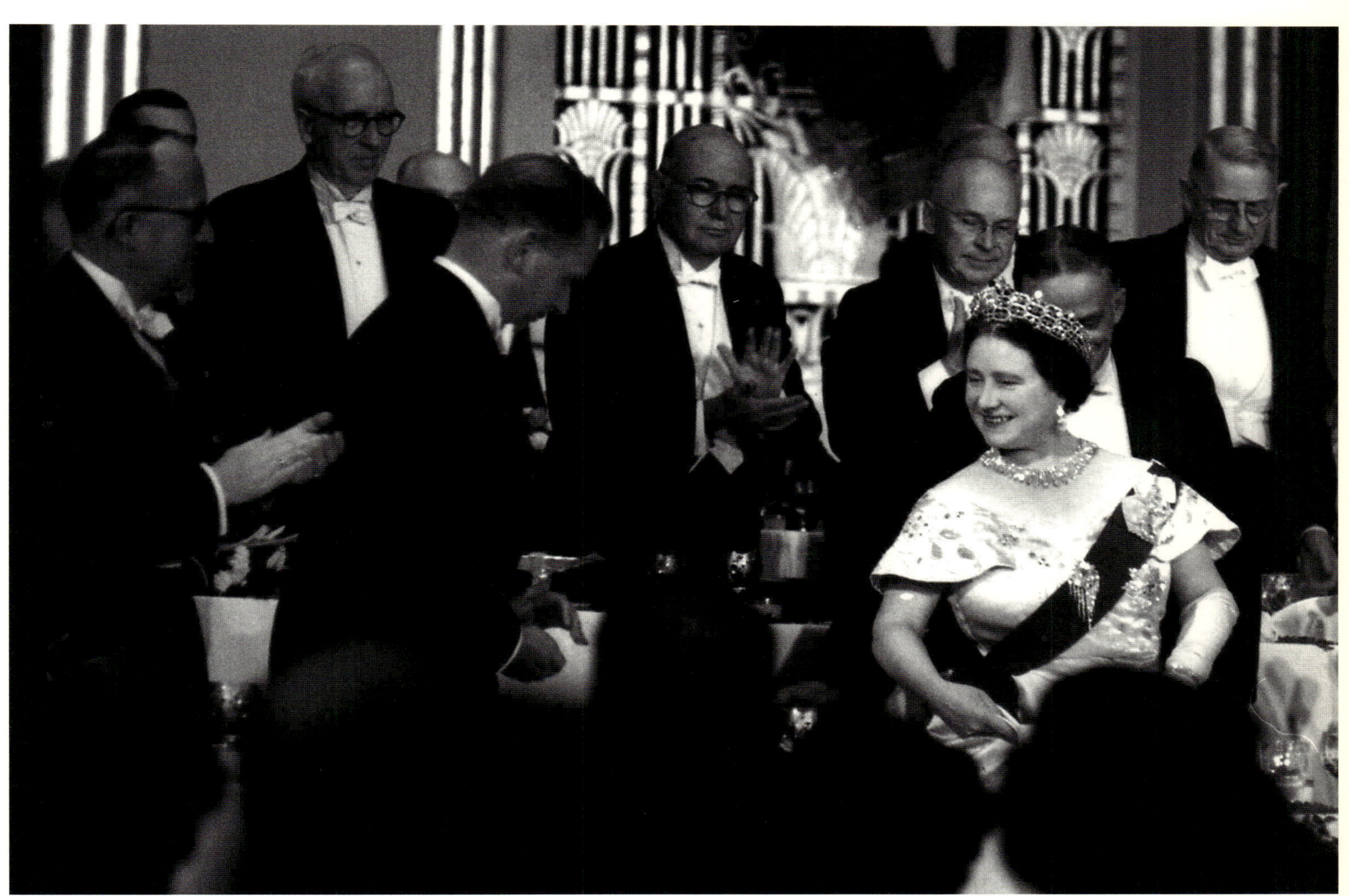

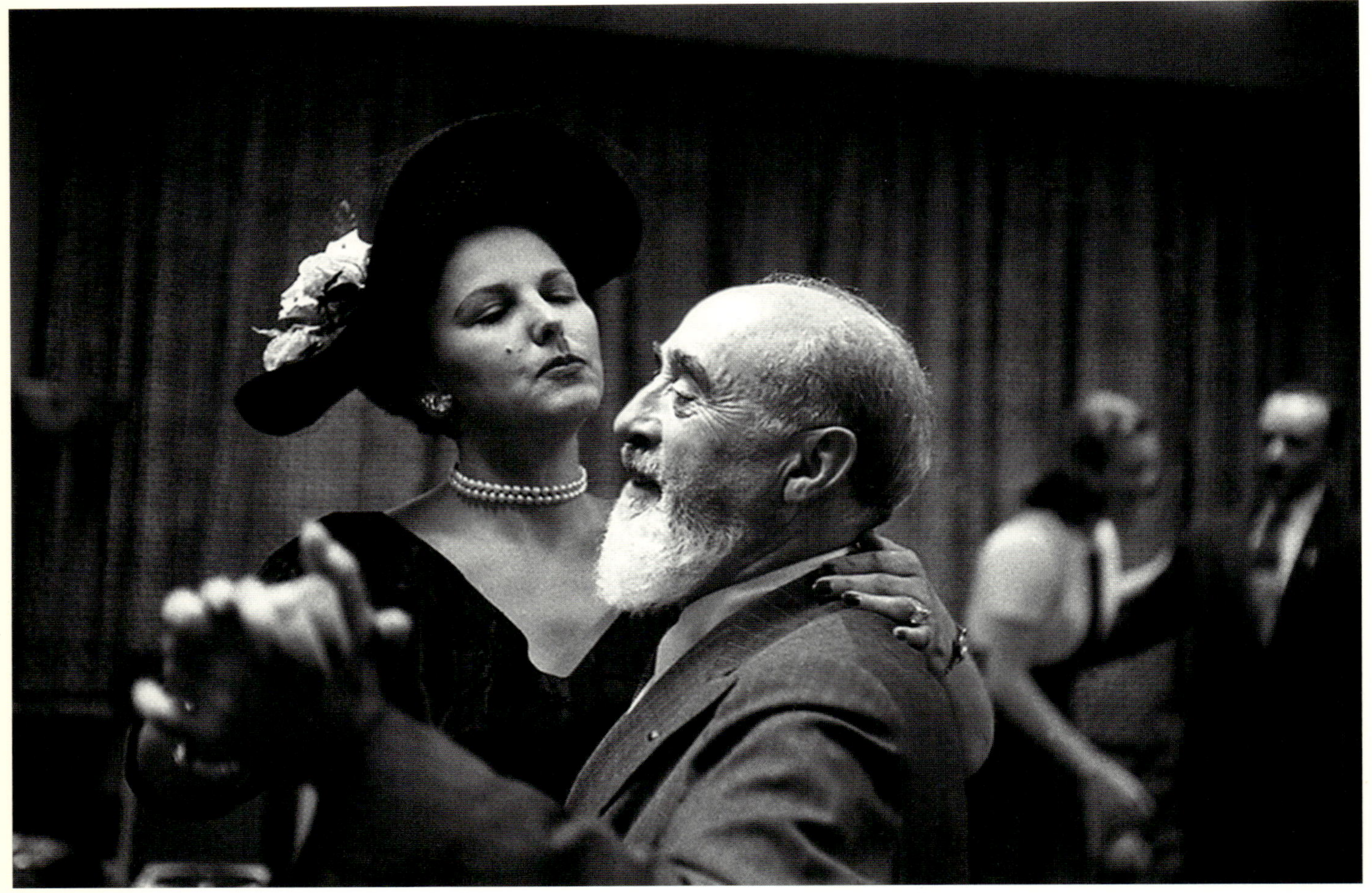

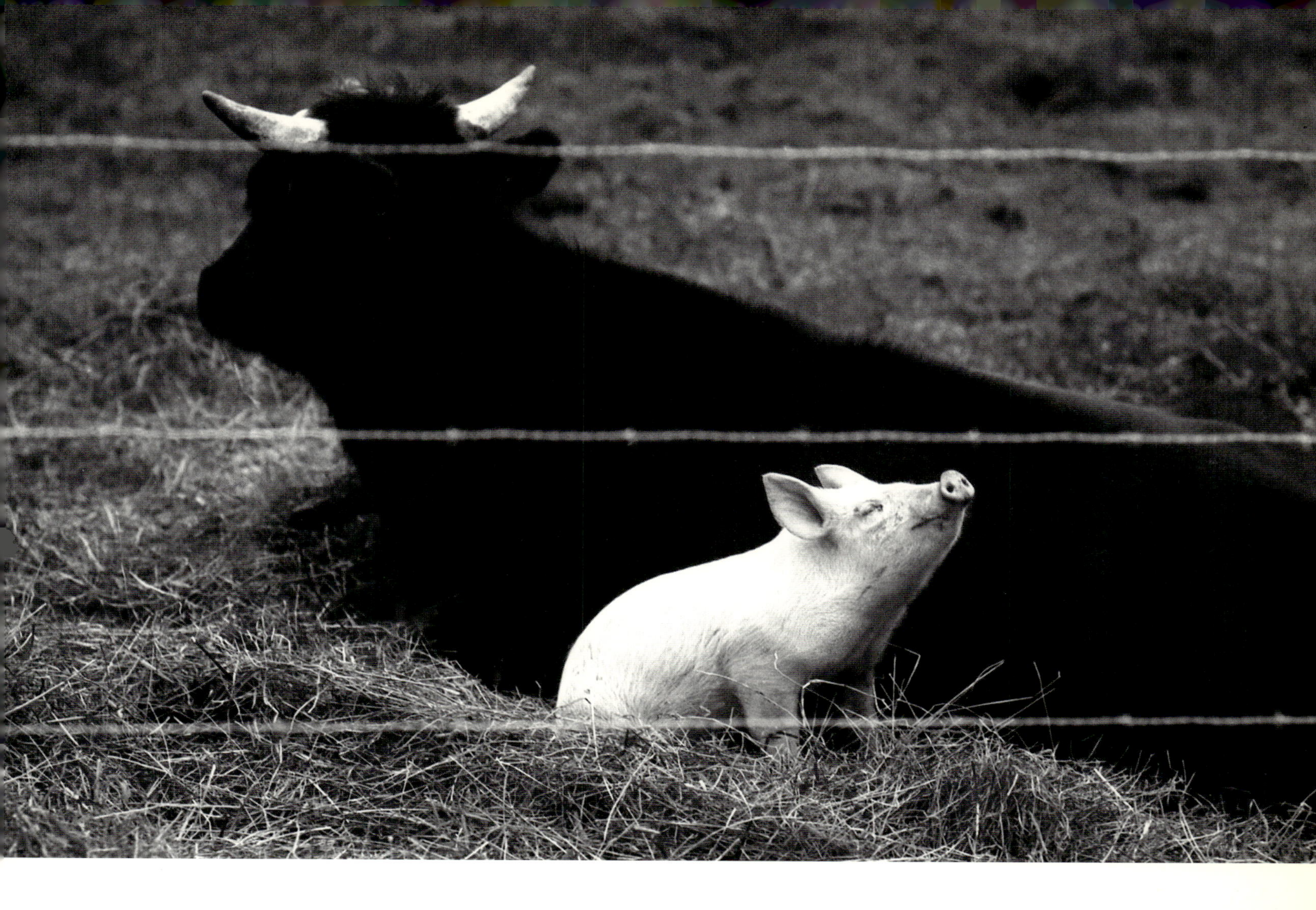

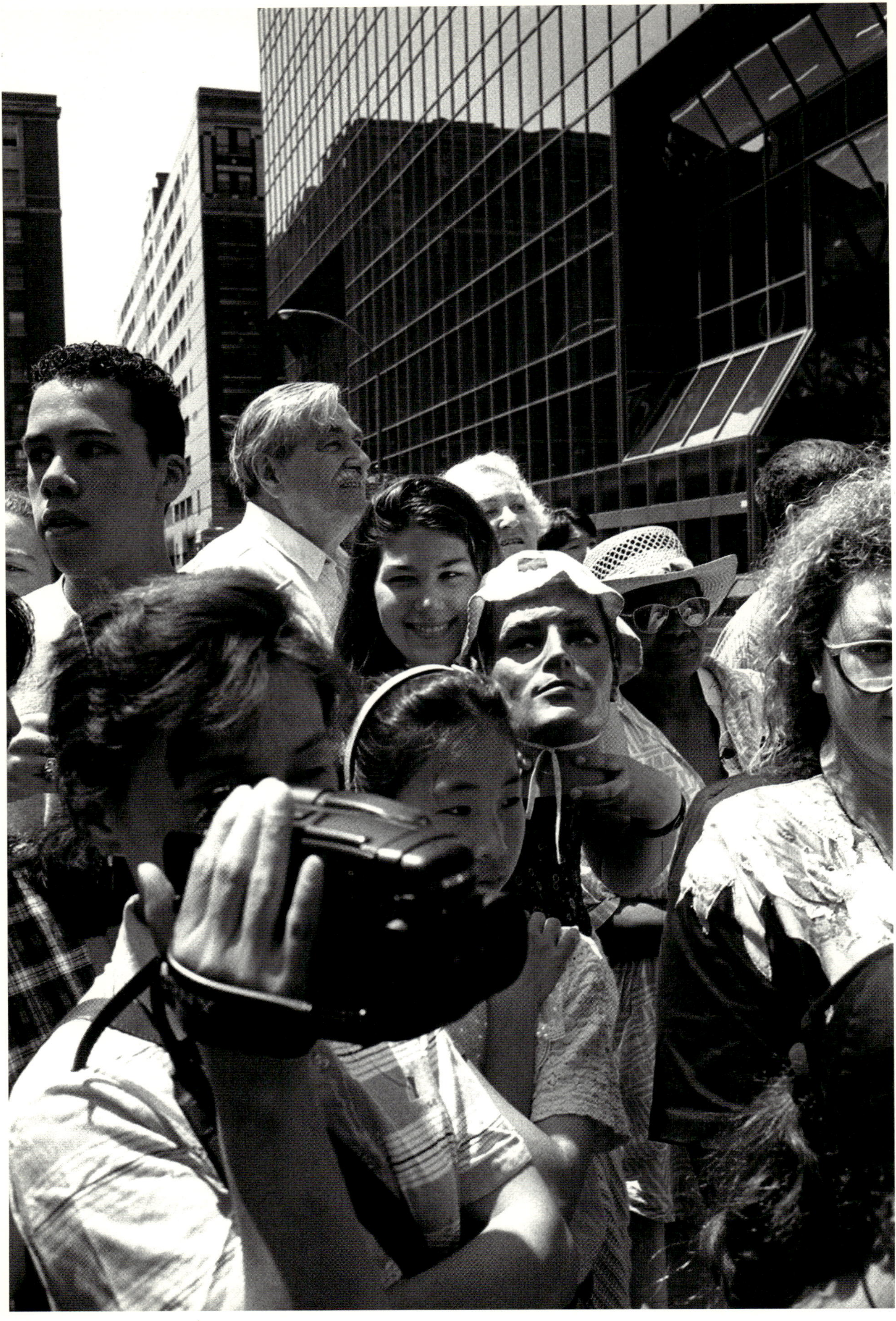

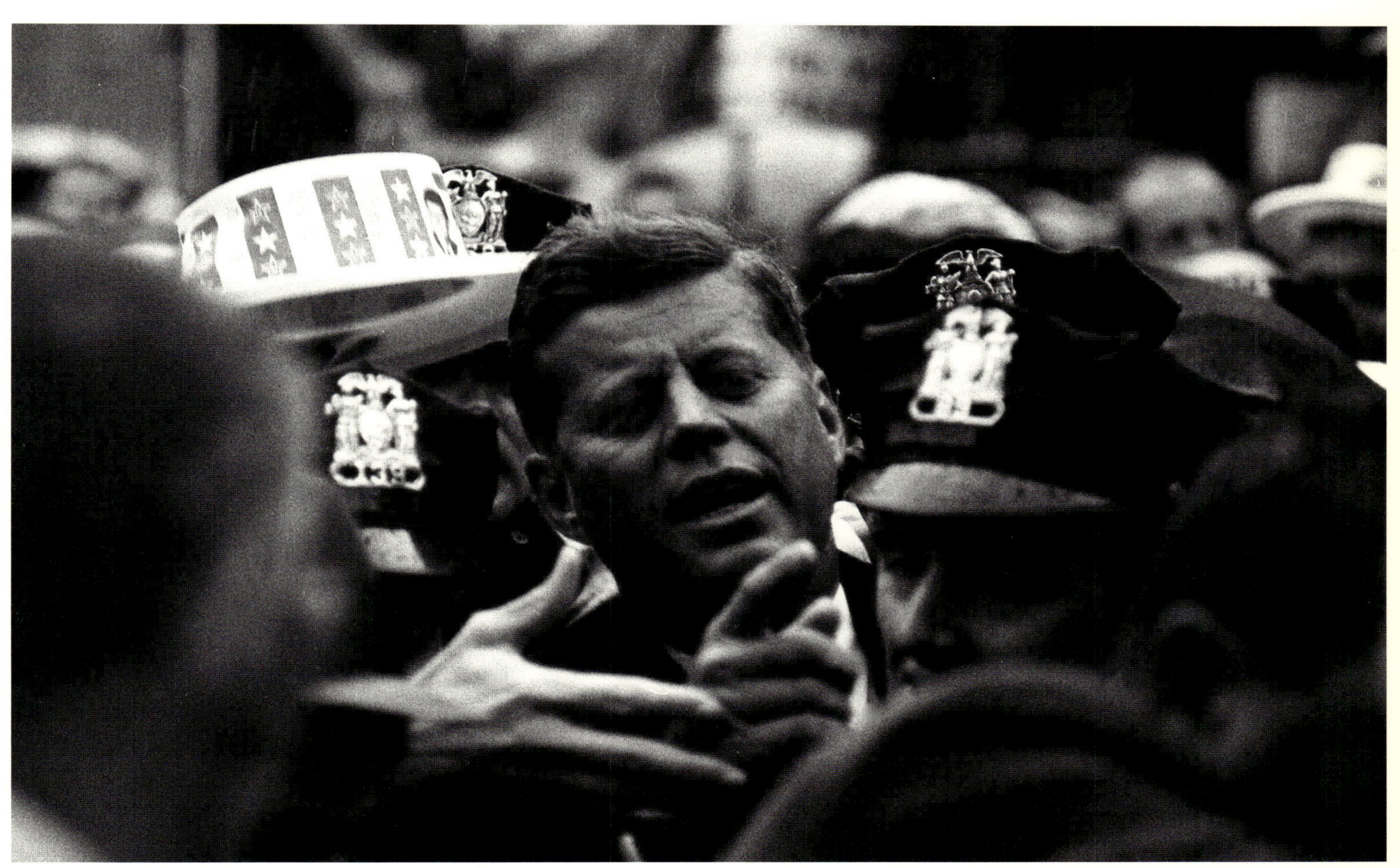

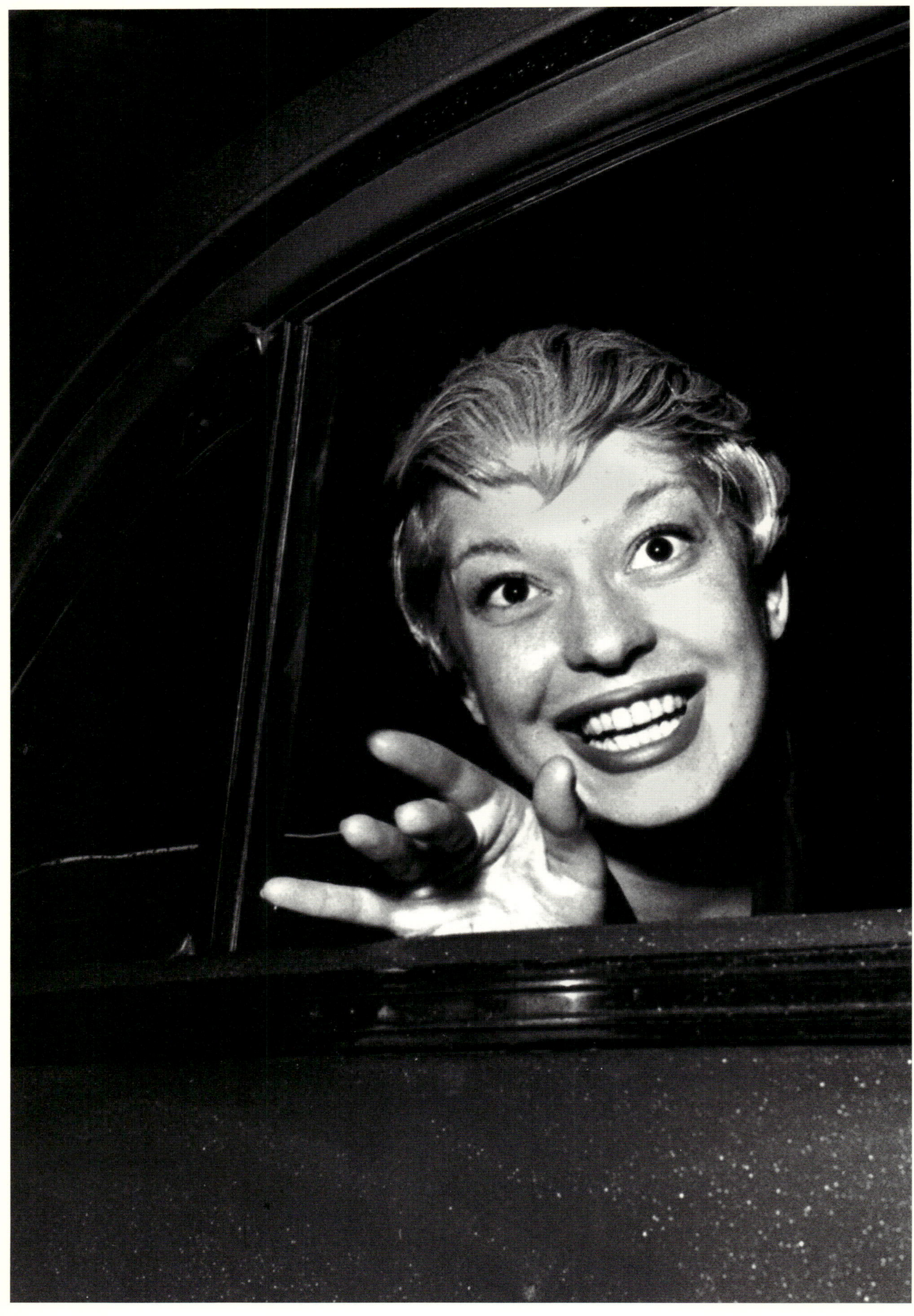

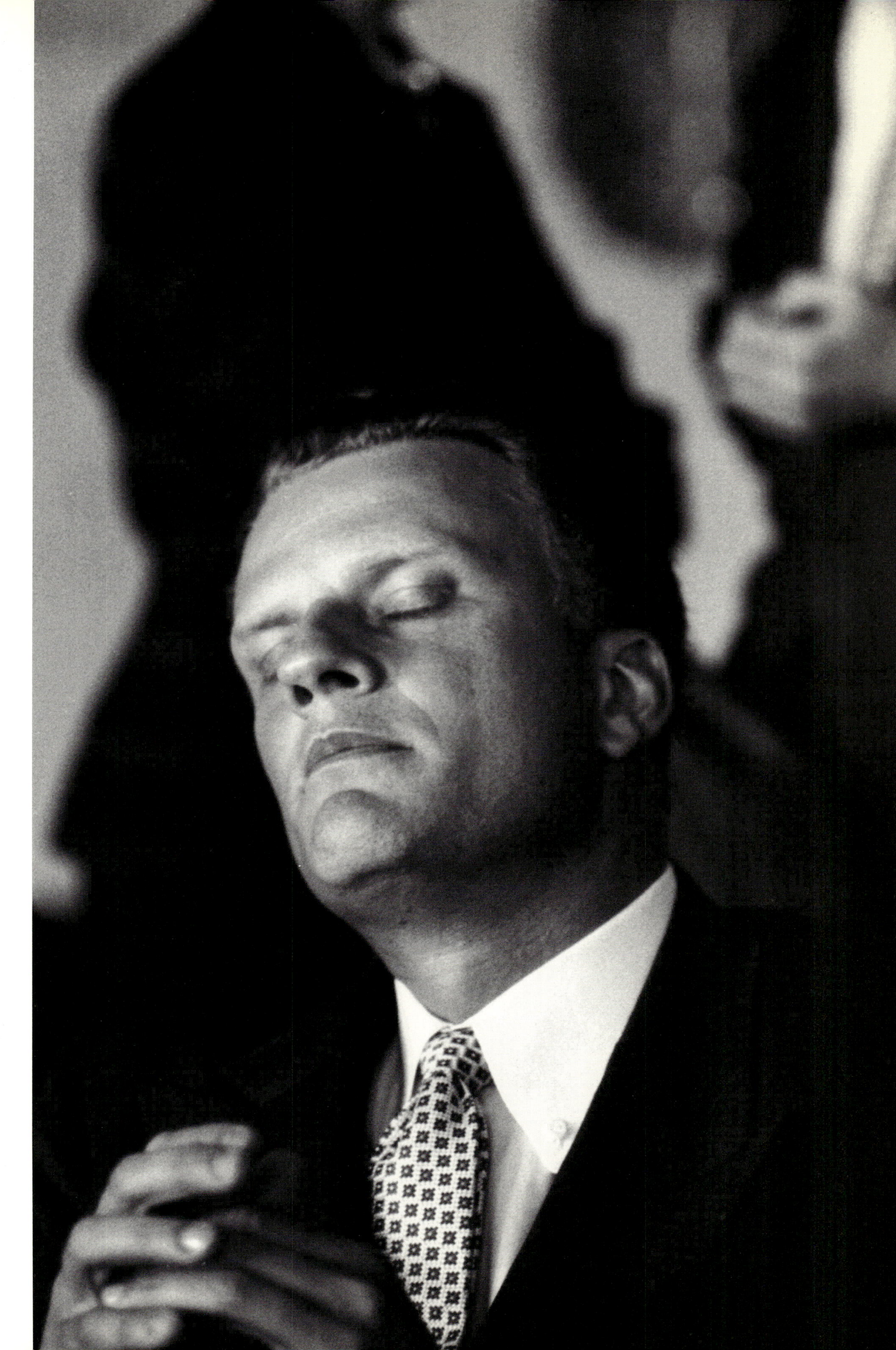

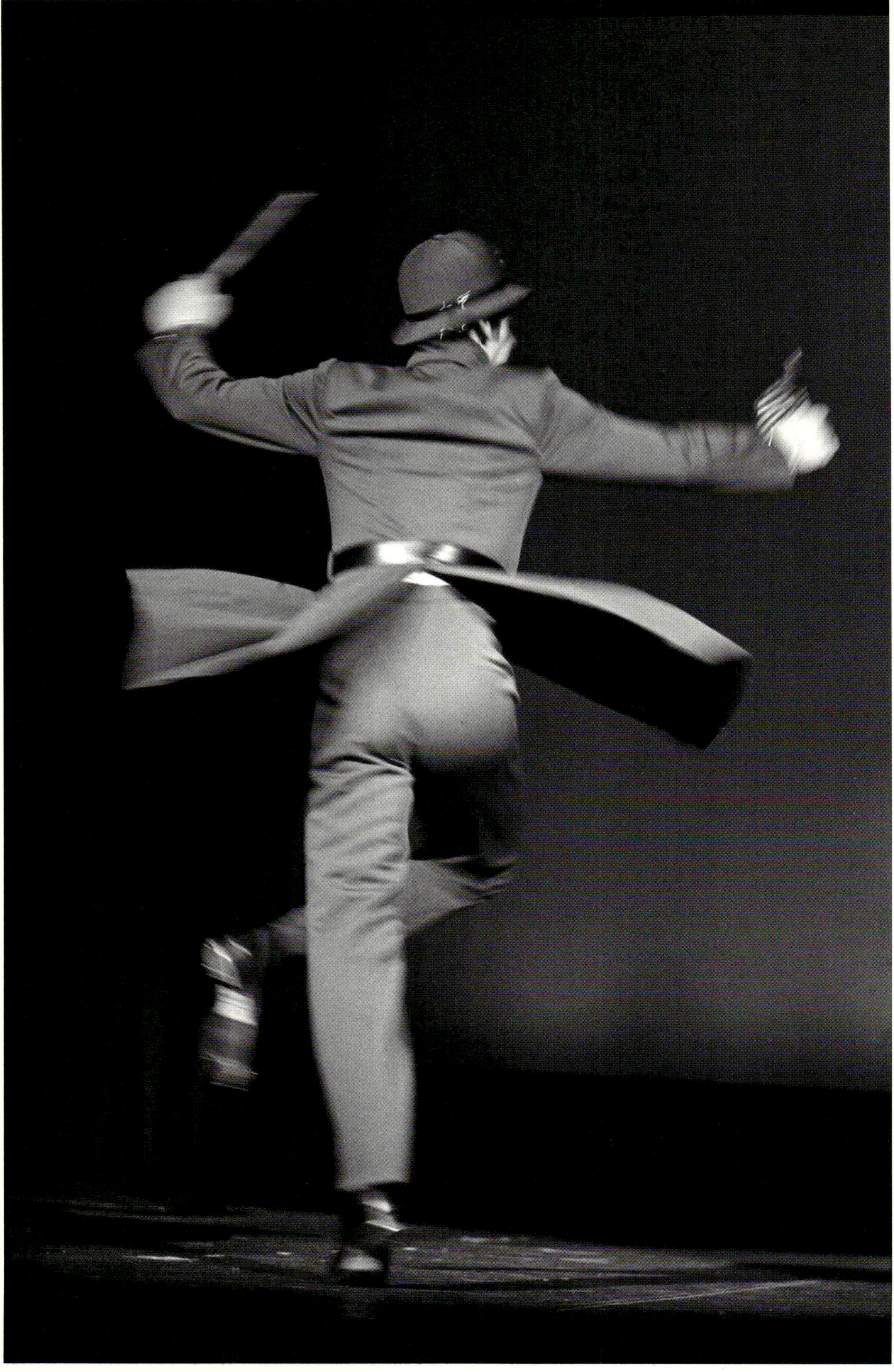

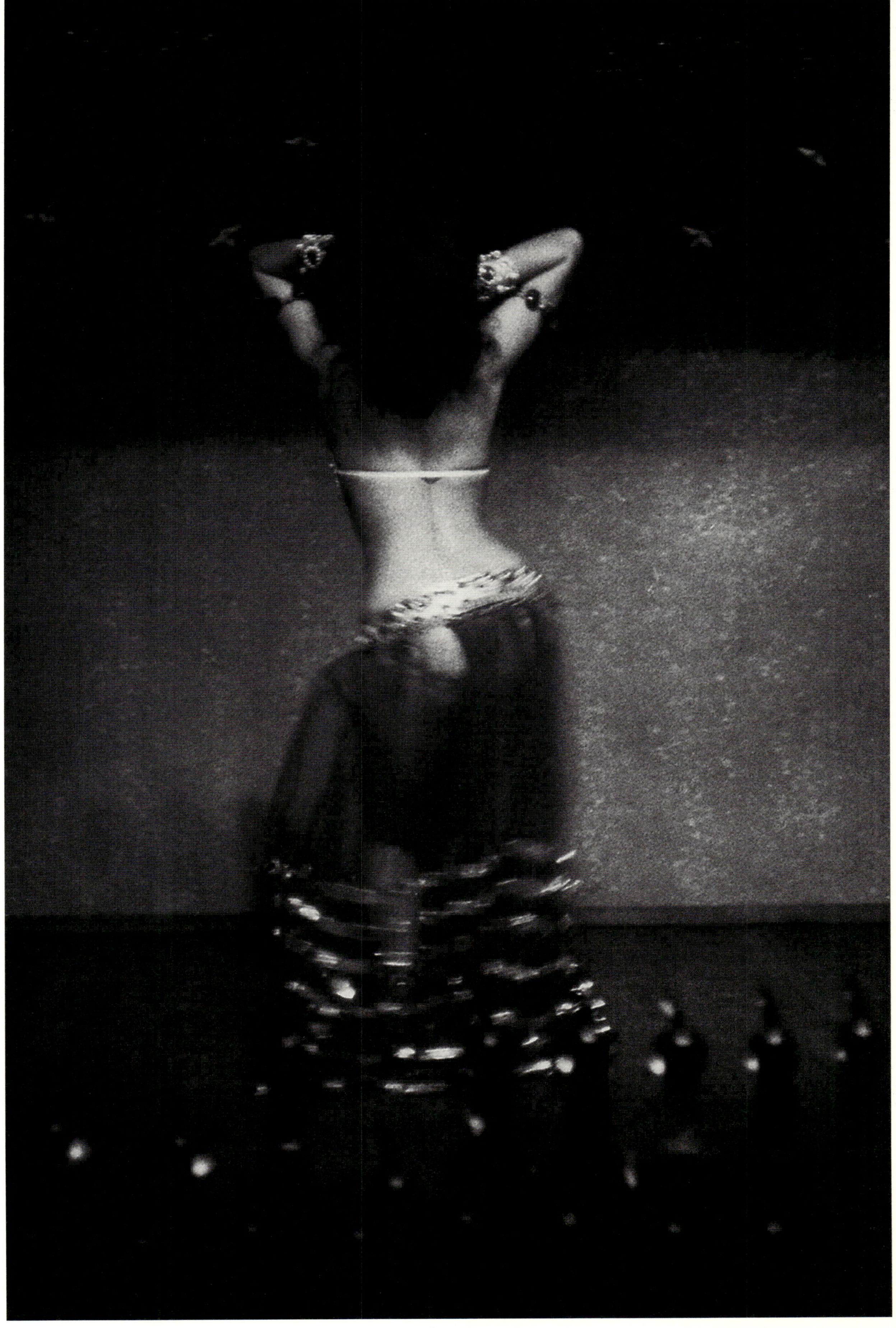

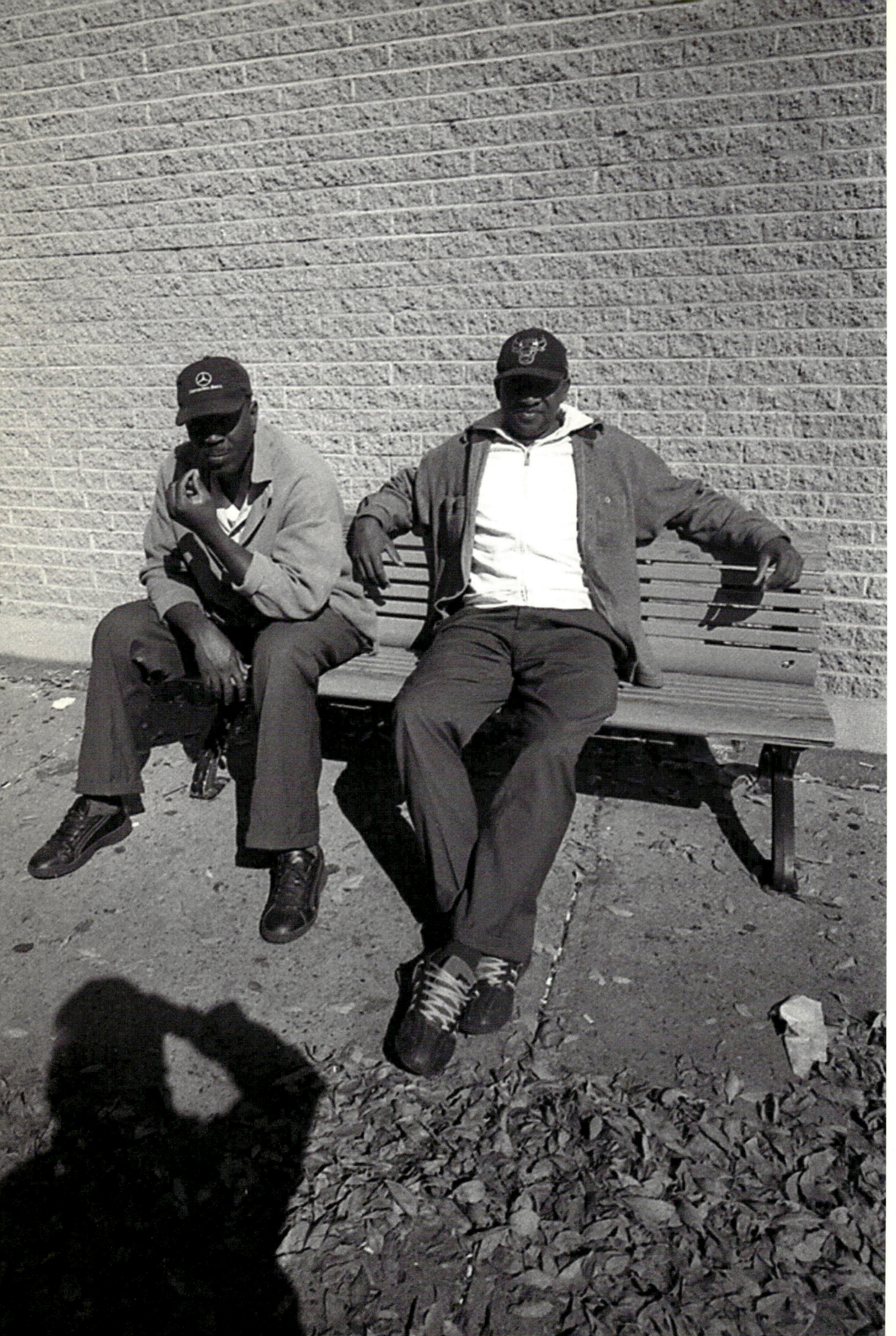

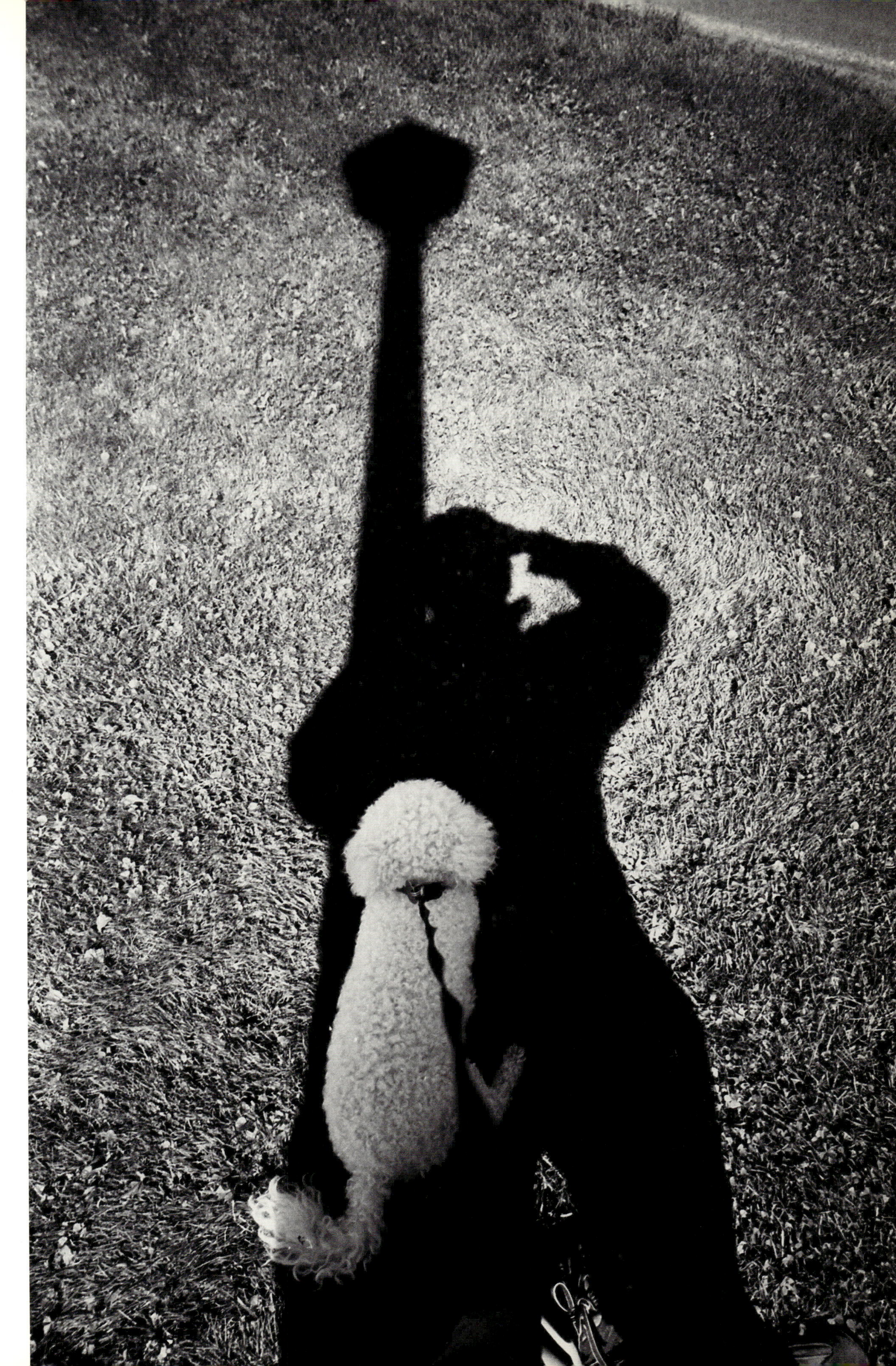

He gives us the impression that we are with him when he took the picture. You see his photographs with shadows and you think, 'where's my shadow?'

Diane Charbonneau, Curator of Photography, Montreal Museum of Fine Arts

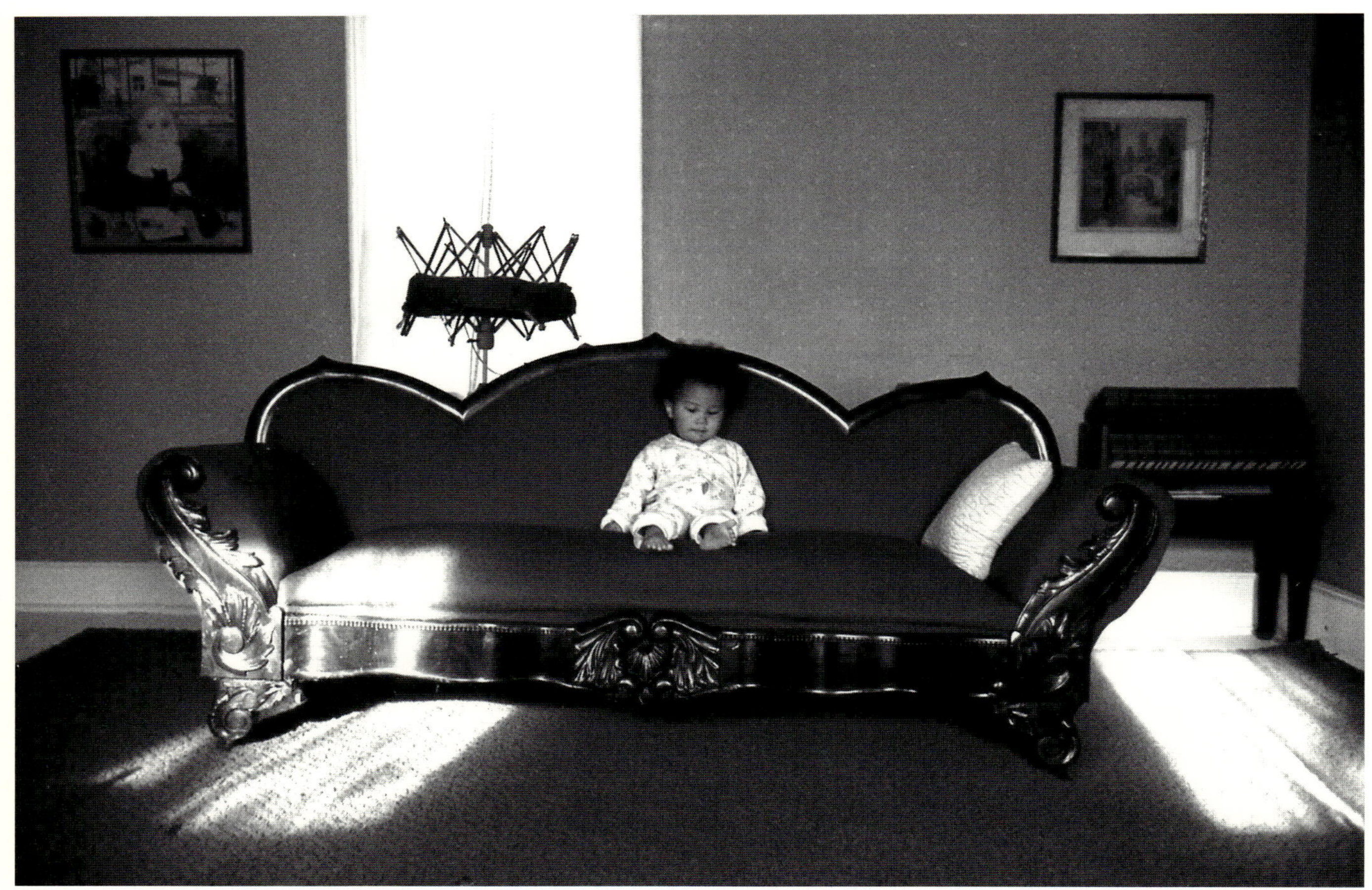

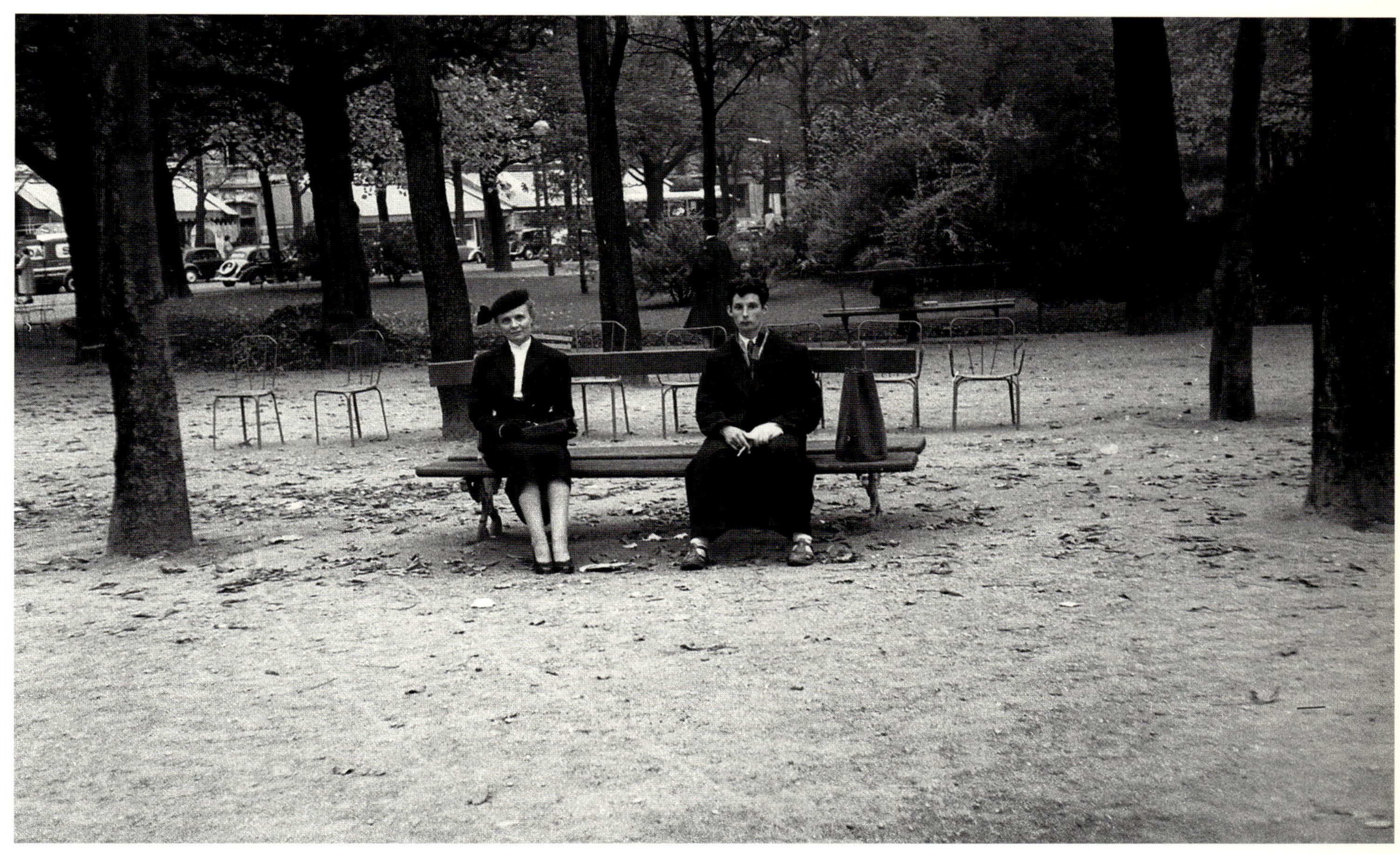

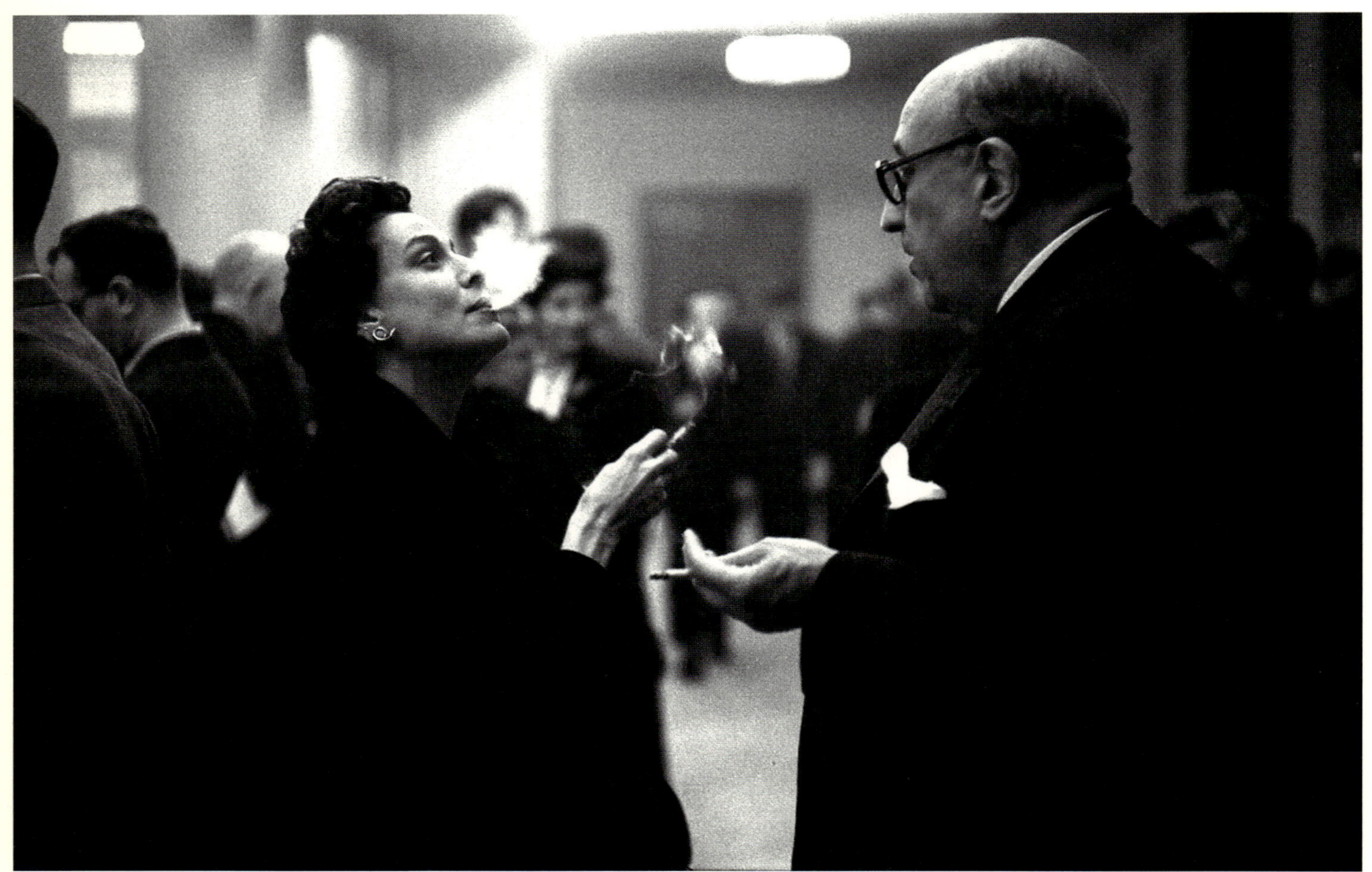

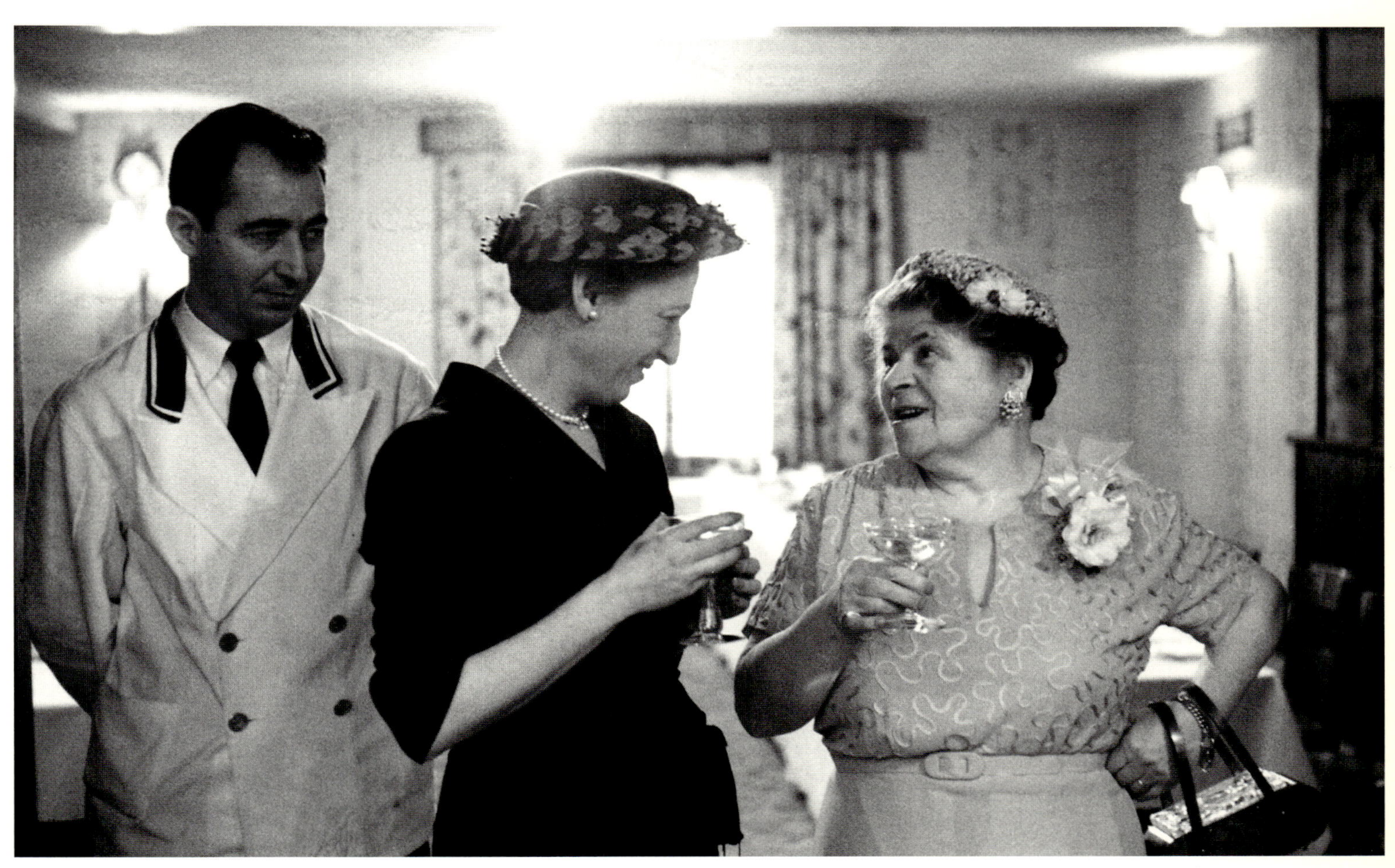

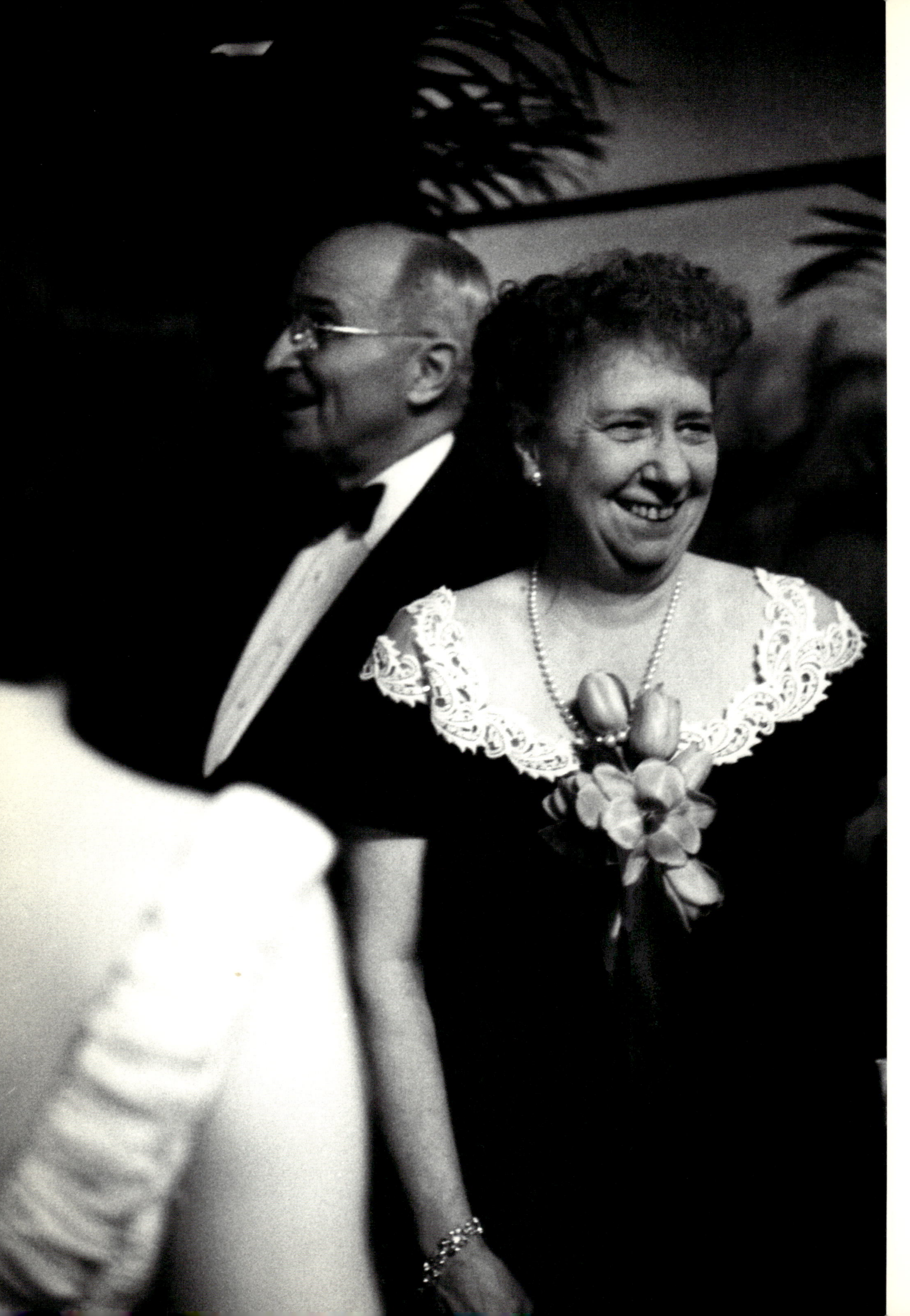

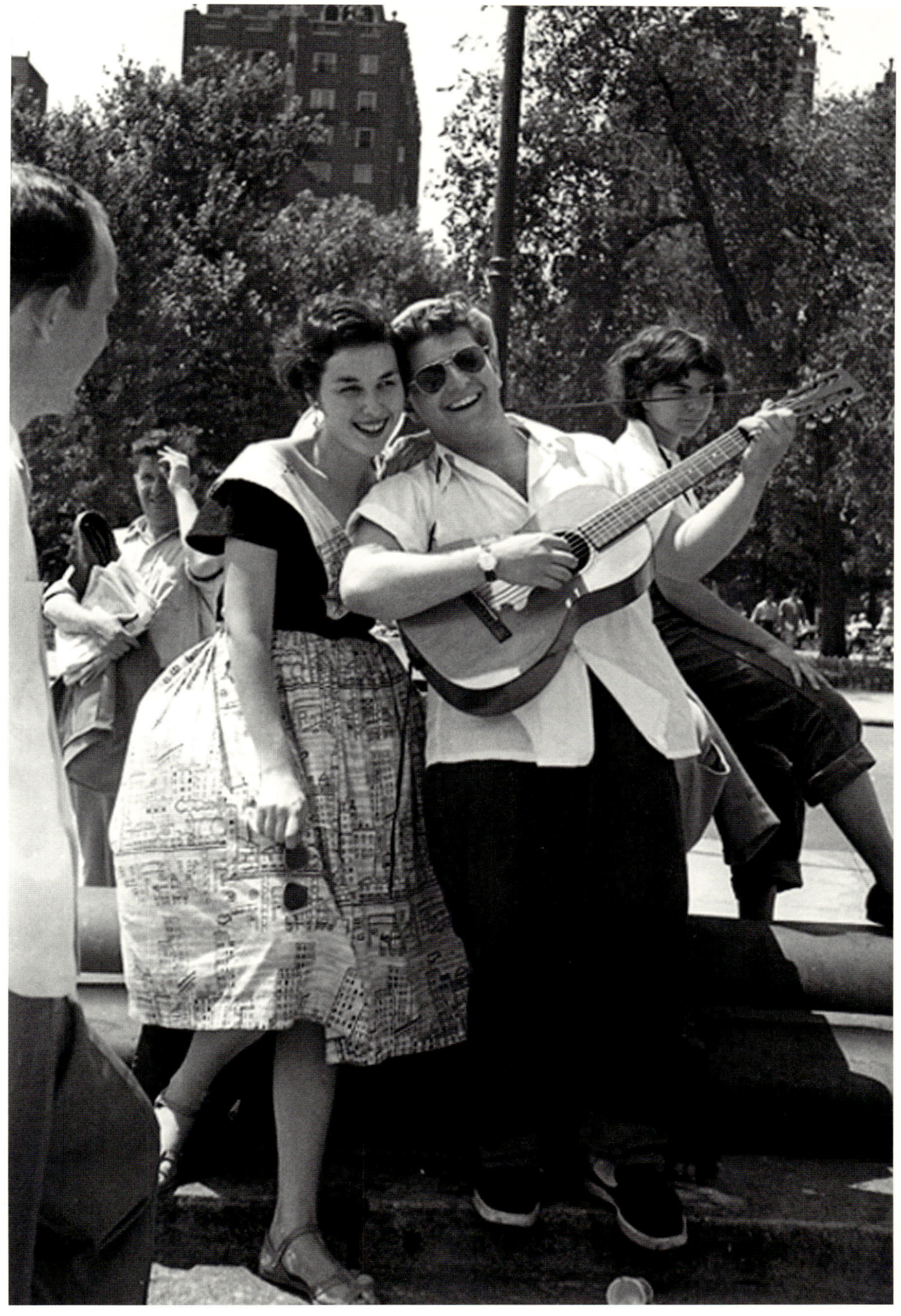

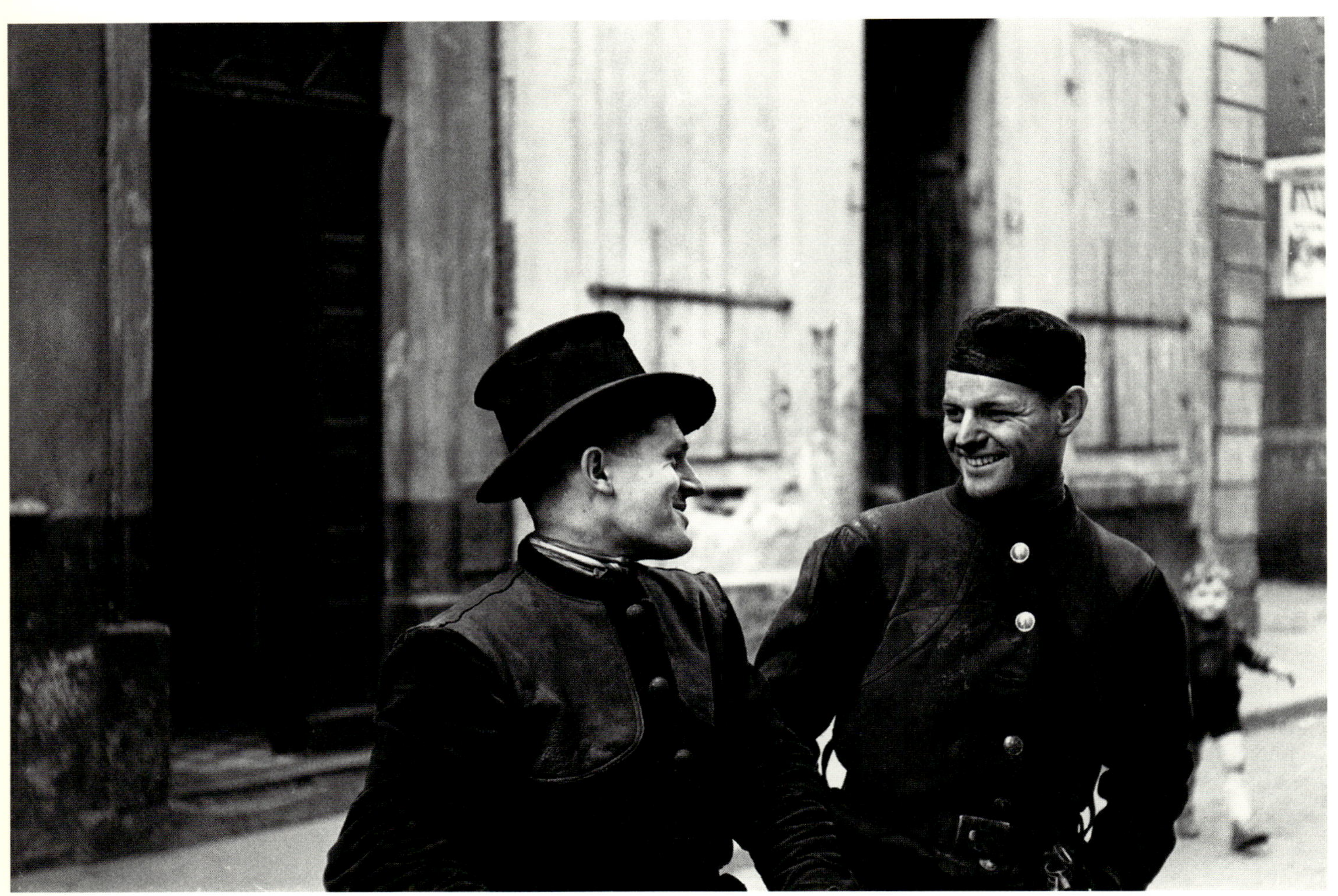

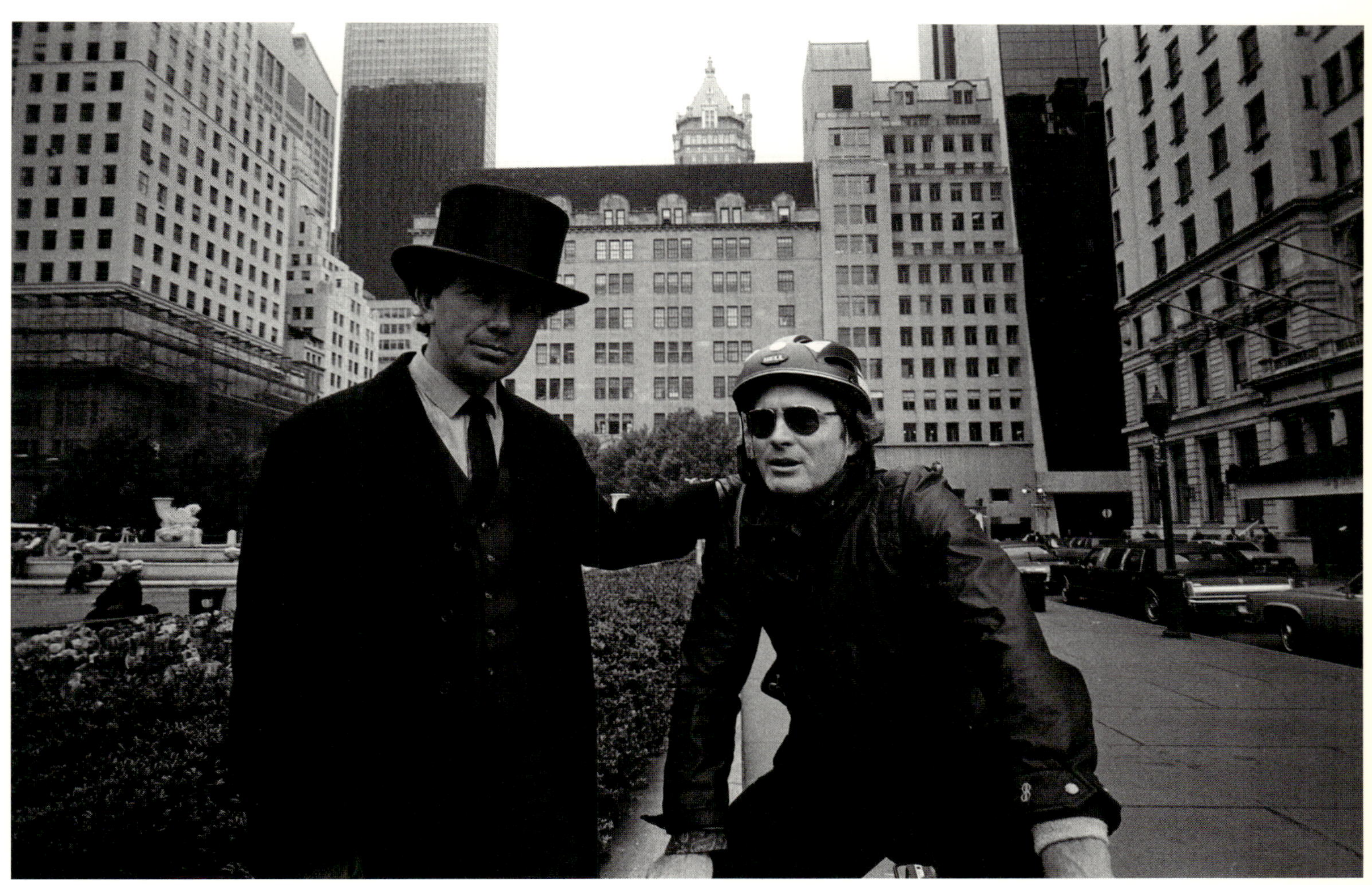

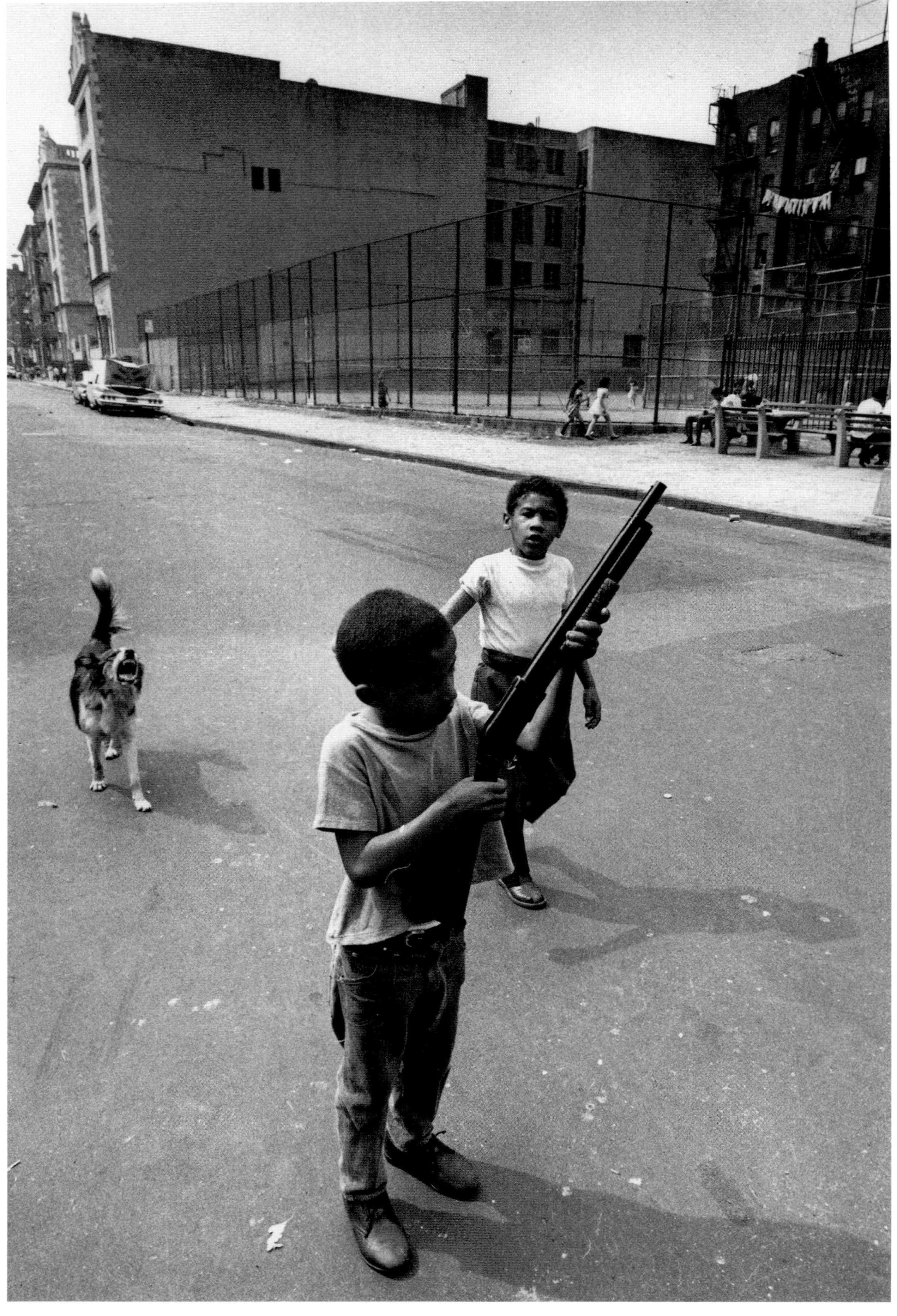

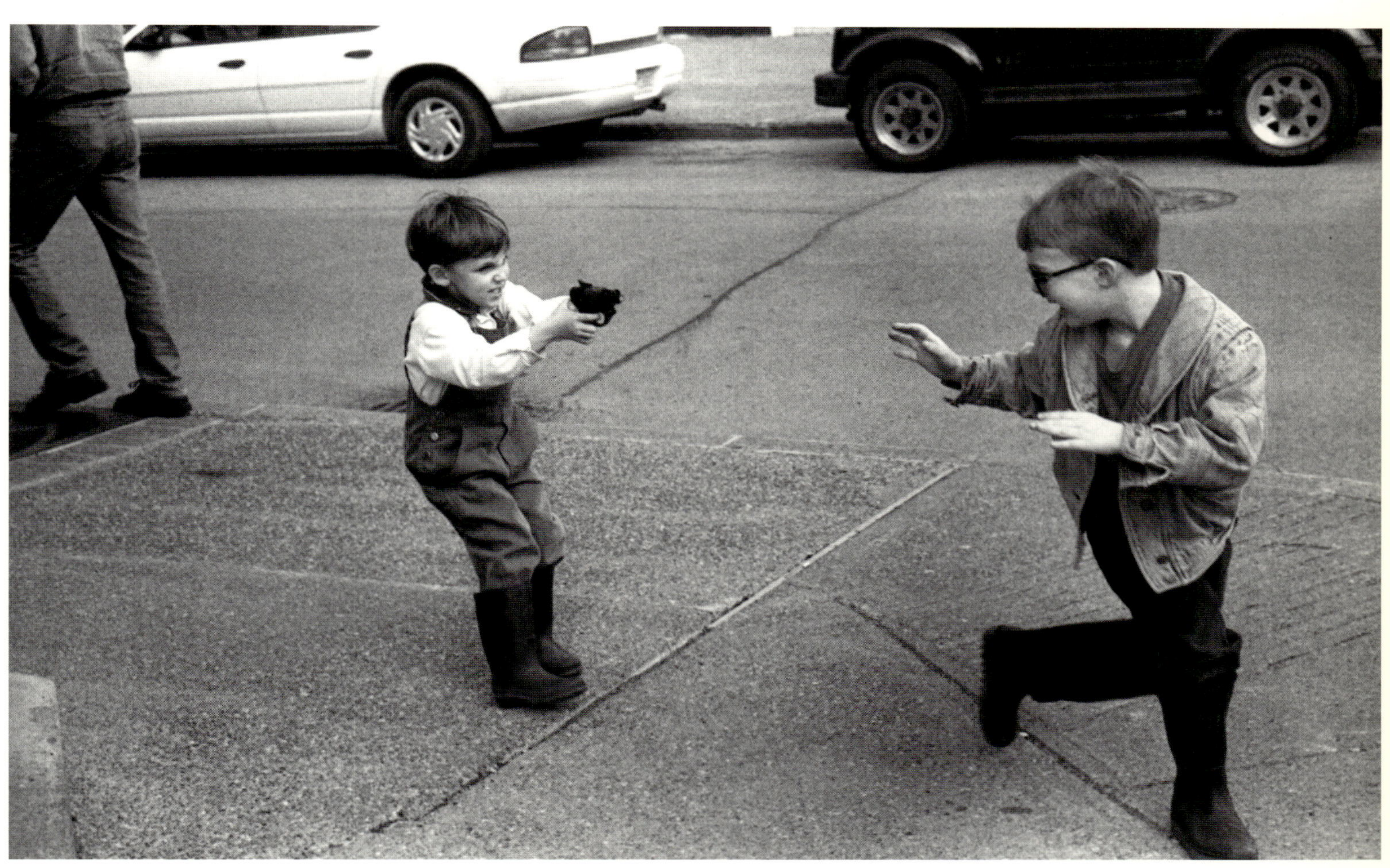

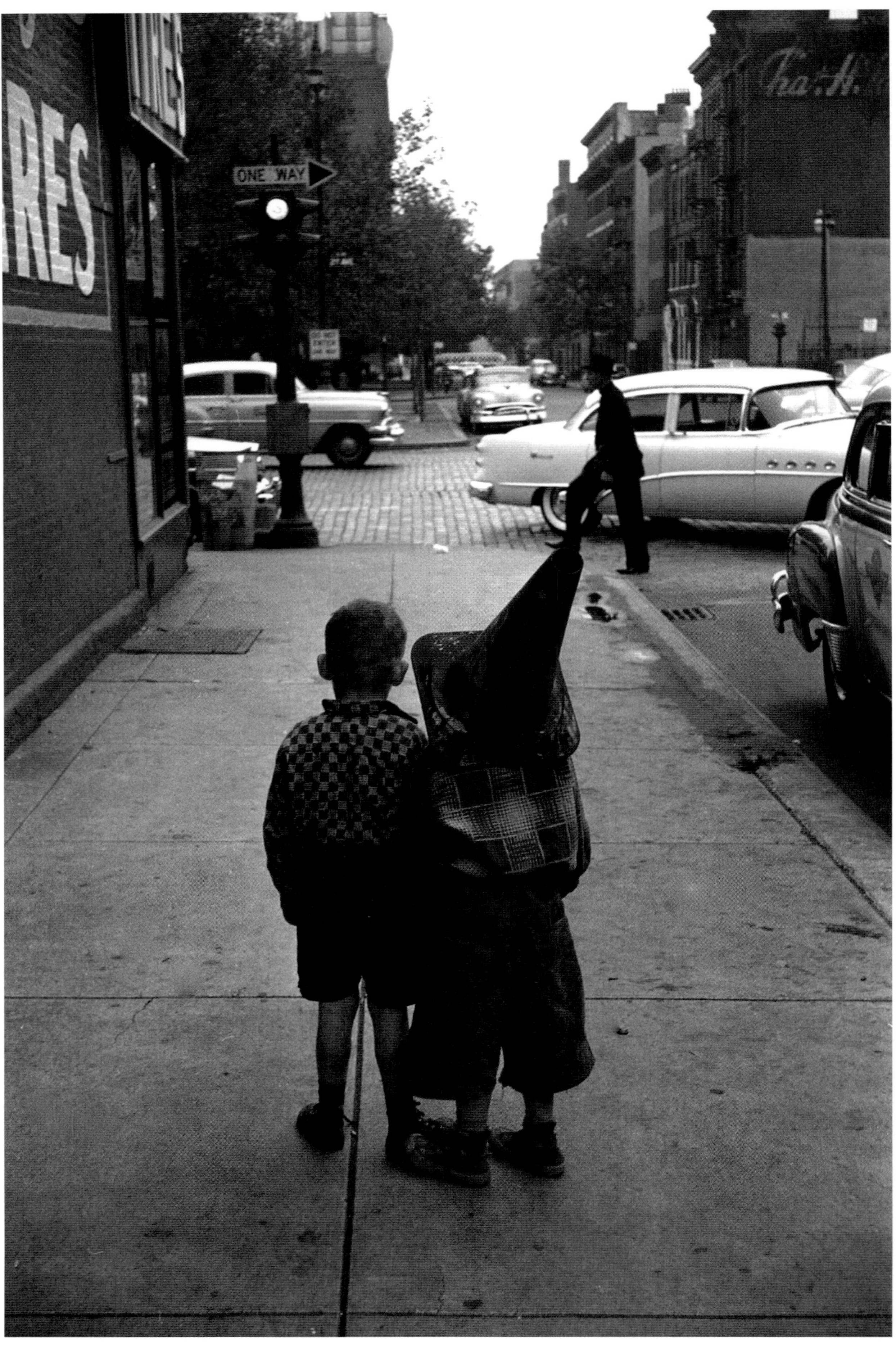
ONE WAY

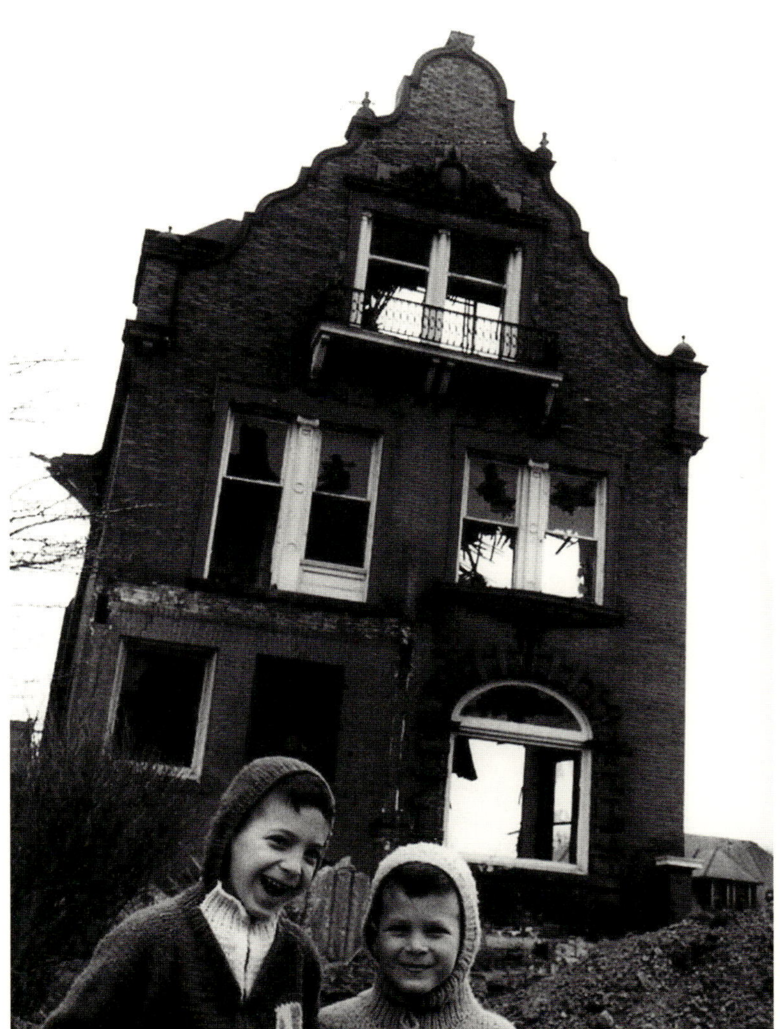

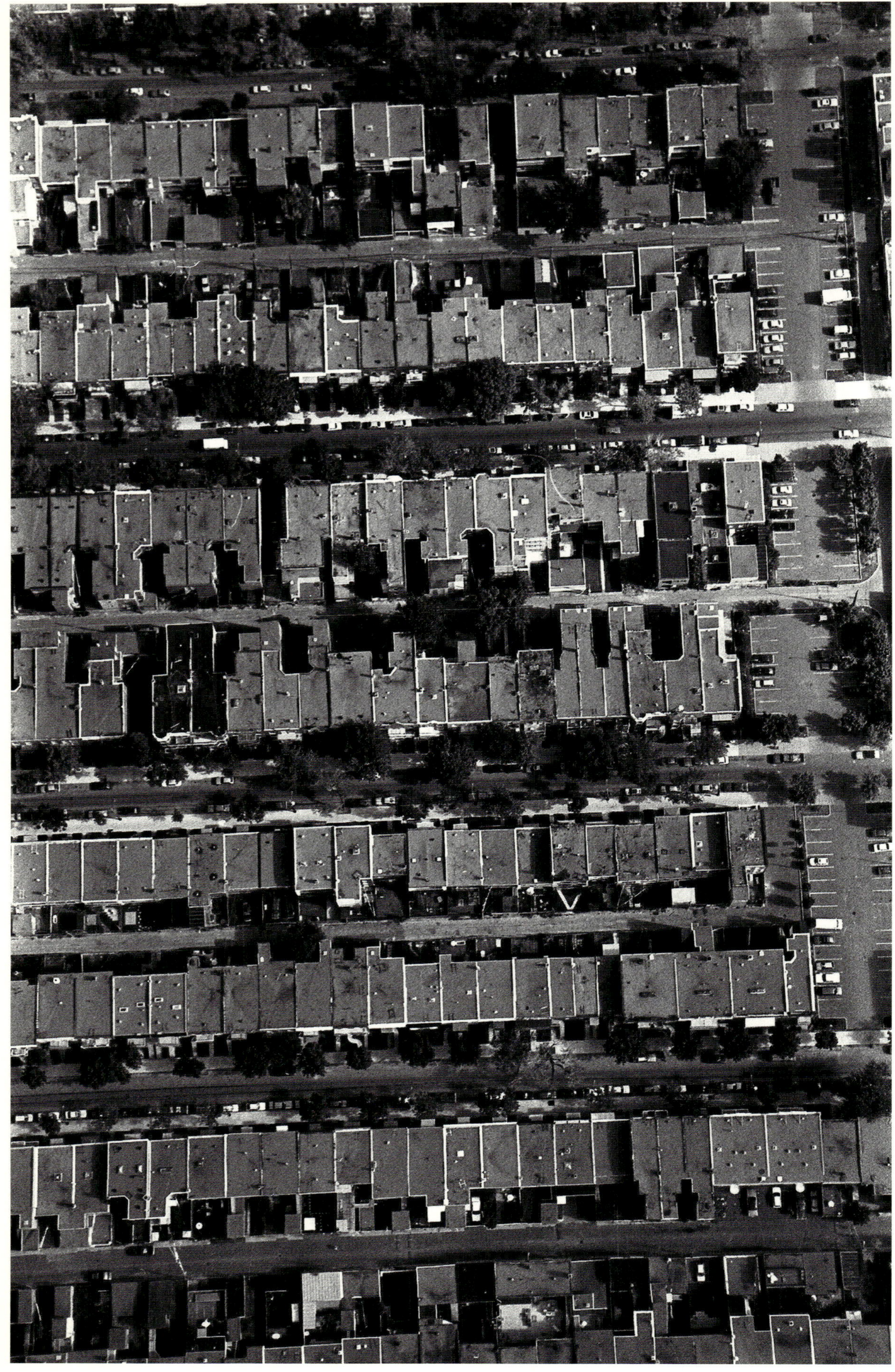

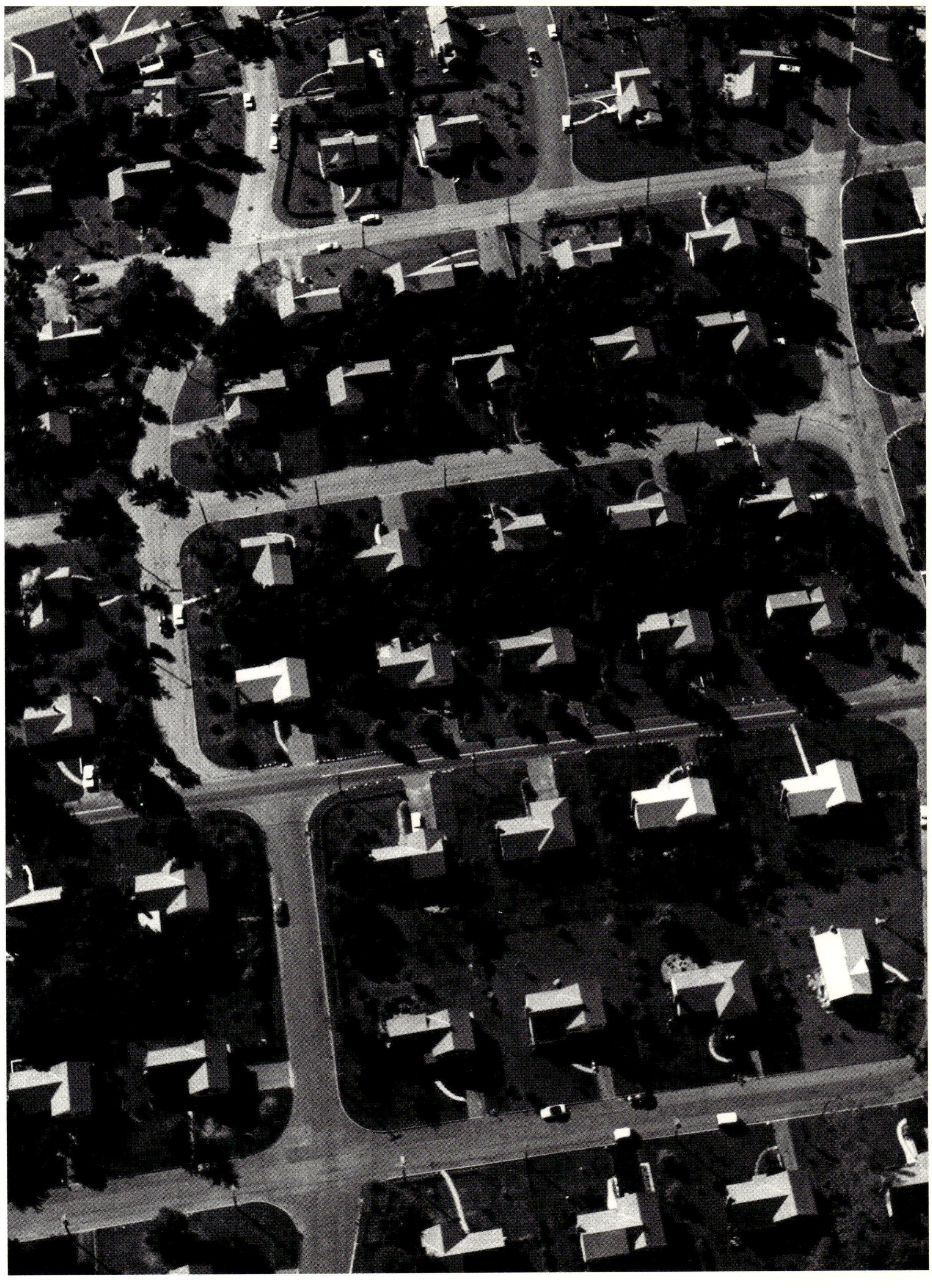

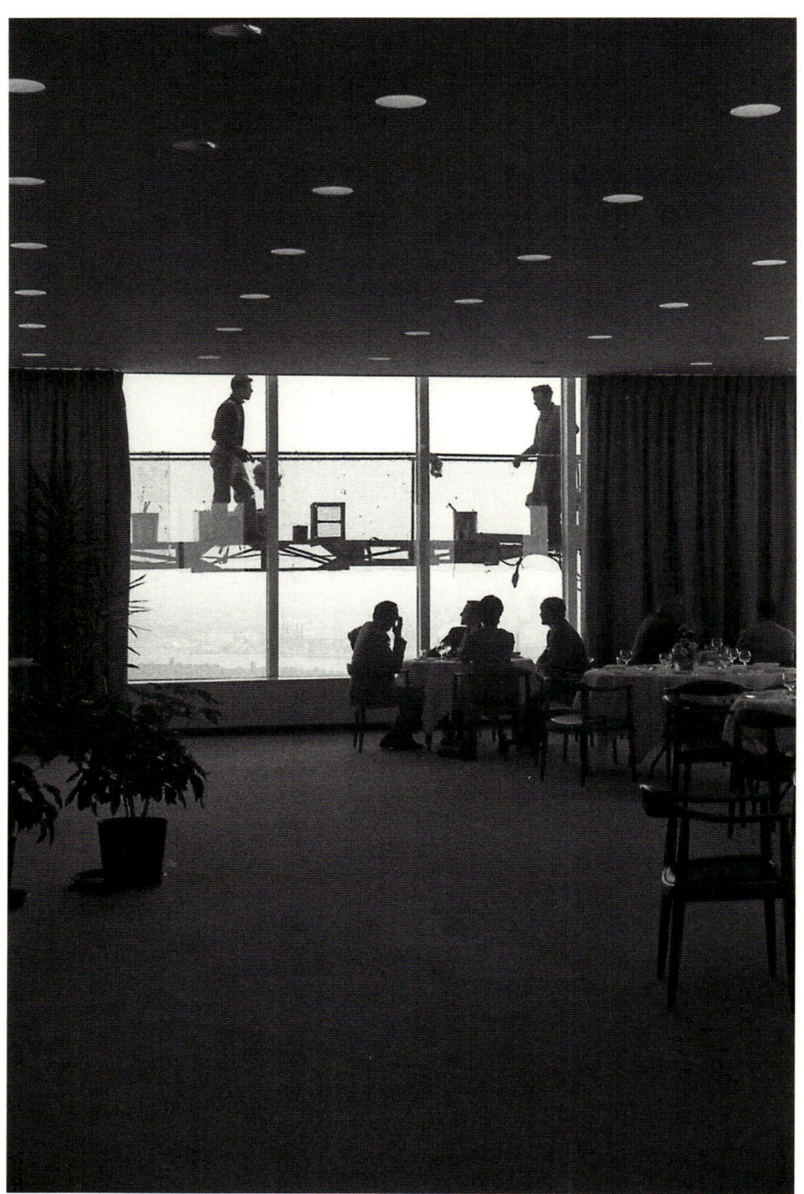

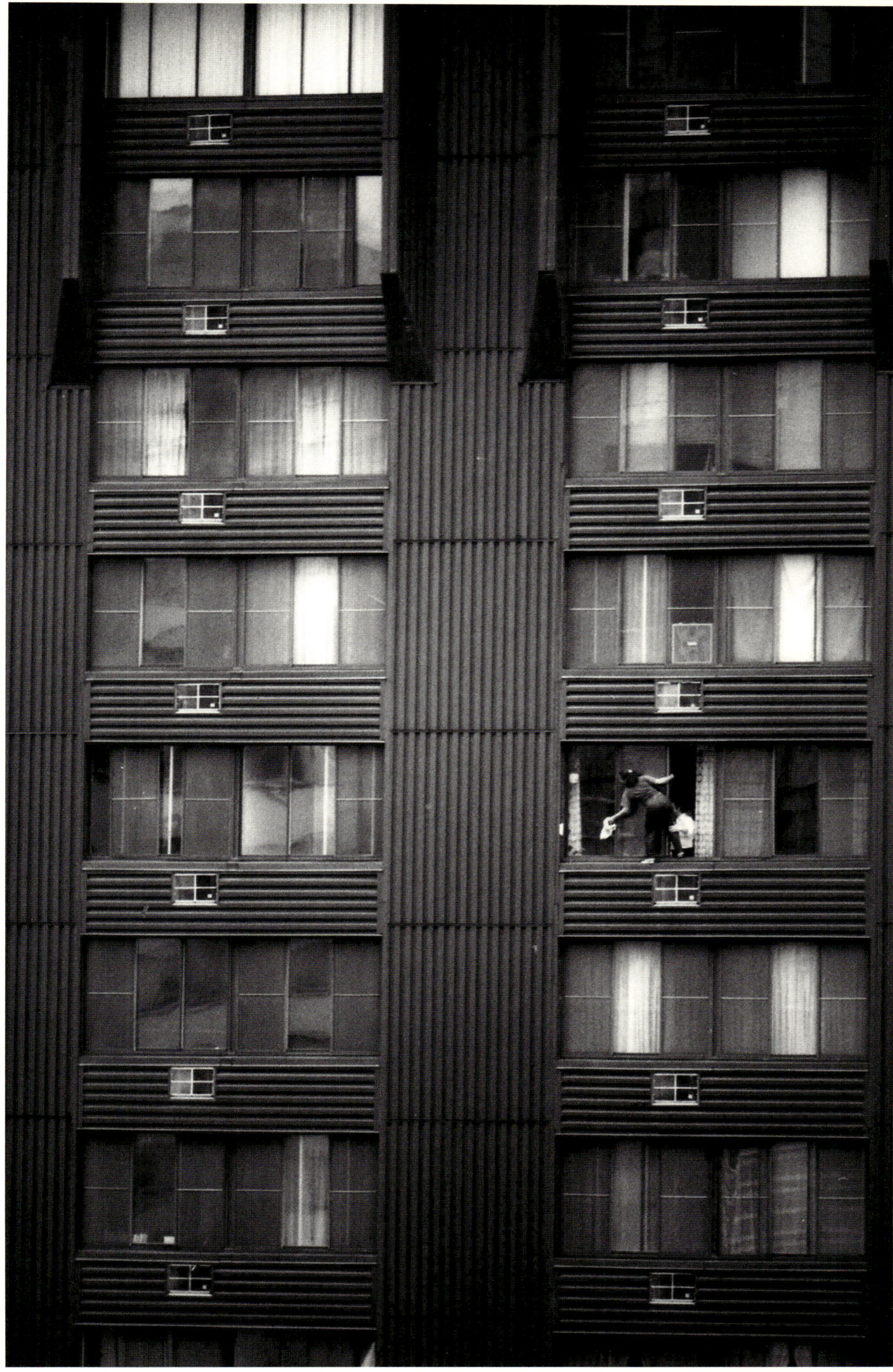

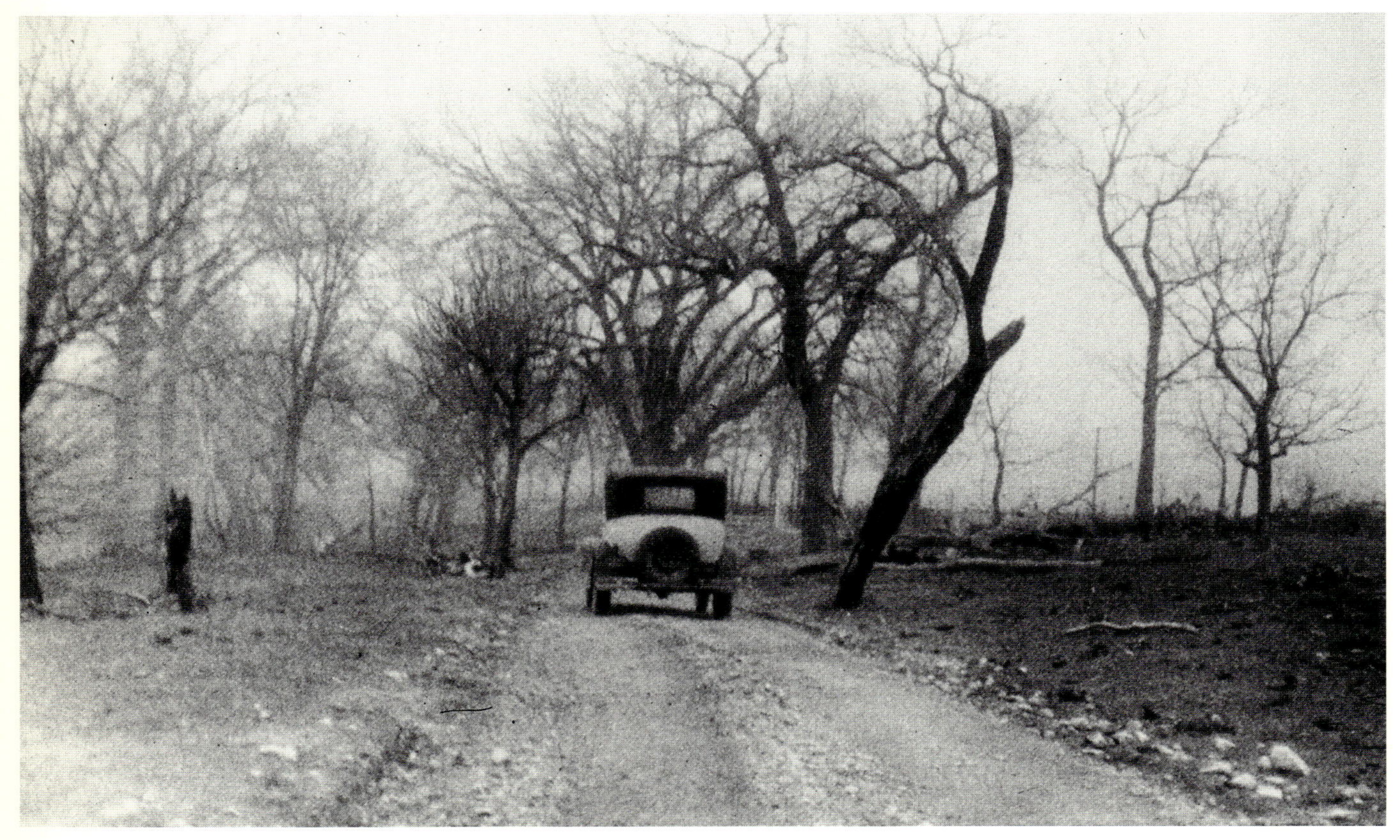

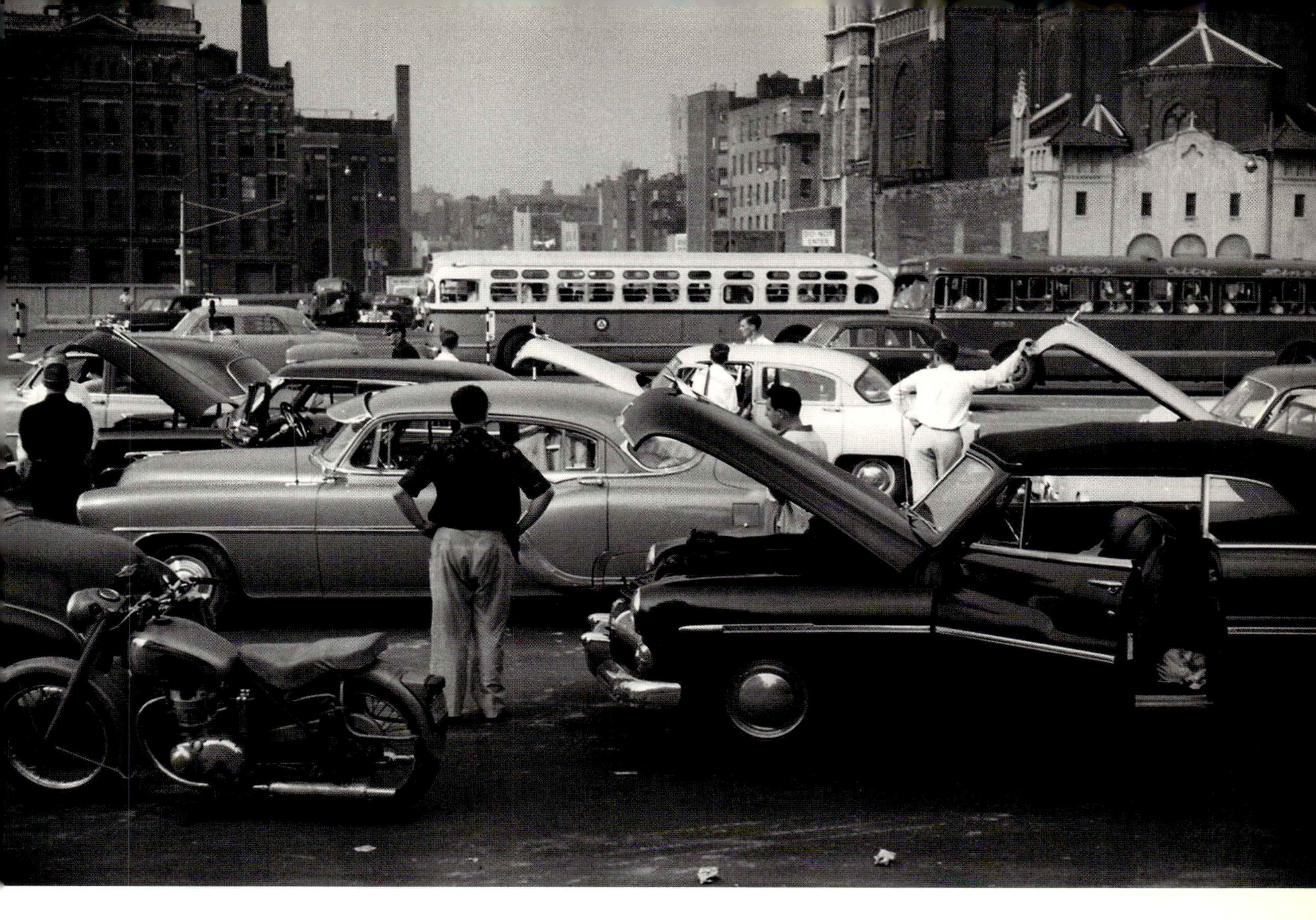
DO NOT
ENTER

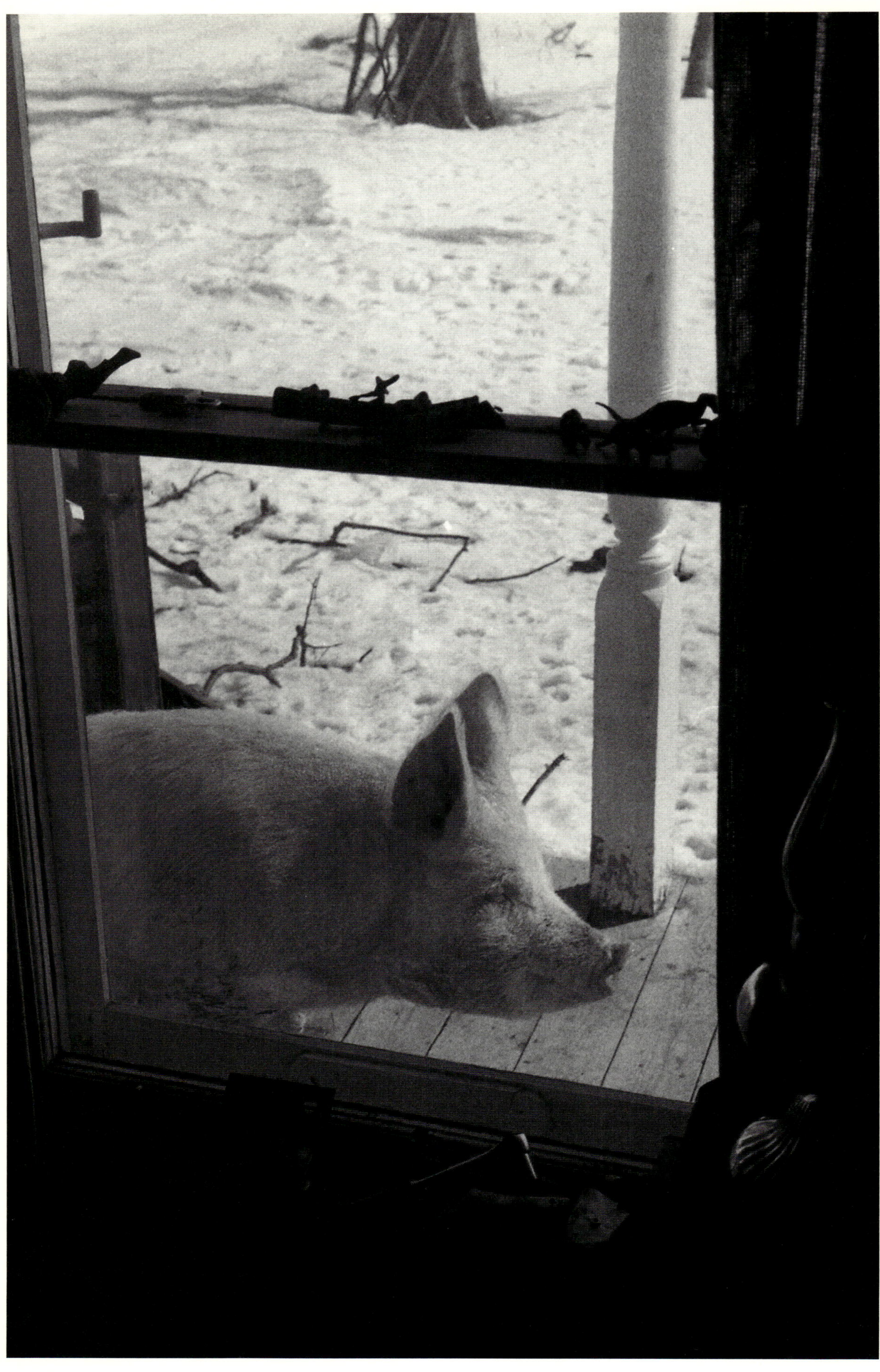

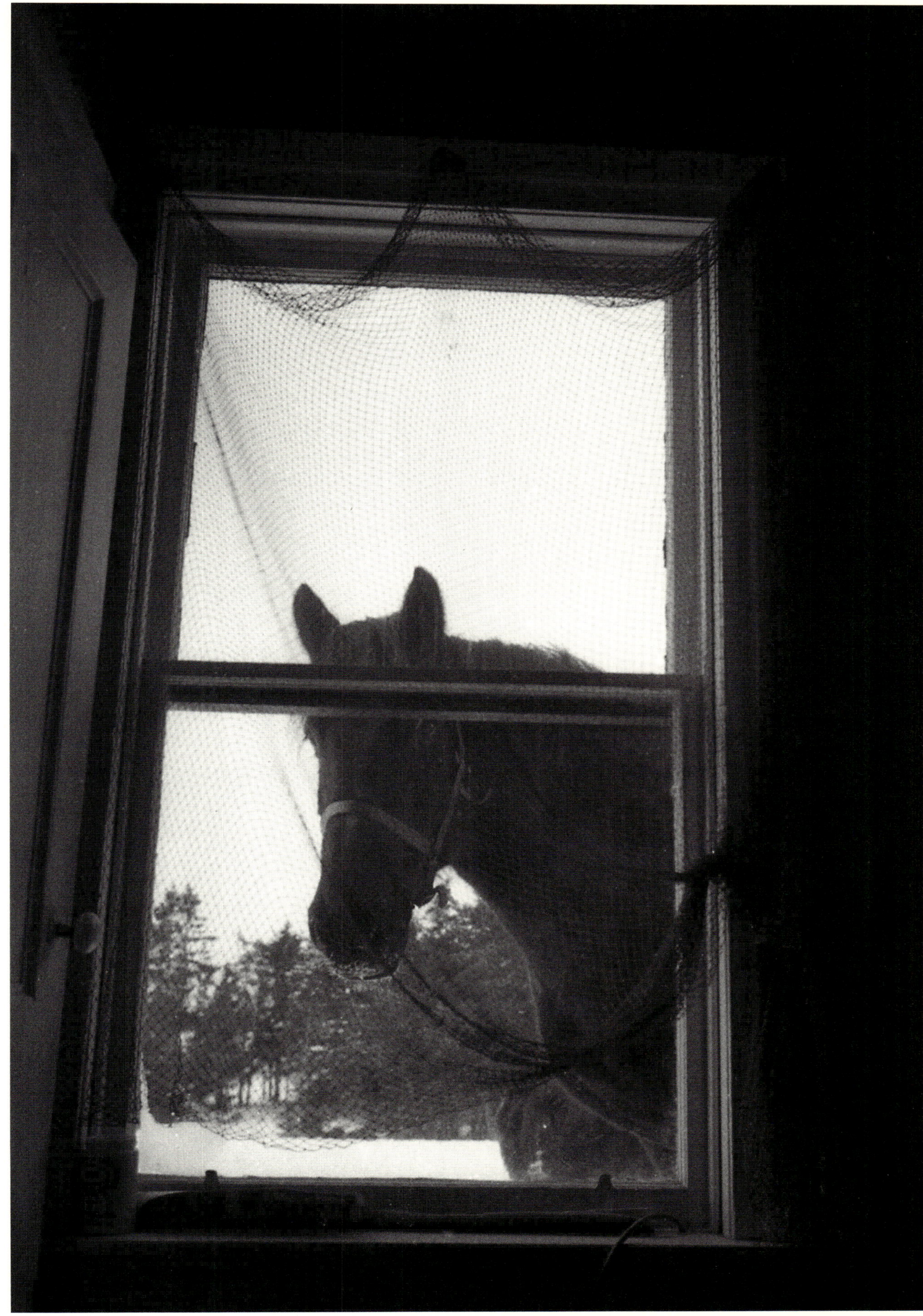

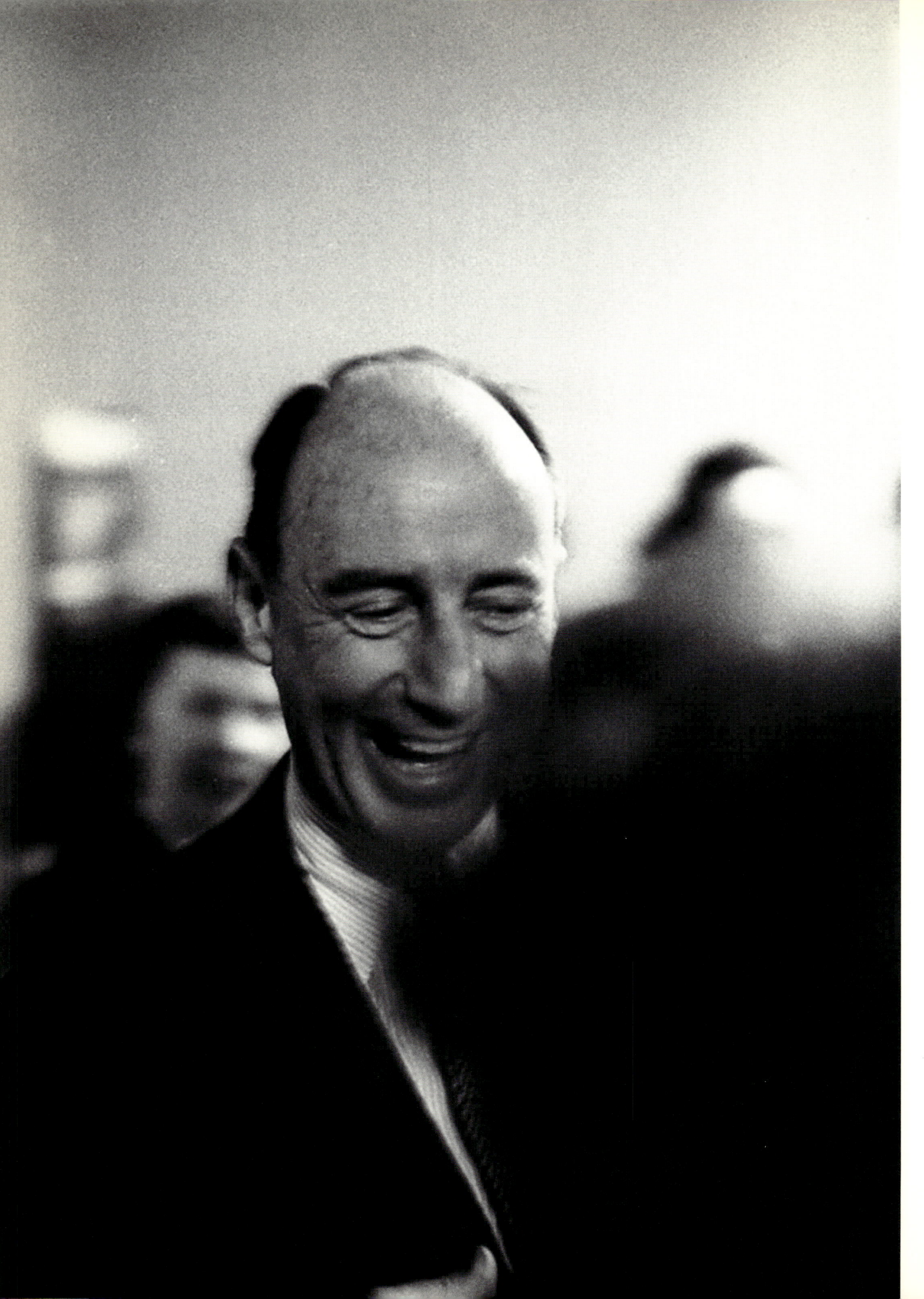

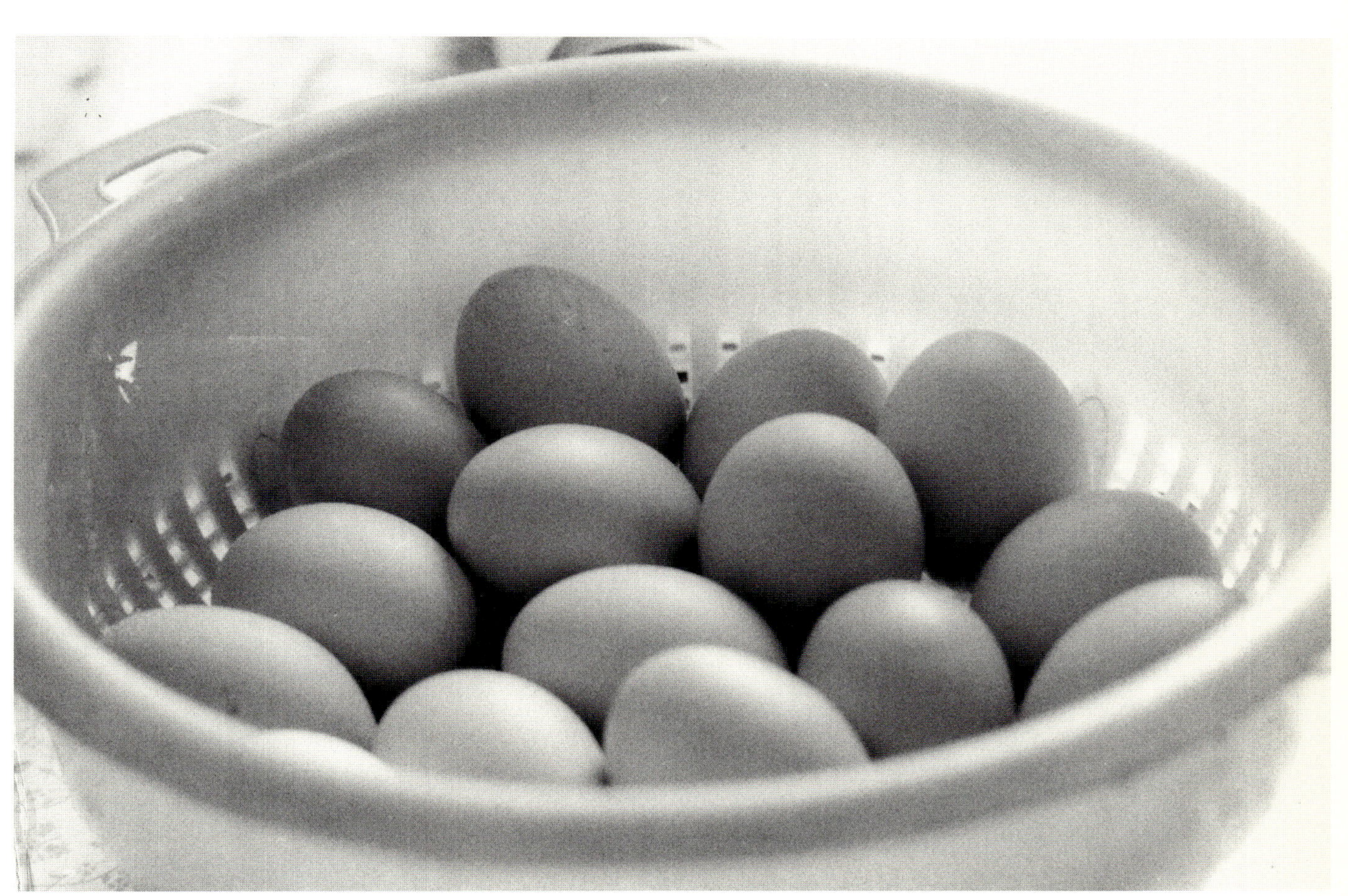

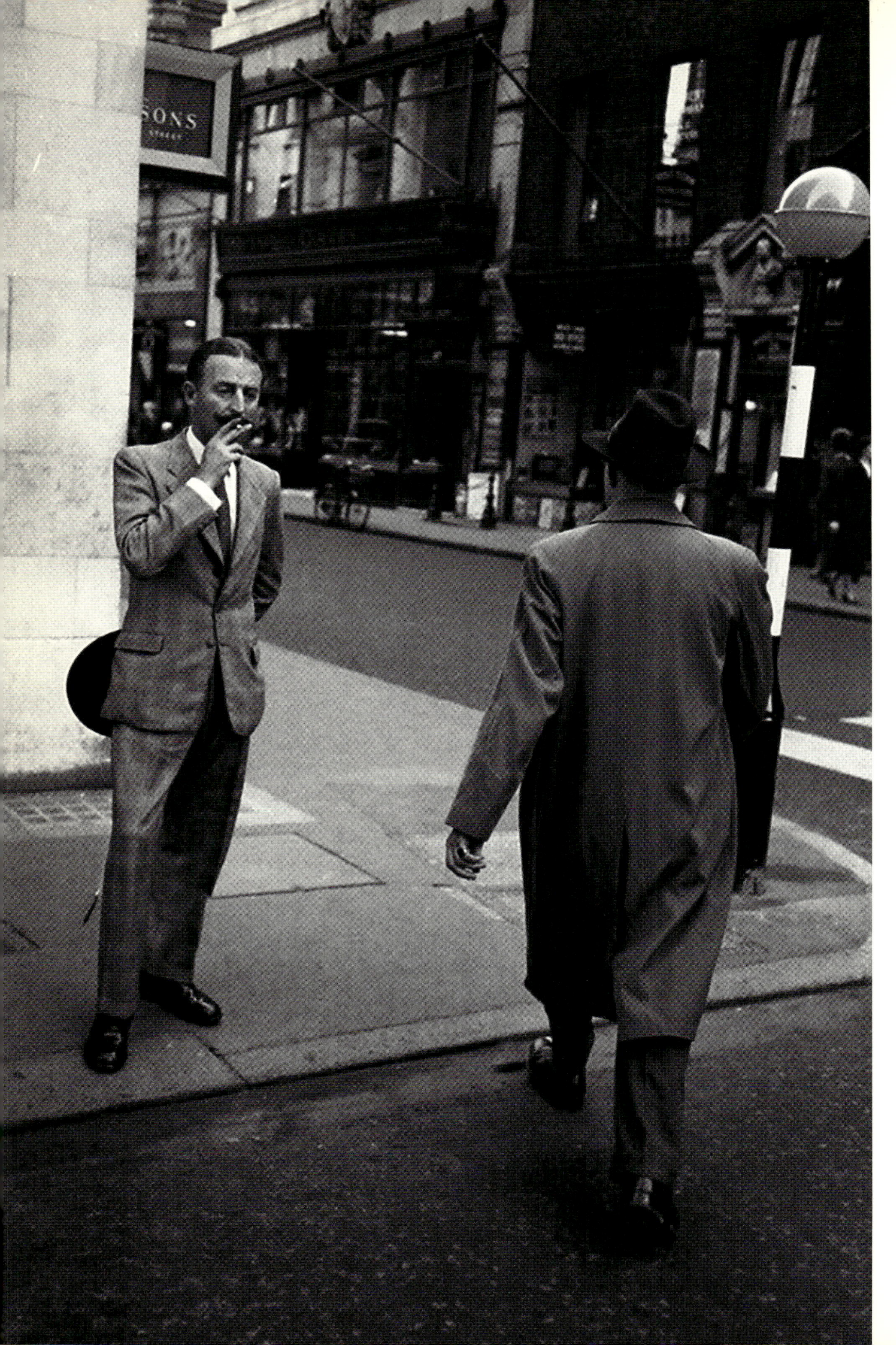
SONS

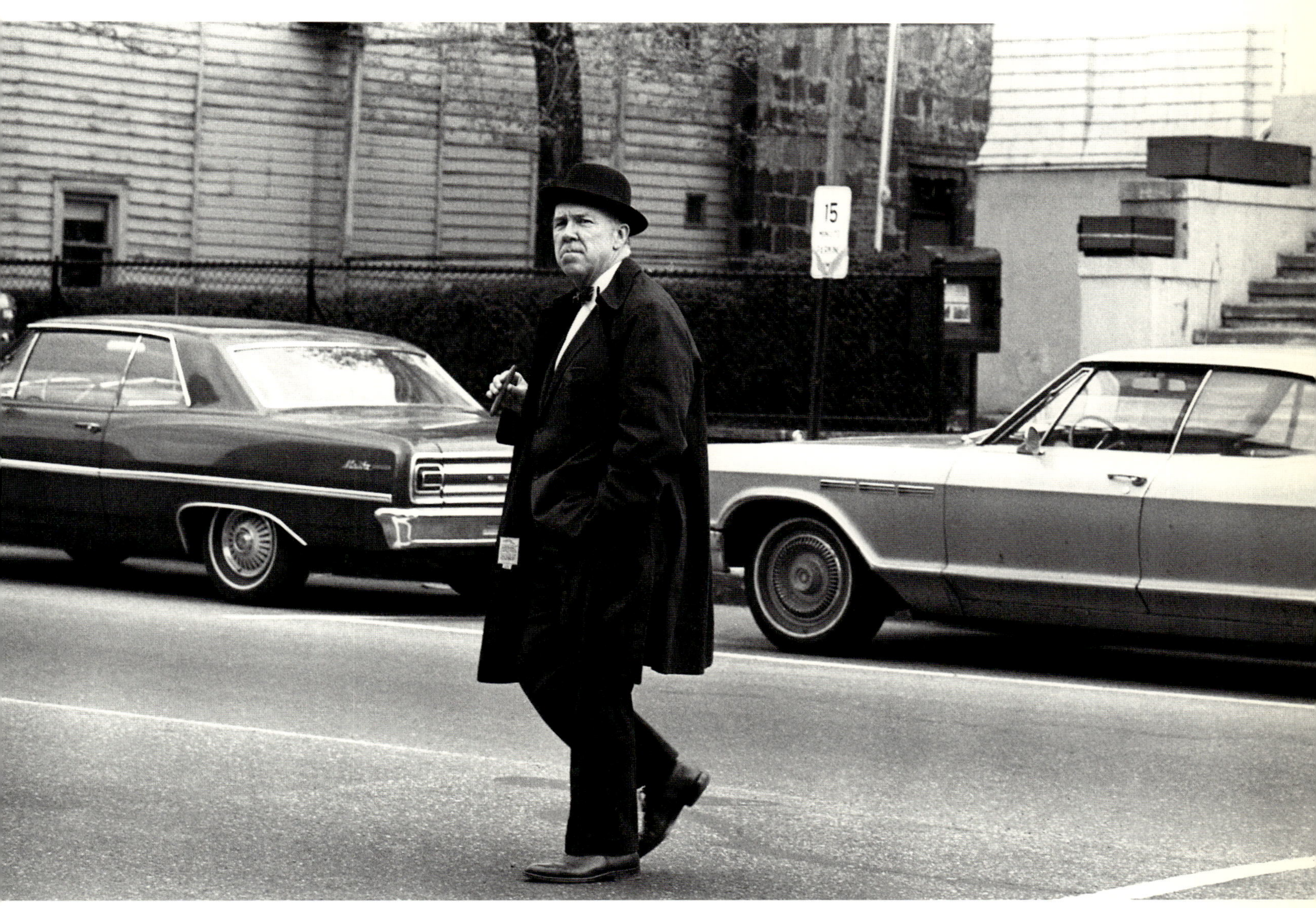
15

Whether it's about a person being contemplative or joking around or working hard or just crossing the street, George has a great eye for revealing gestures.

Anne Tucker, Founding Curator the Department of Photography, Museum of Fine Arts Houston

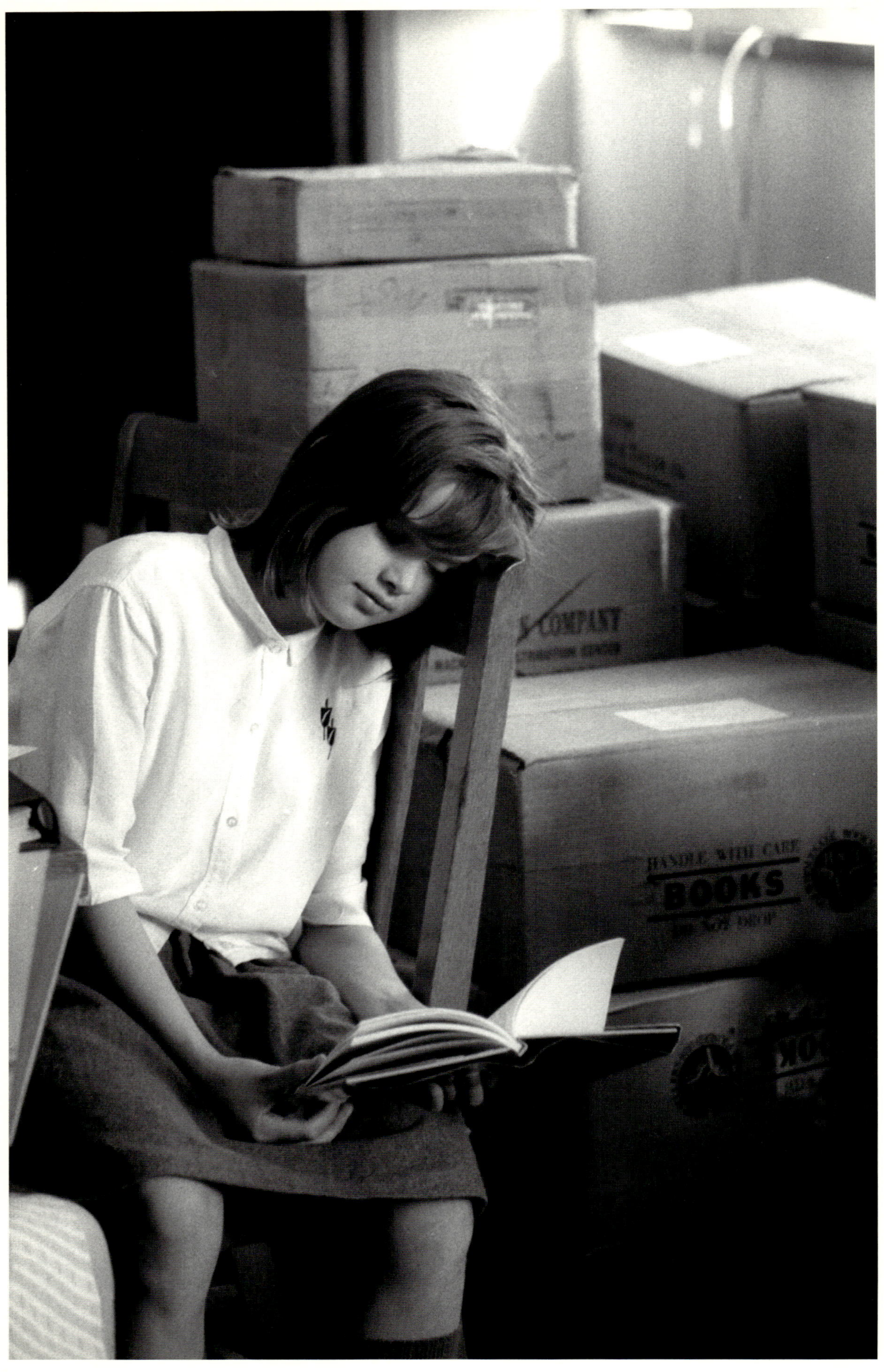
COMPANY
BOOKS

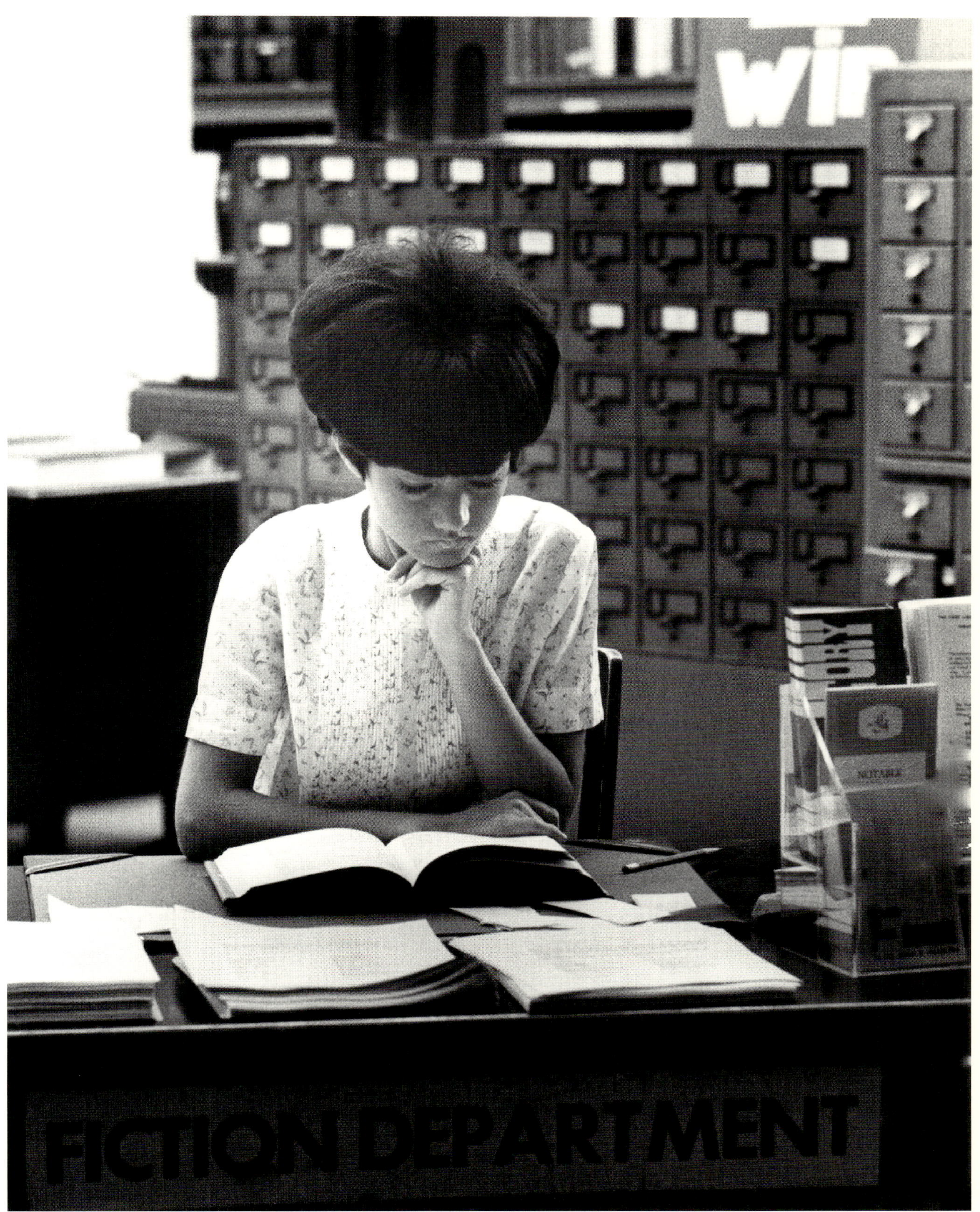
FICTION DEPARTMENT
NOTABLE

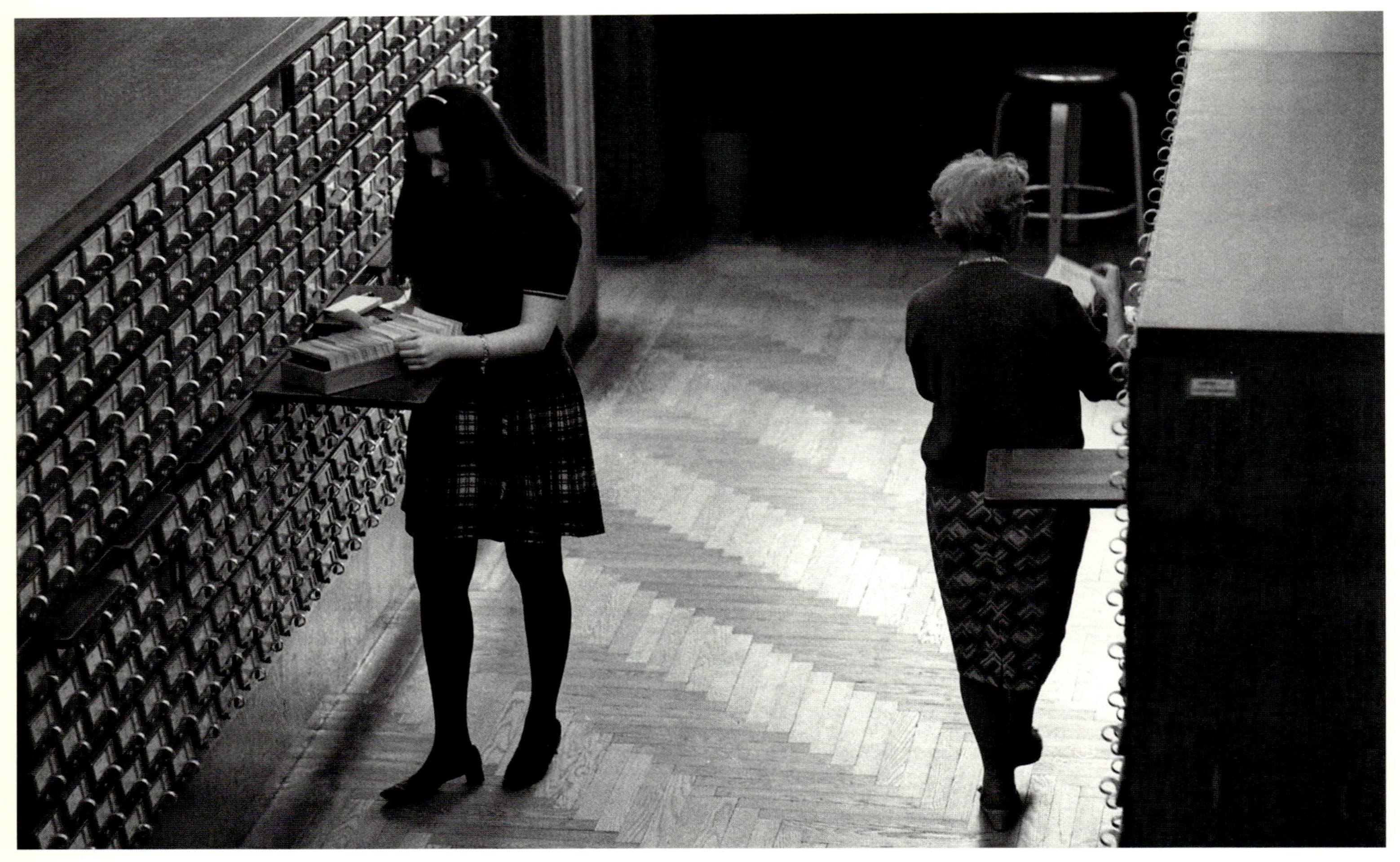

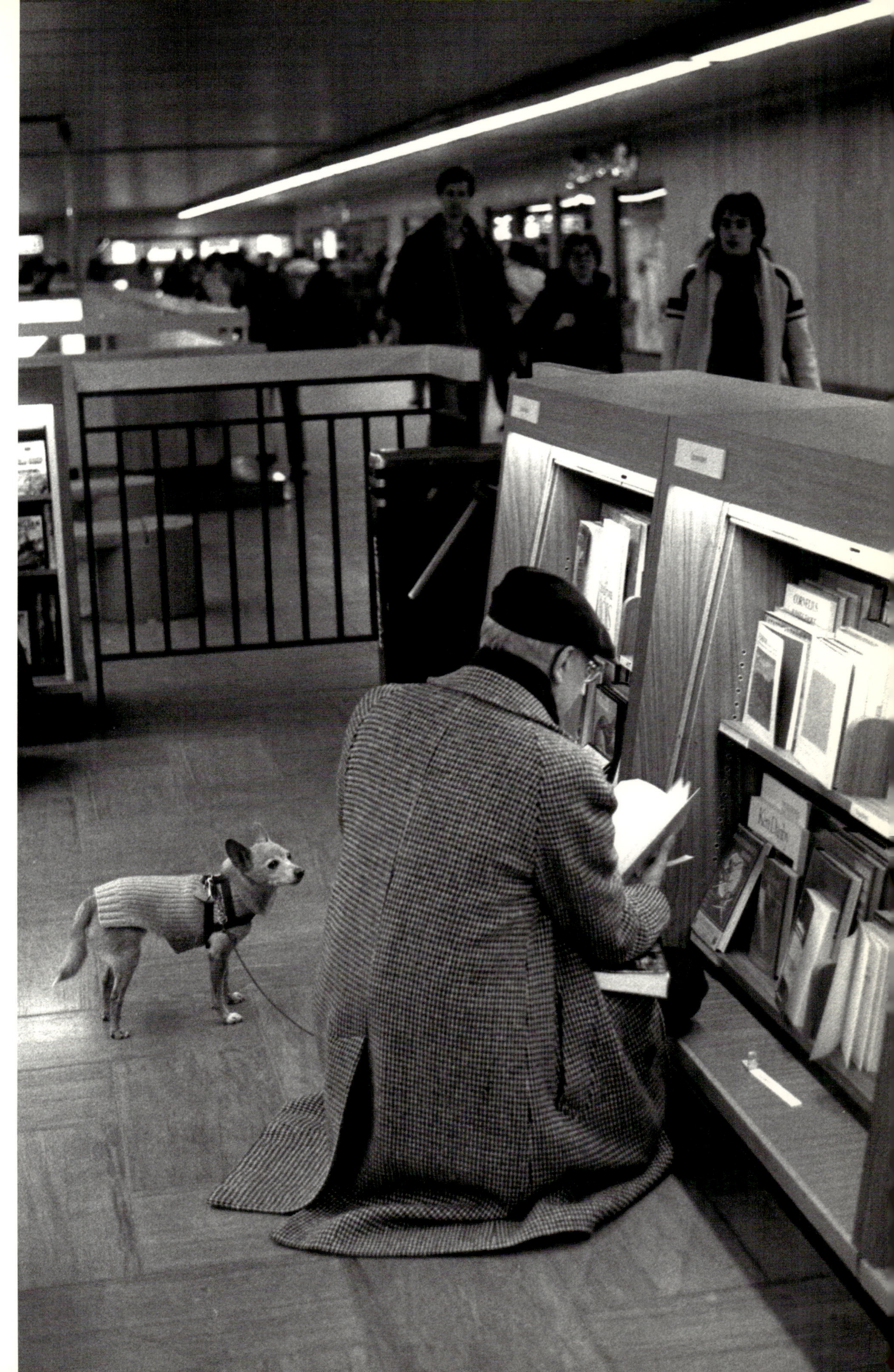

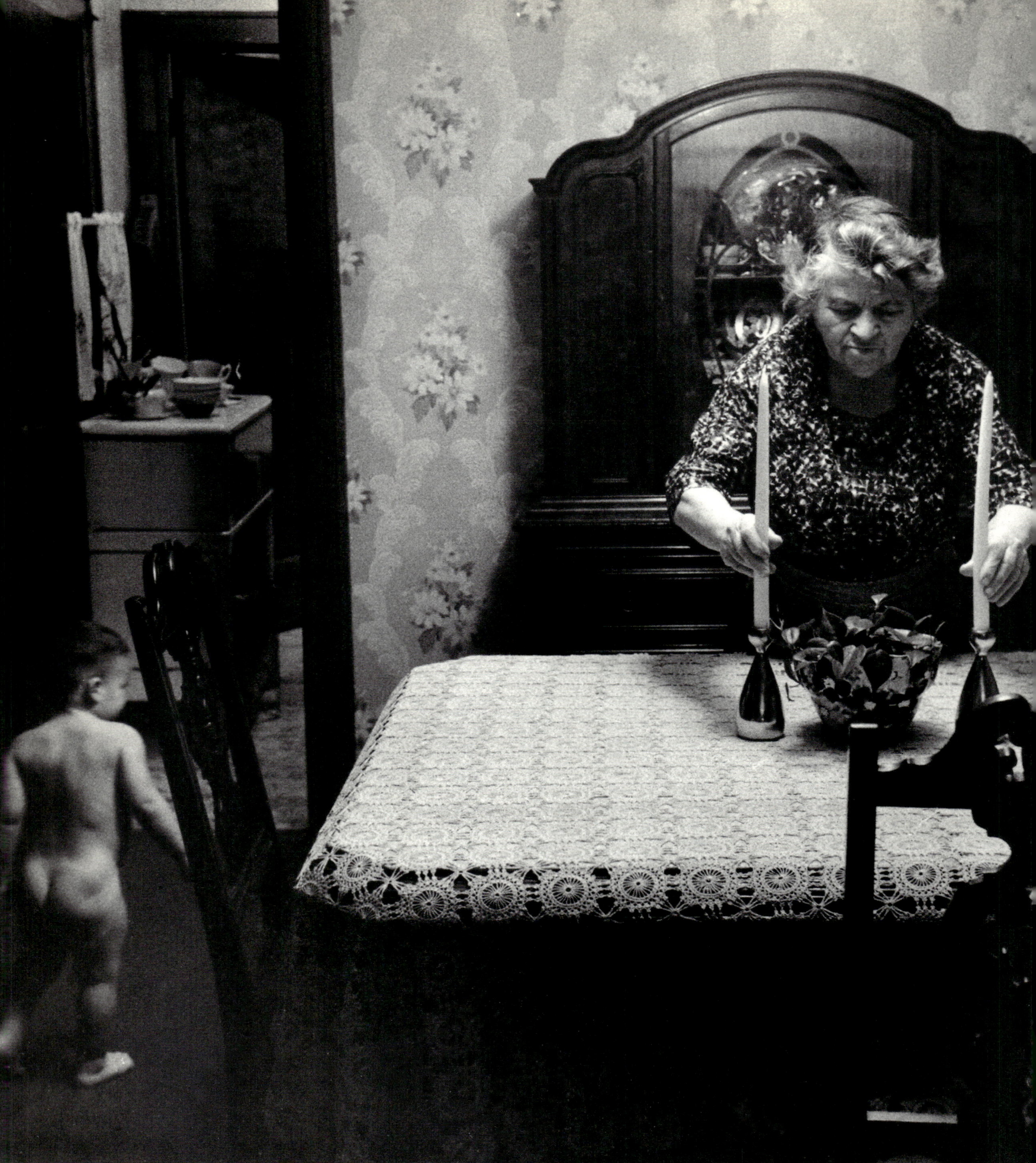

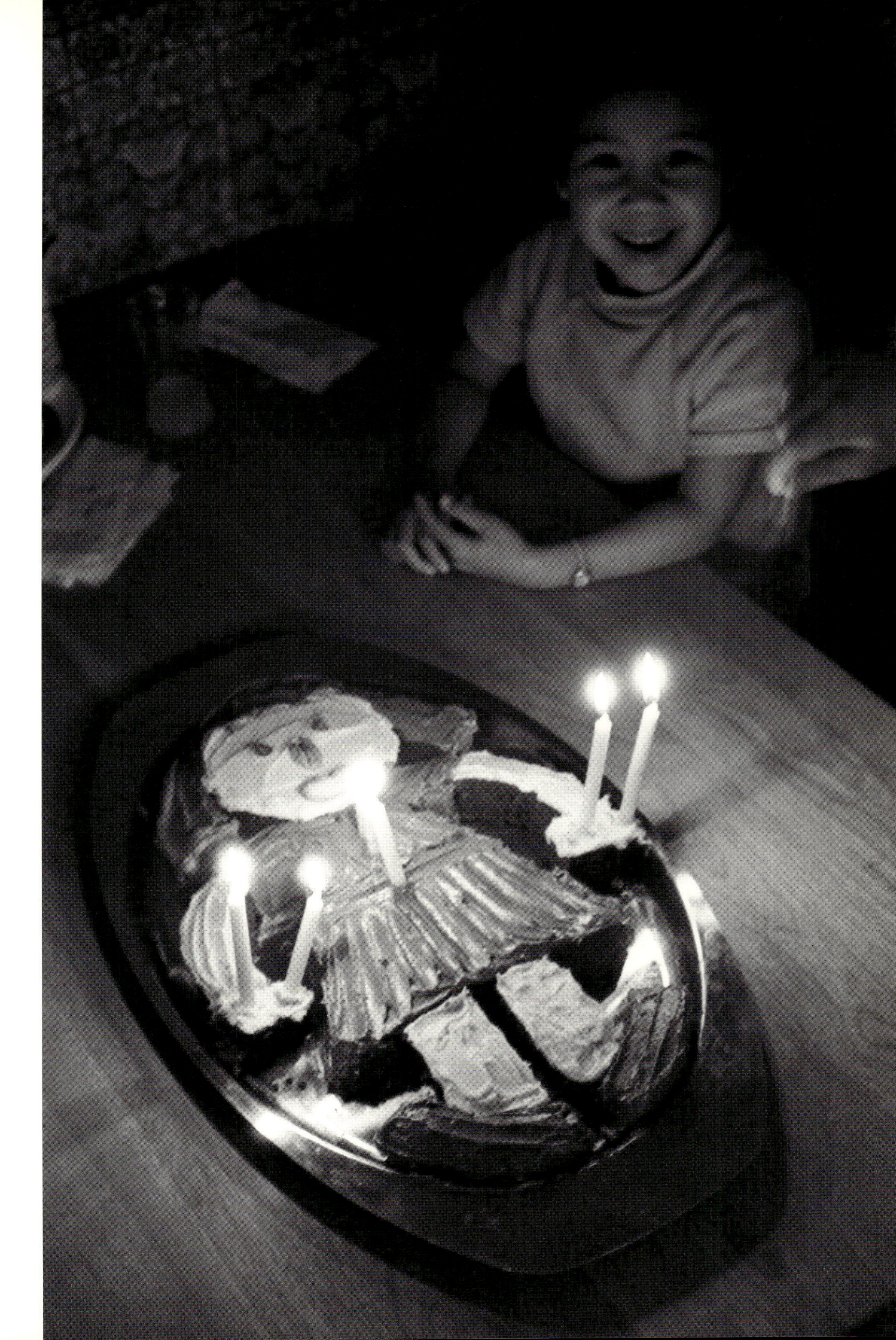

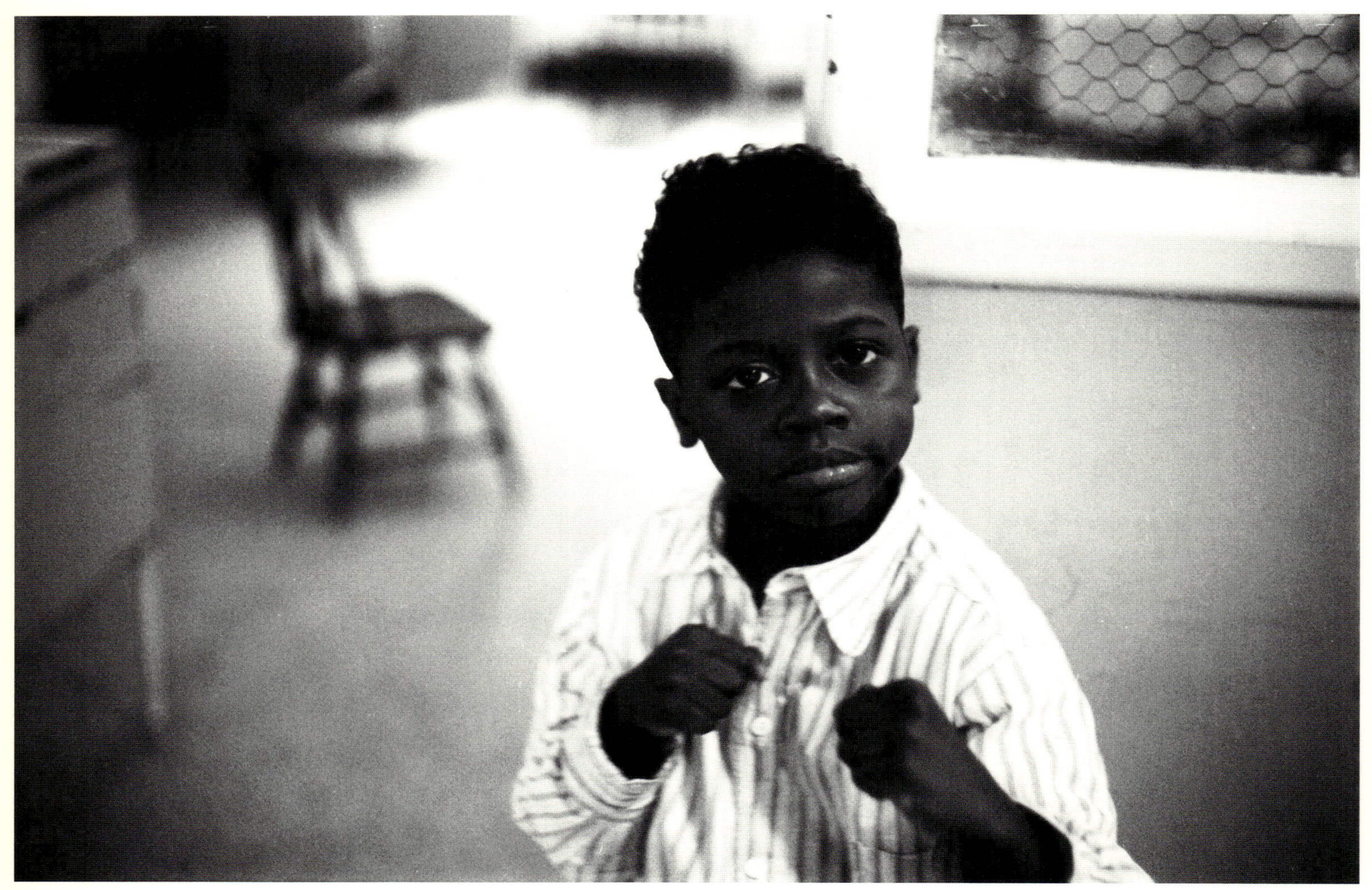

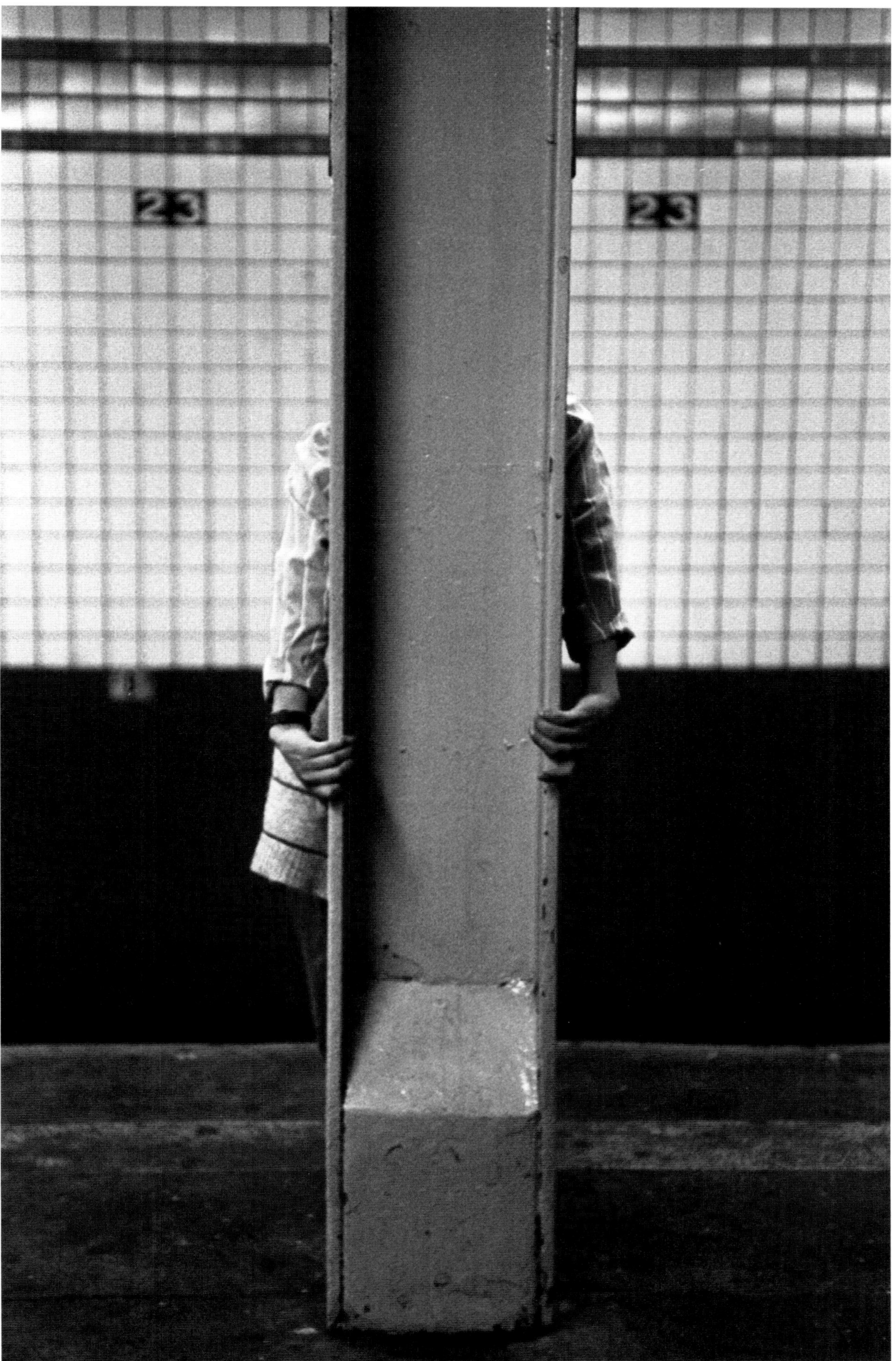
23
23

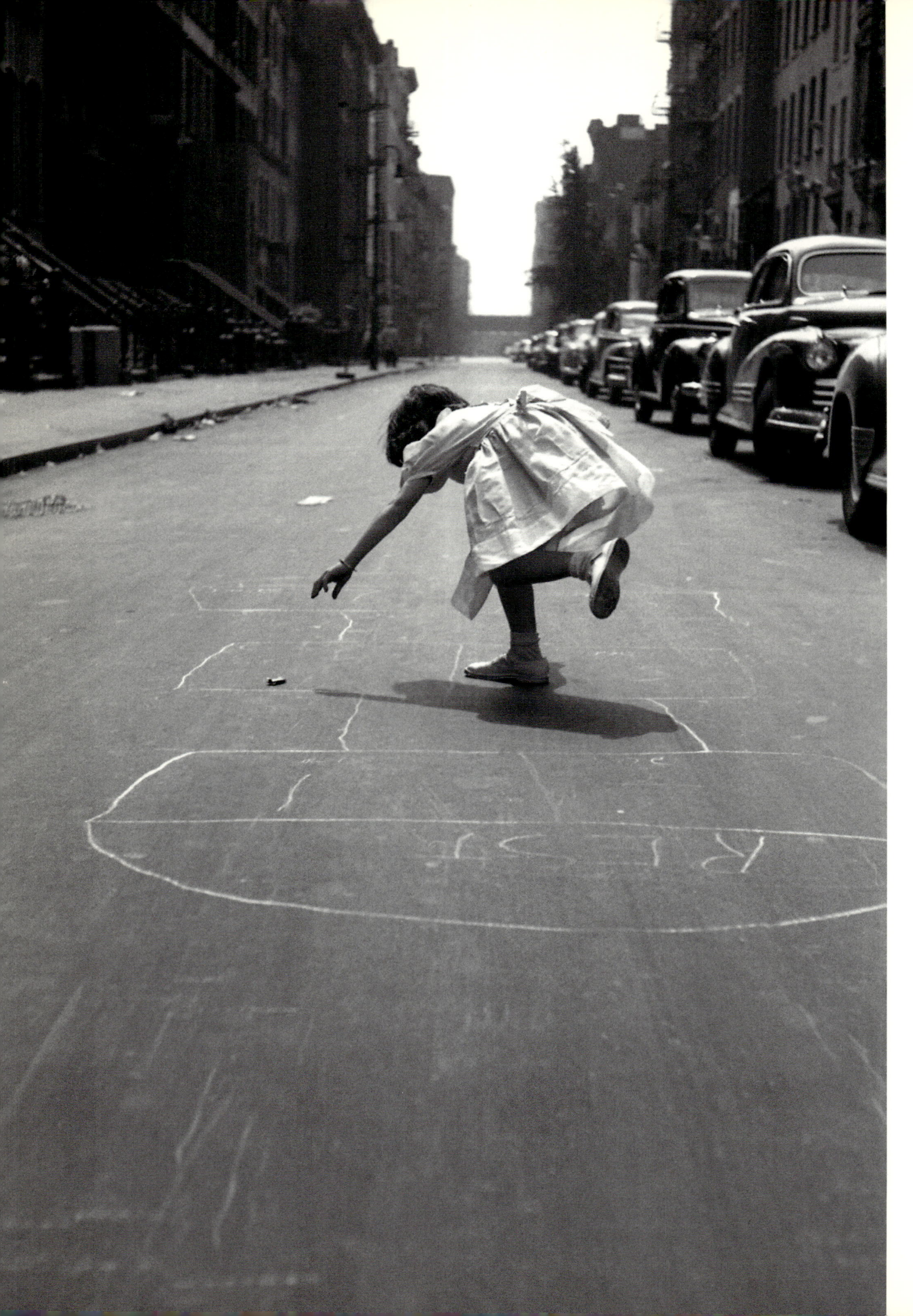

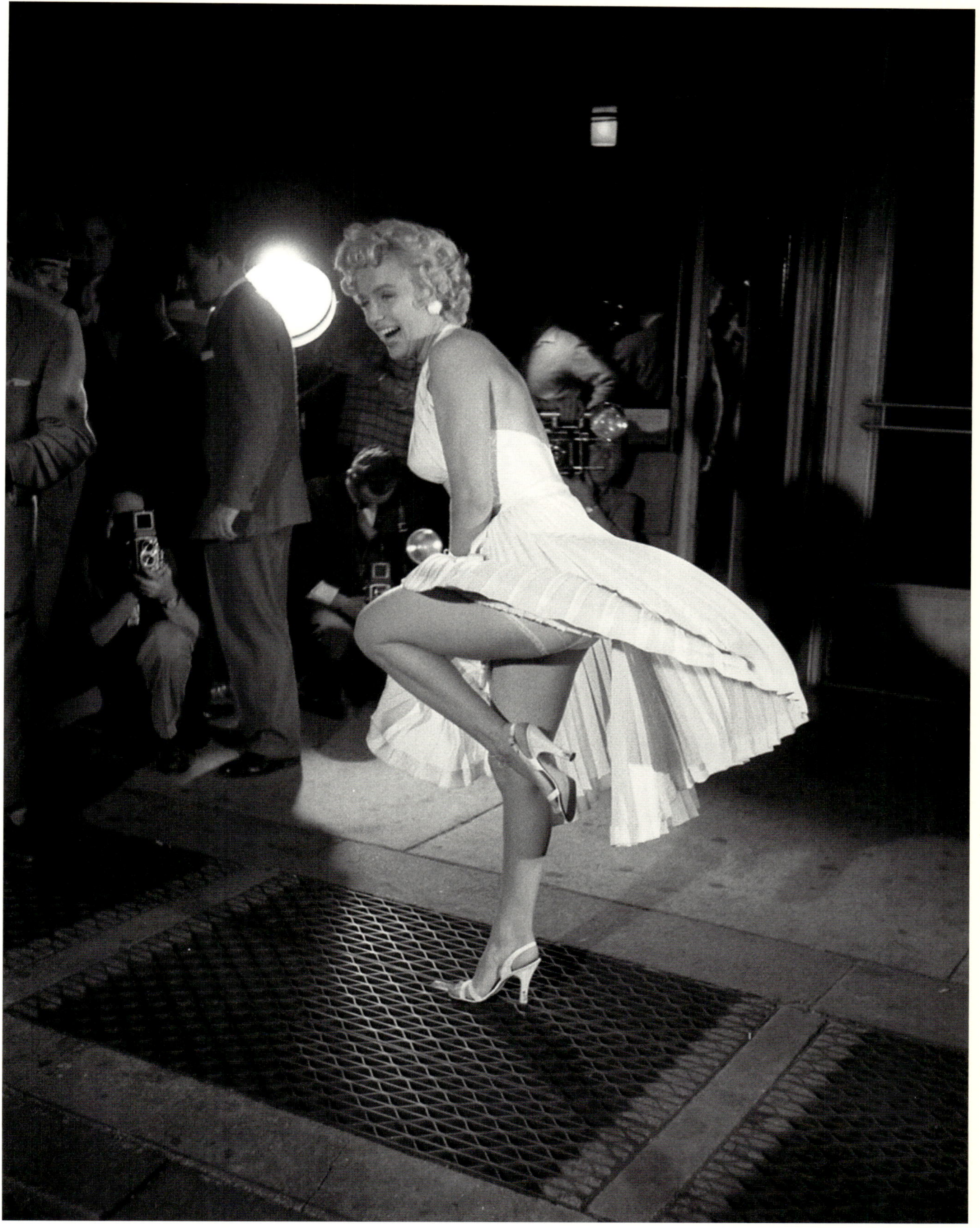

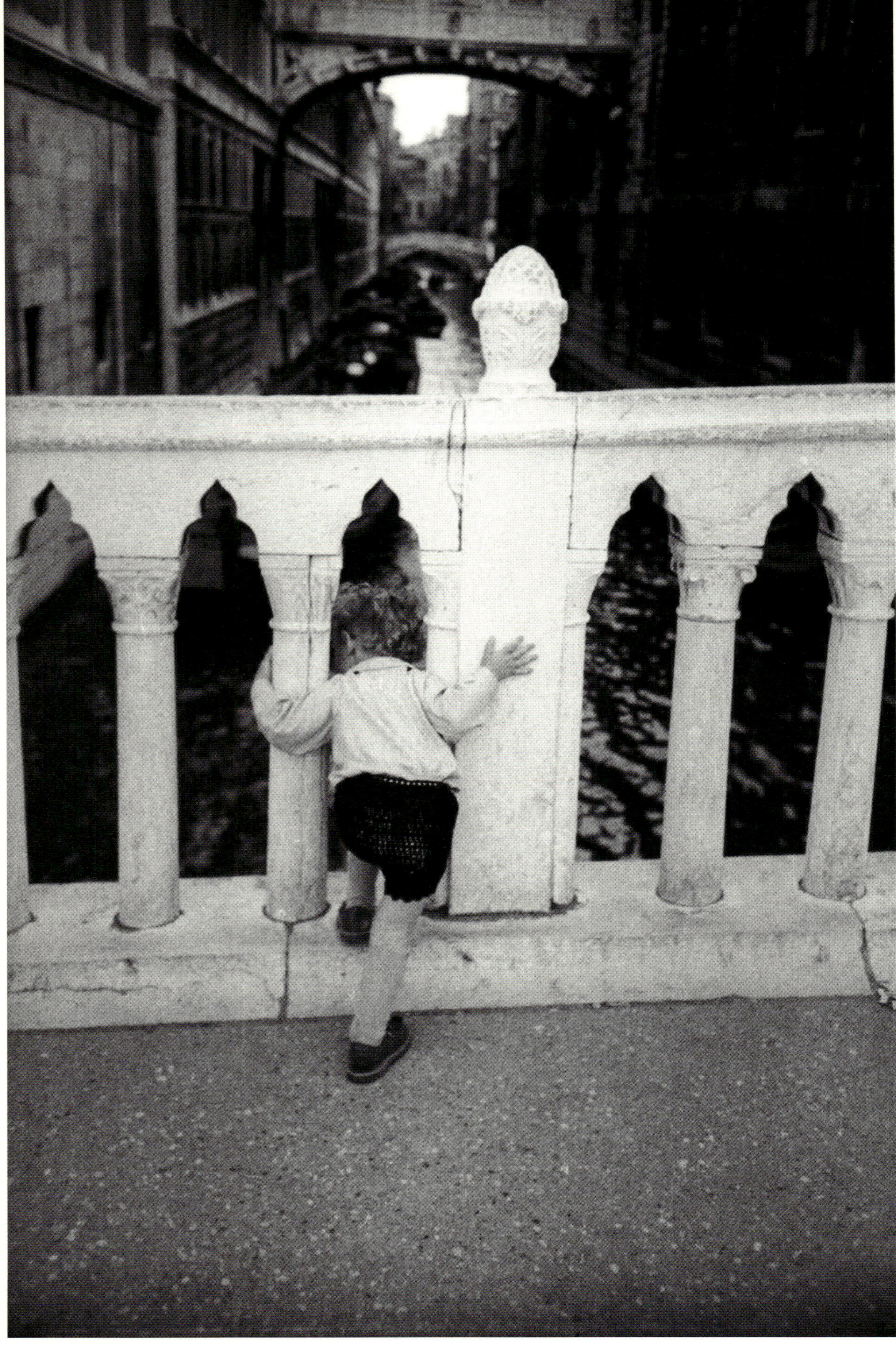

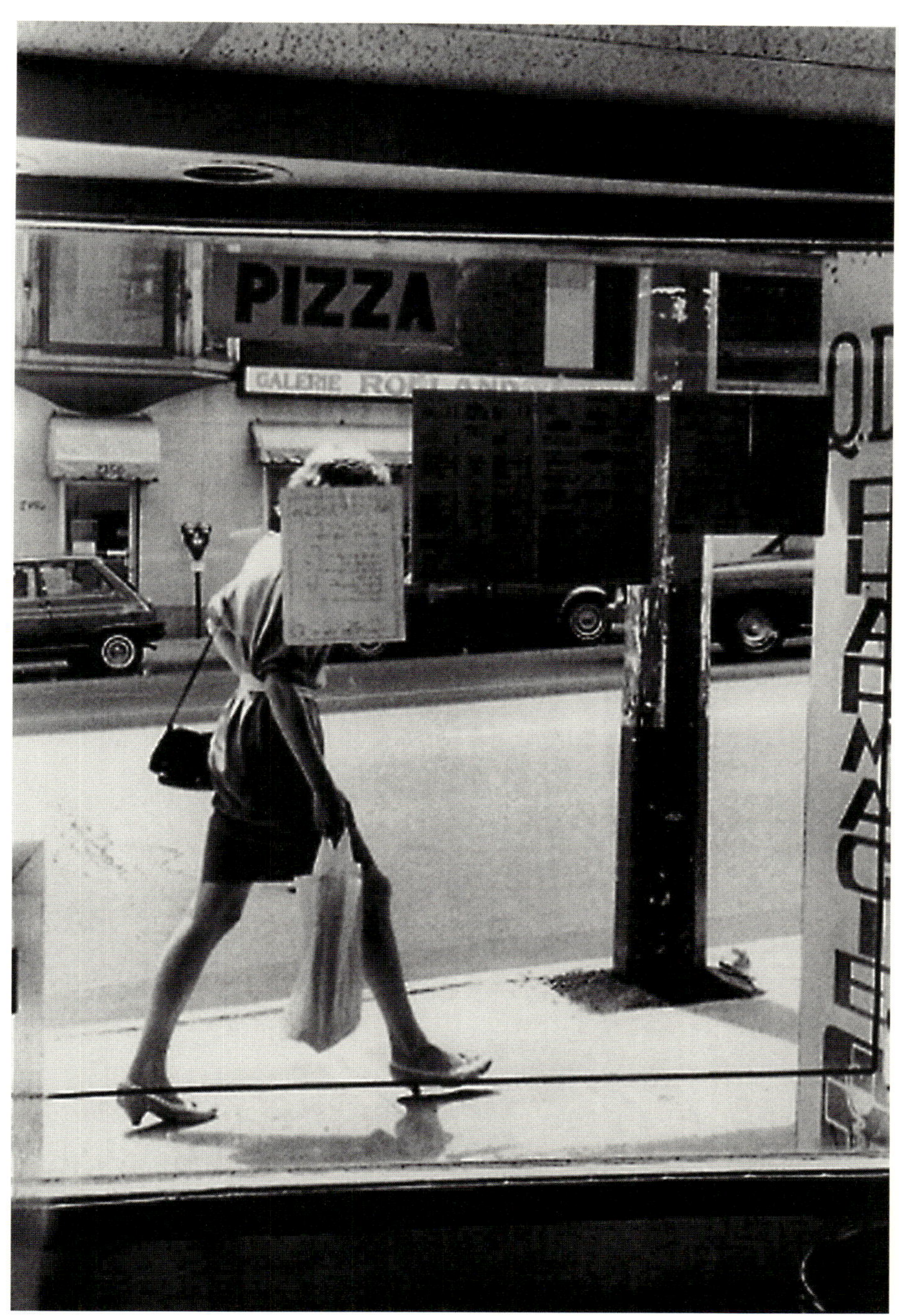
PIZZA
GALERIE

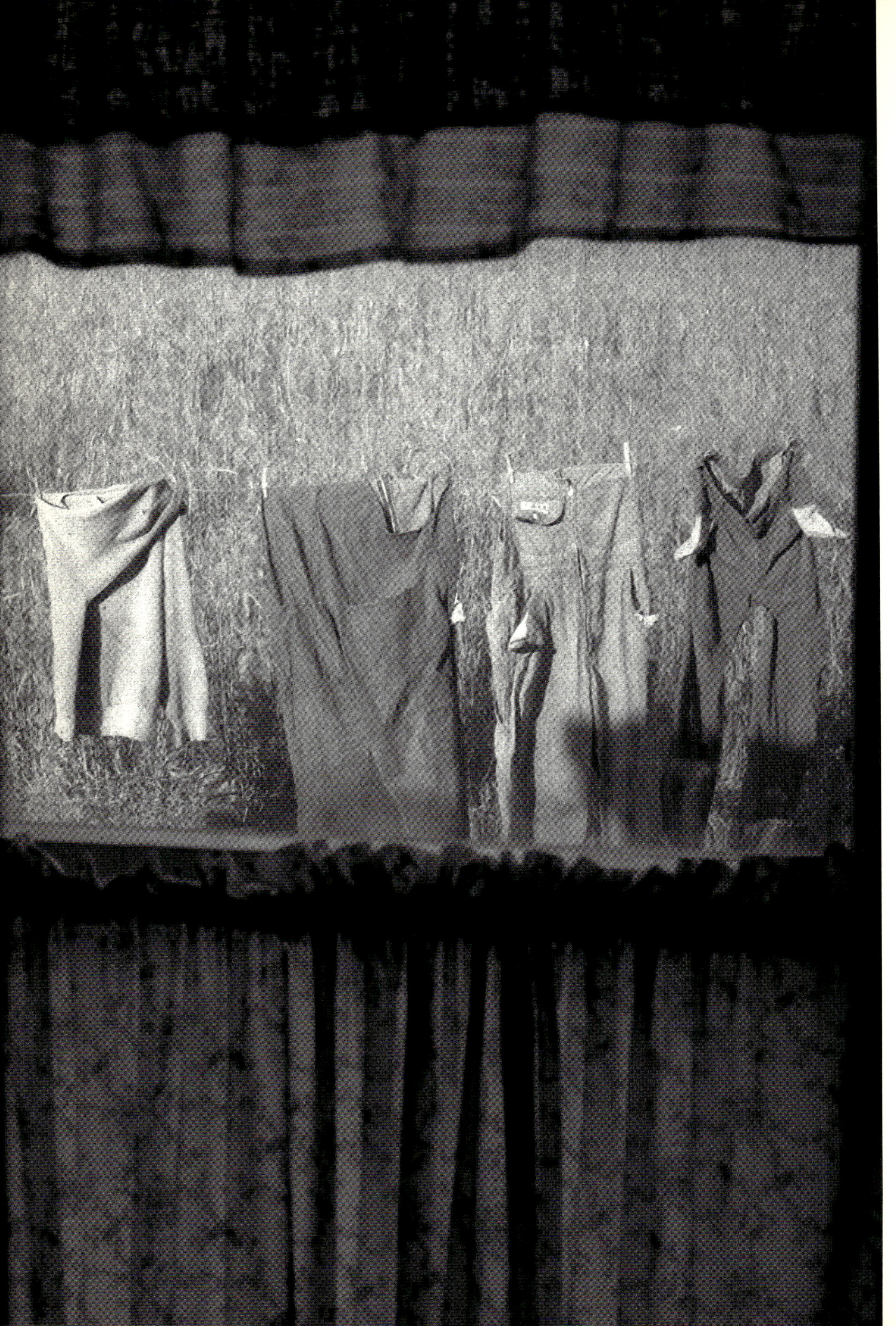

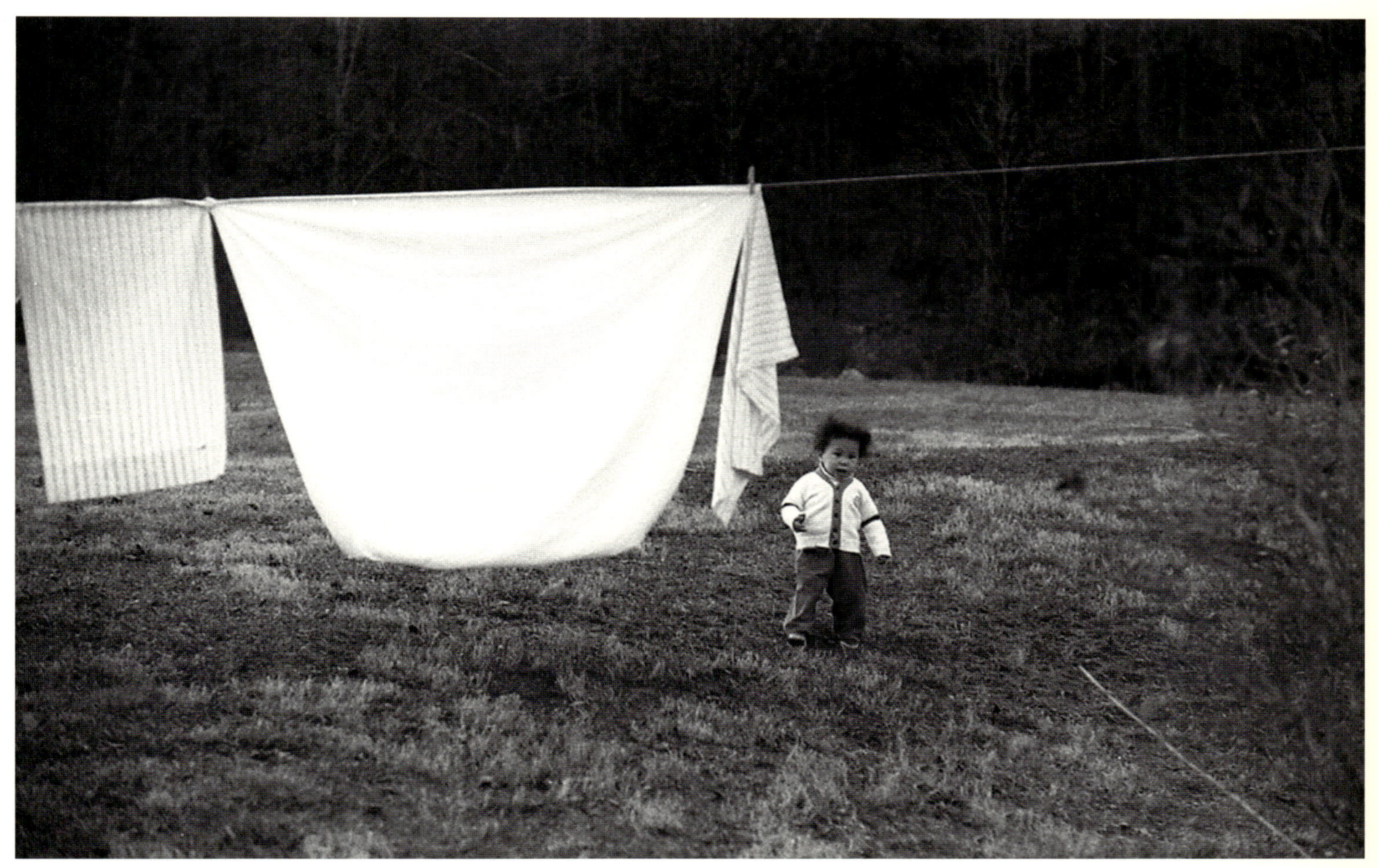

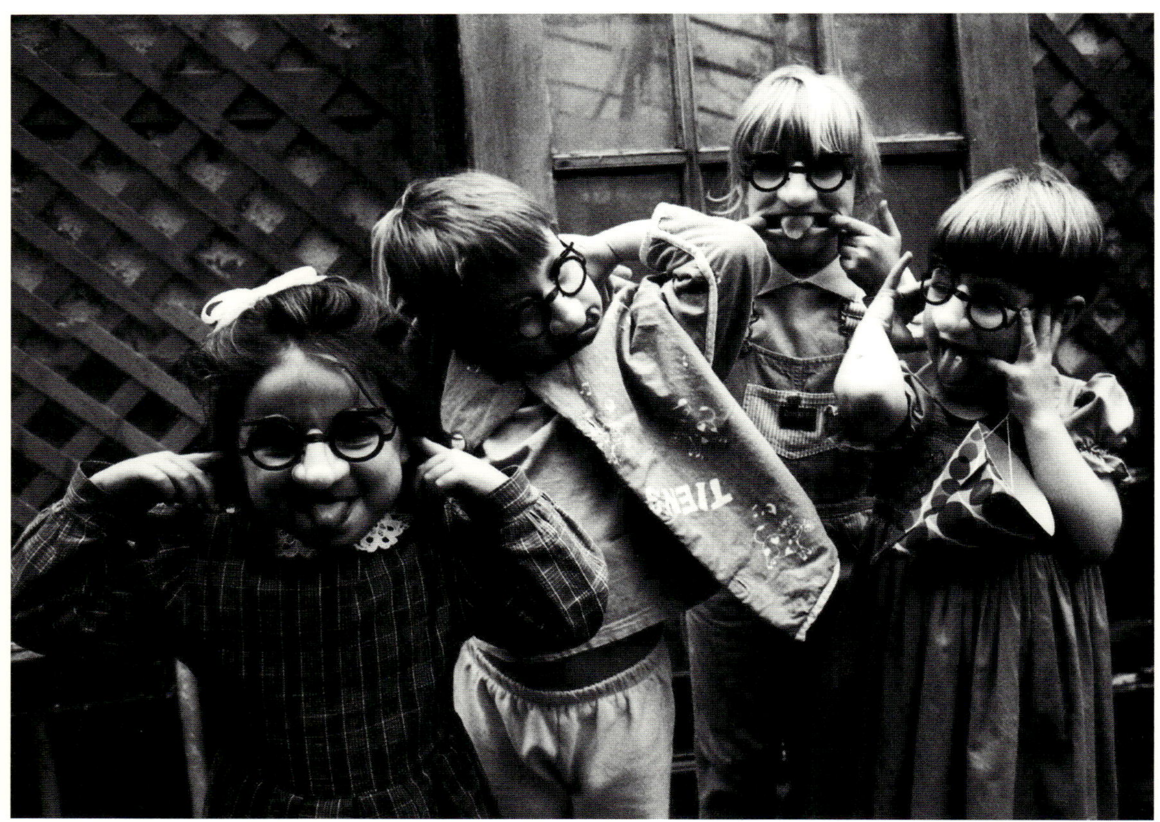

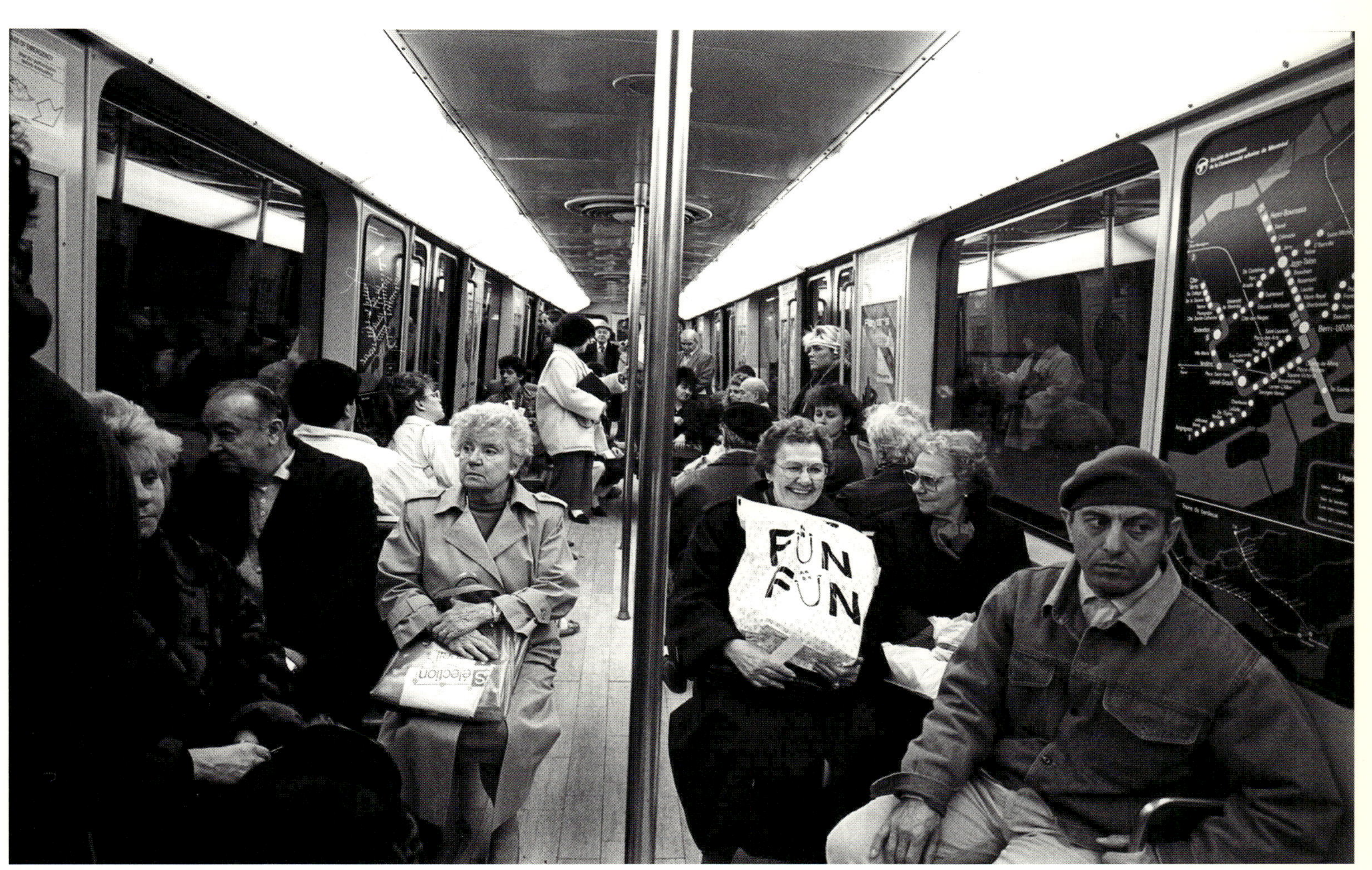
FUN
FUN

You don't feel misery, you don't feel that it's the end of the world, you don't feel that there is no reason to live anymore, it's the opposite.

Jean Bardaji, collector

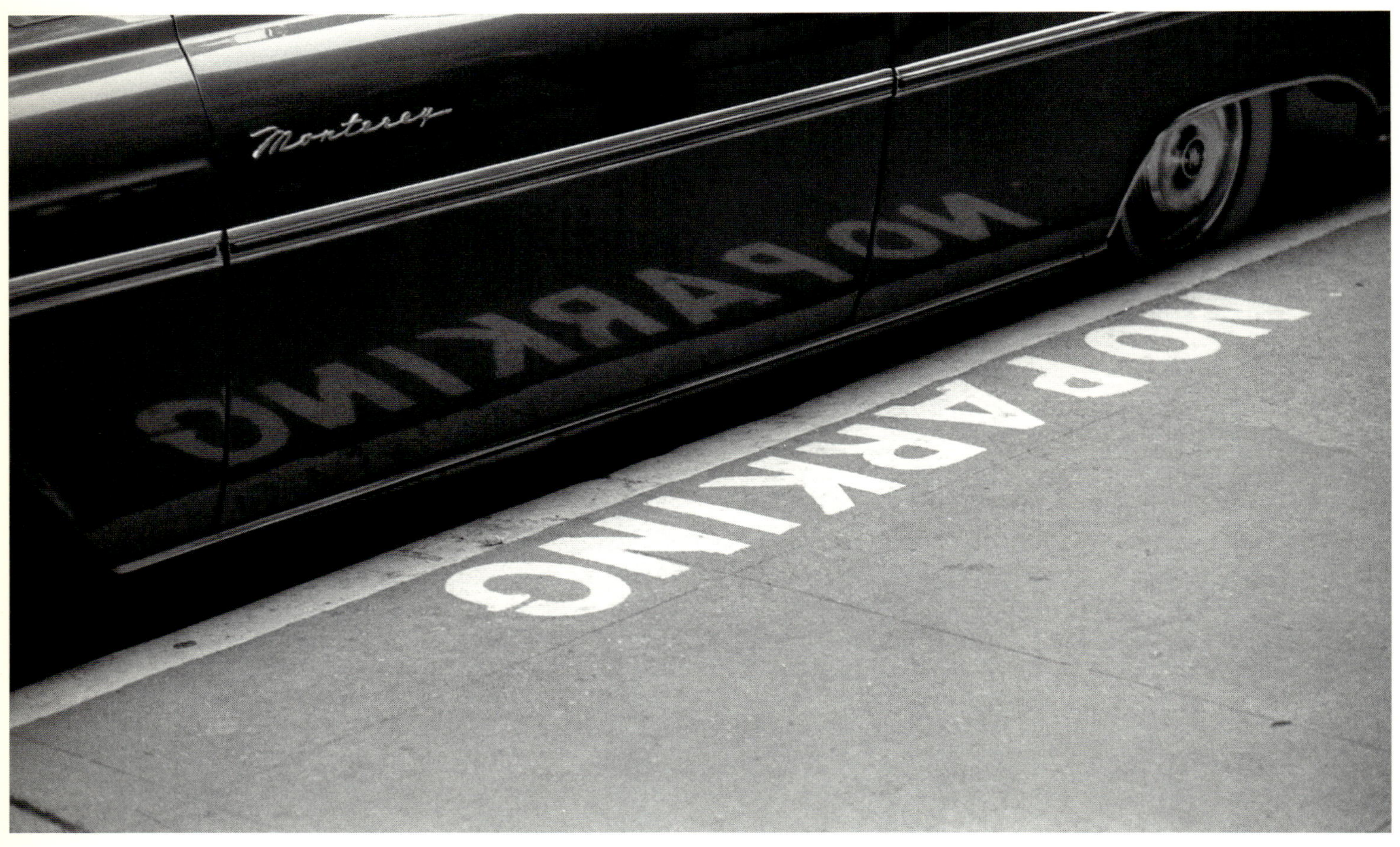
Monterey
NO PARKING

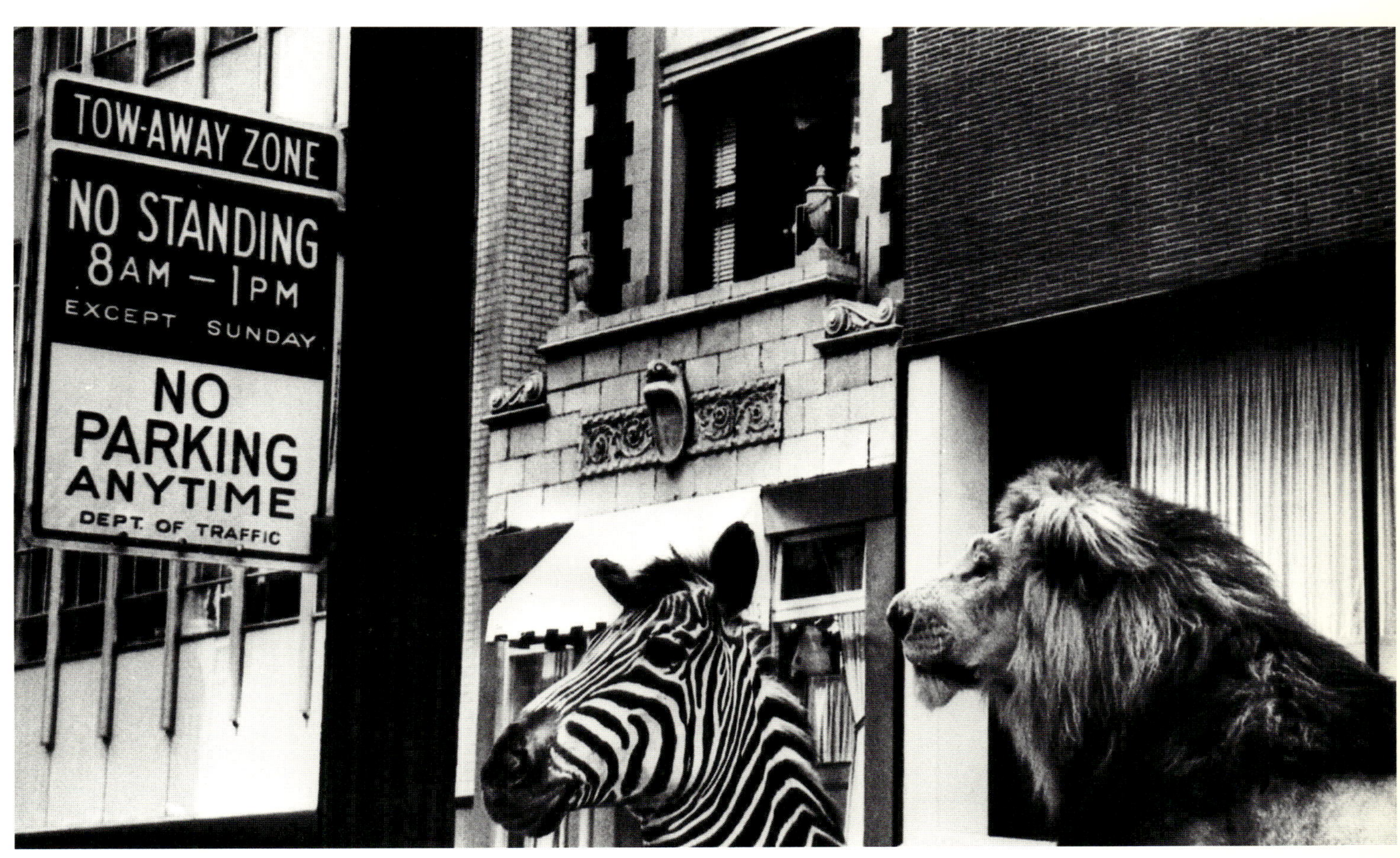
TOW-AWAY ZONE
NO STANDING
8AM – 1PM
EXCEPT SUNDAY
NO
PARKING
ANYTIME
DEPT. OF TRAFFIC

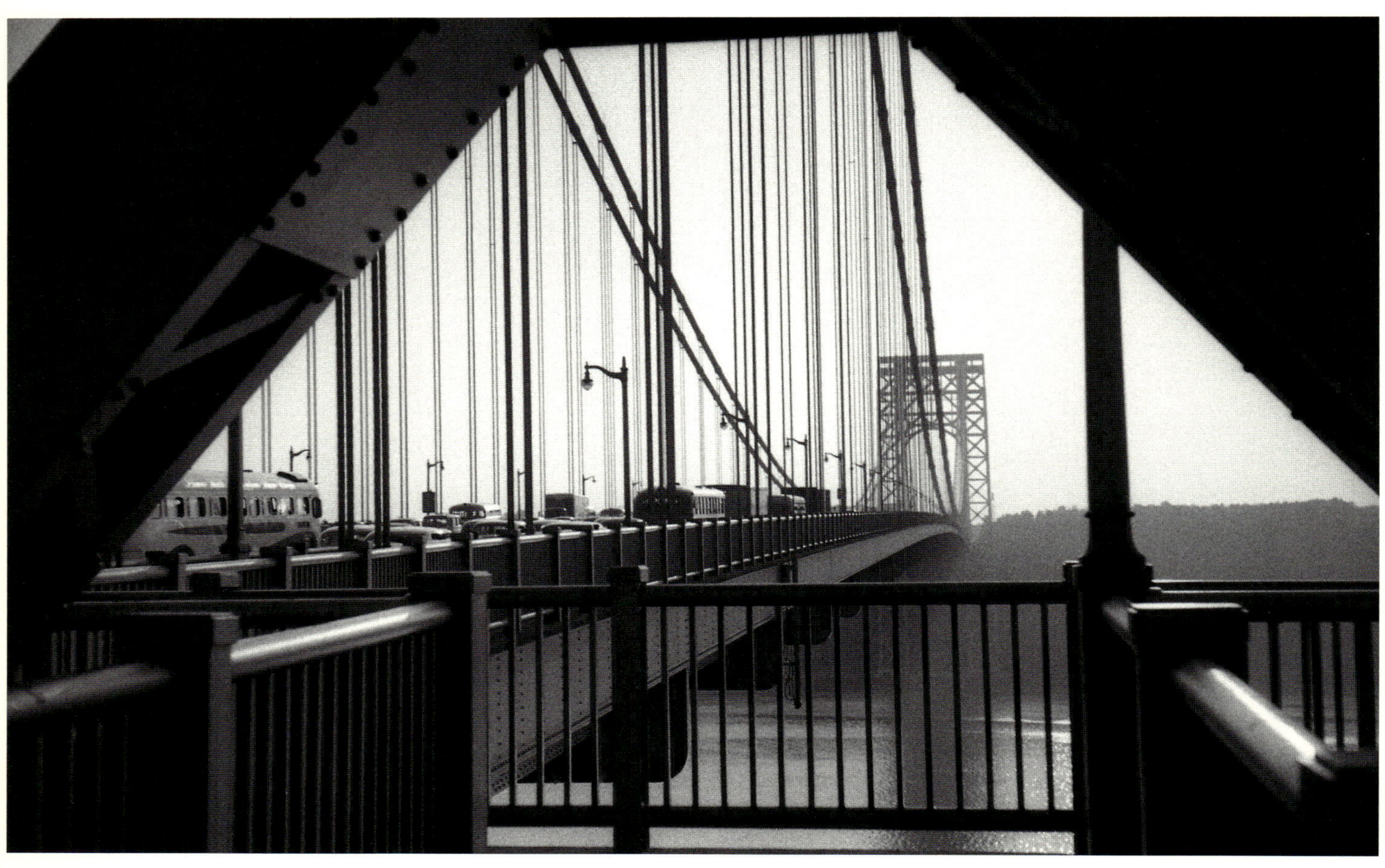

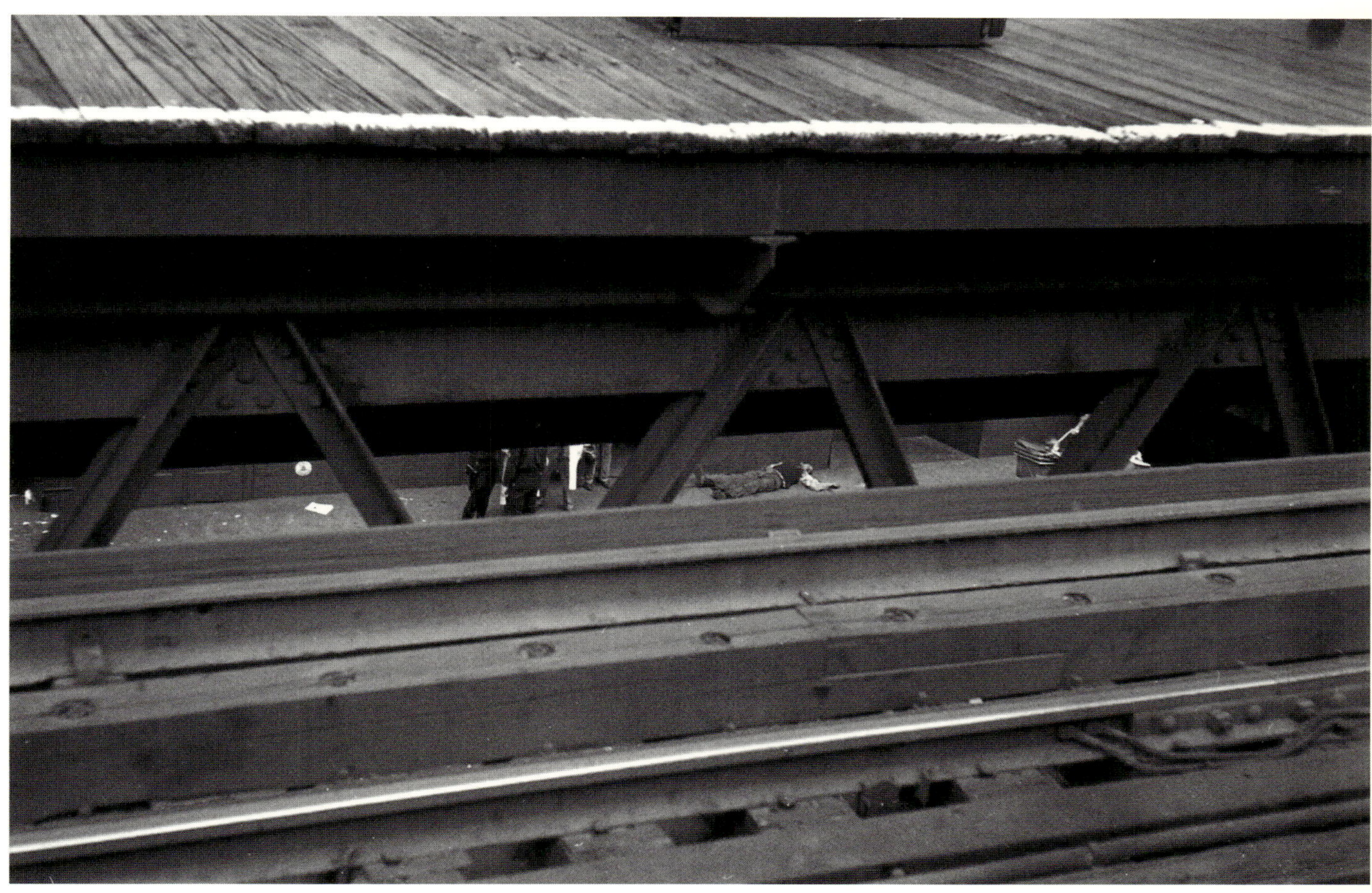

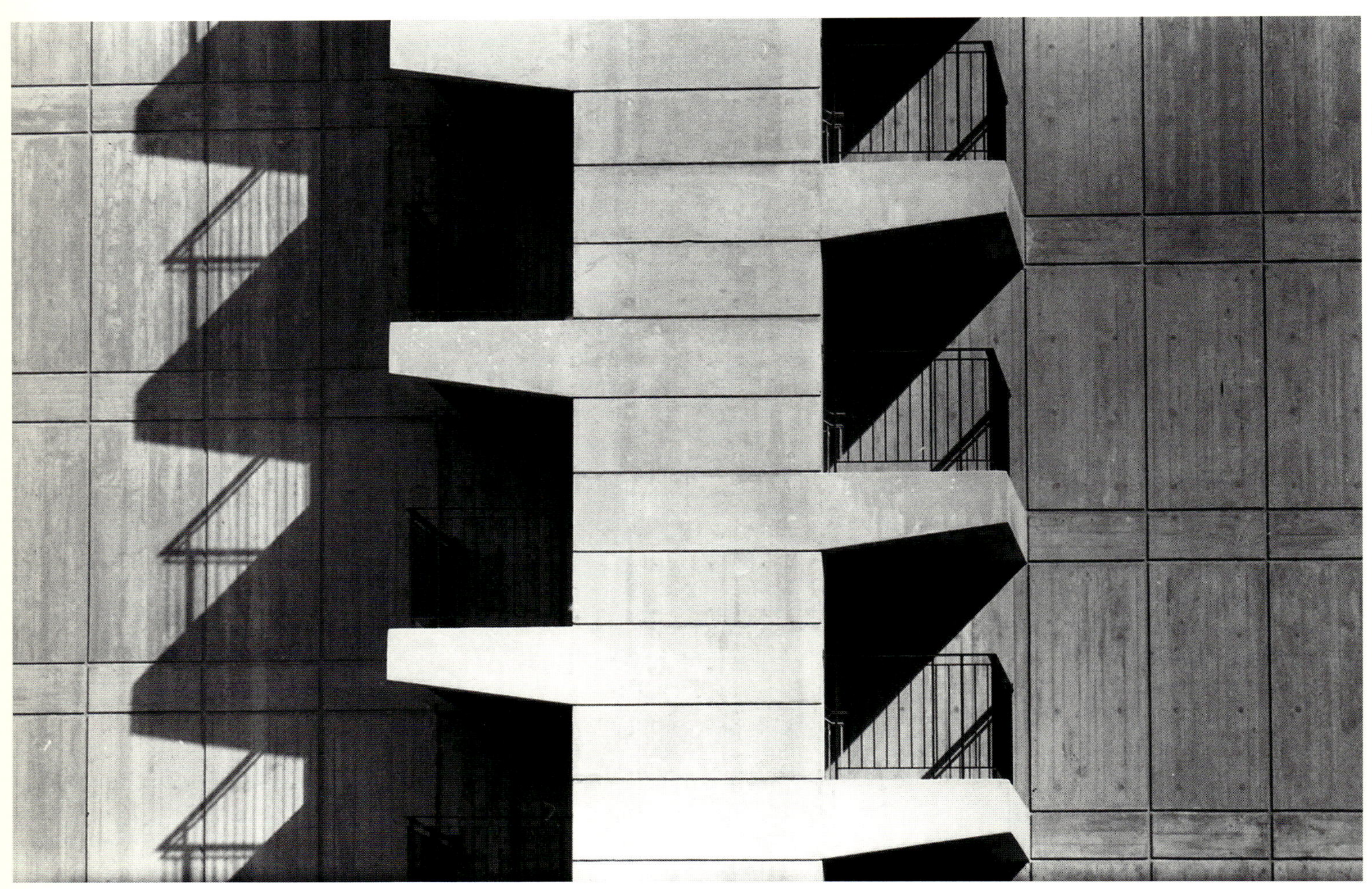

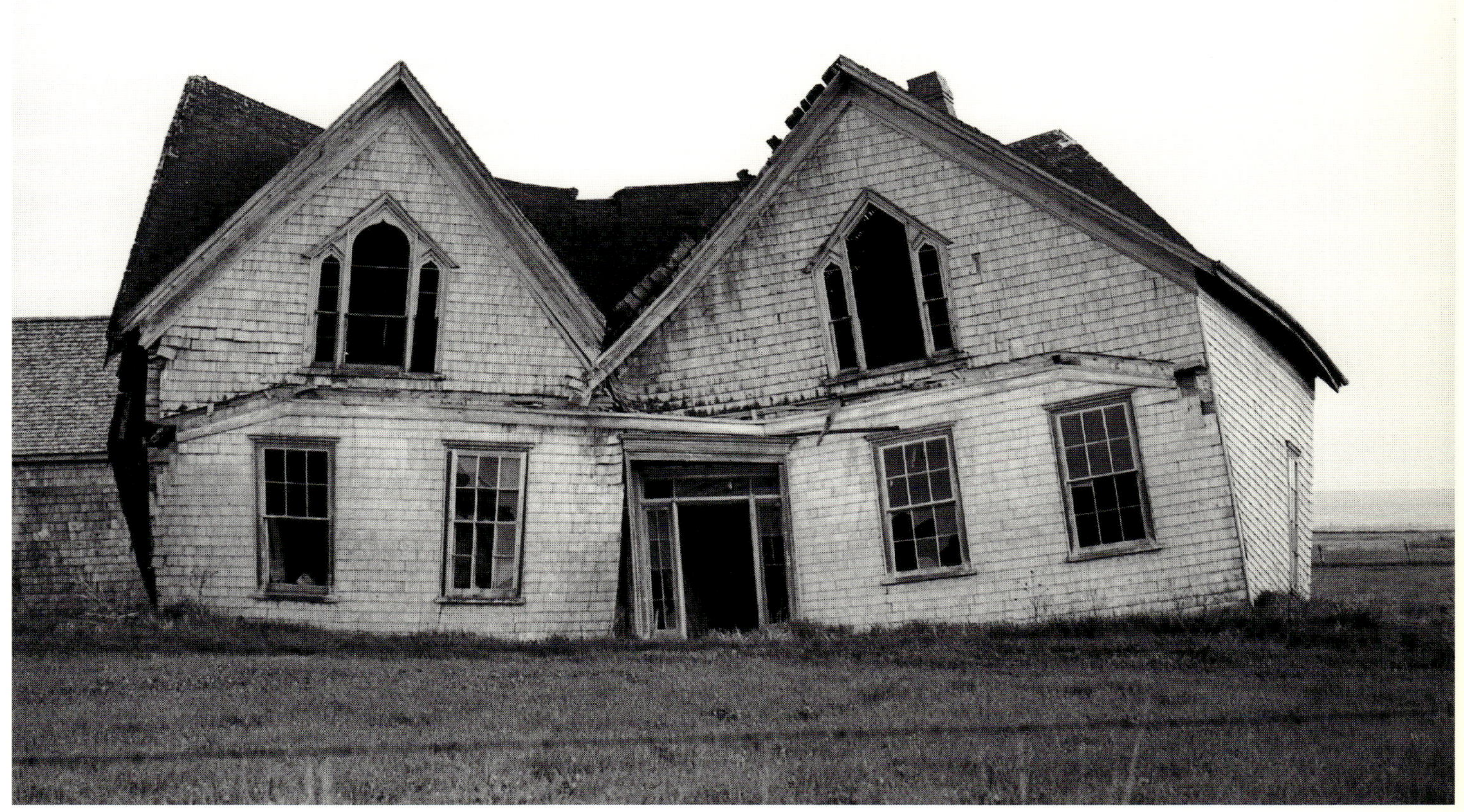

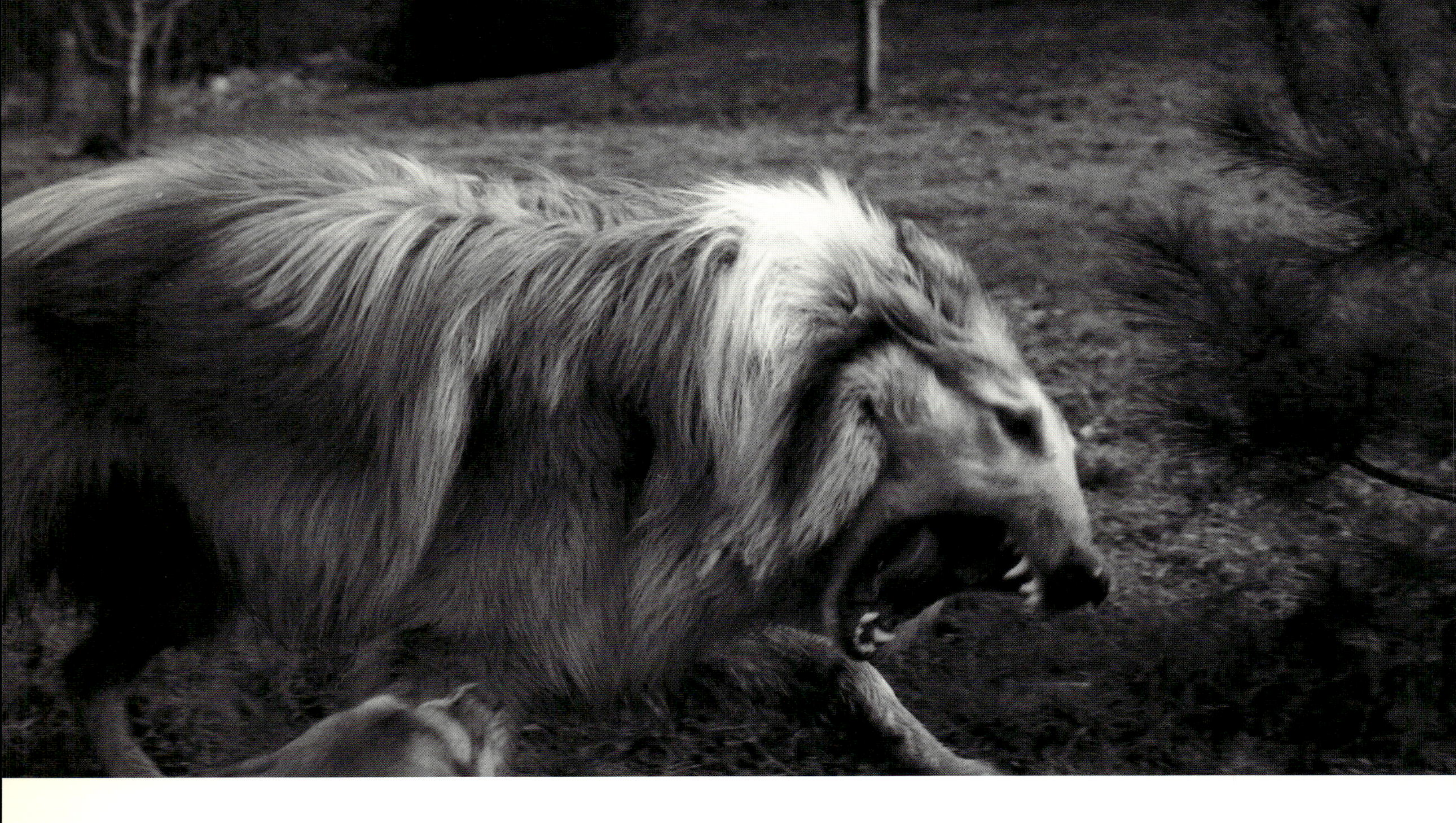

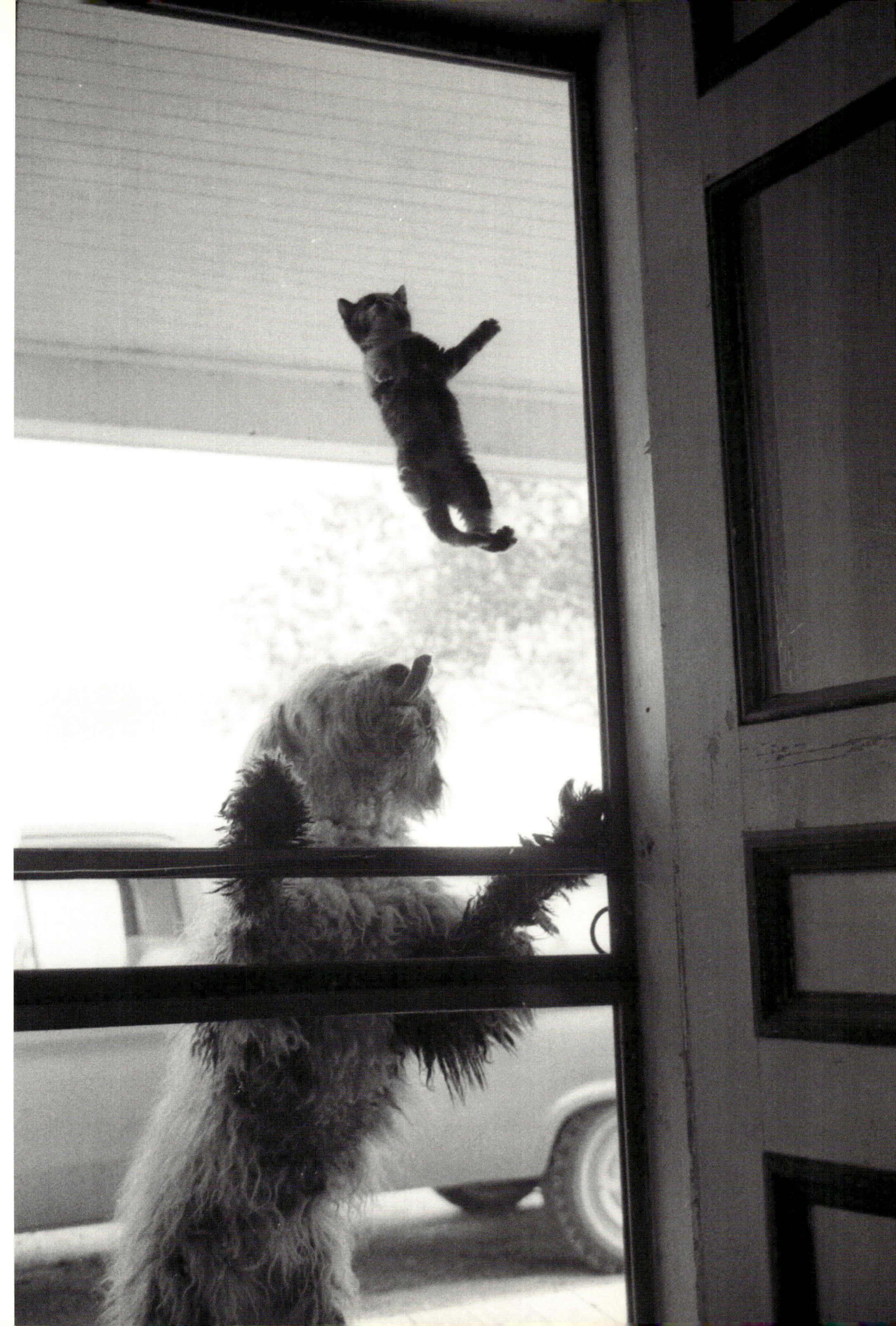

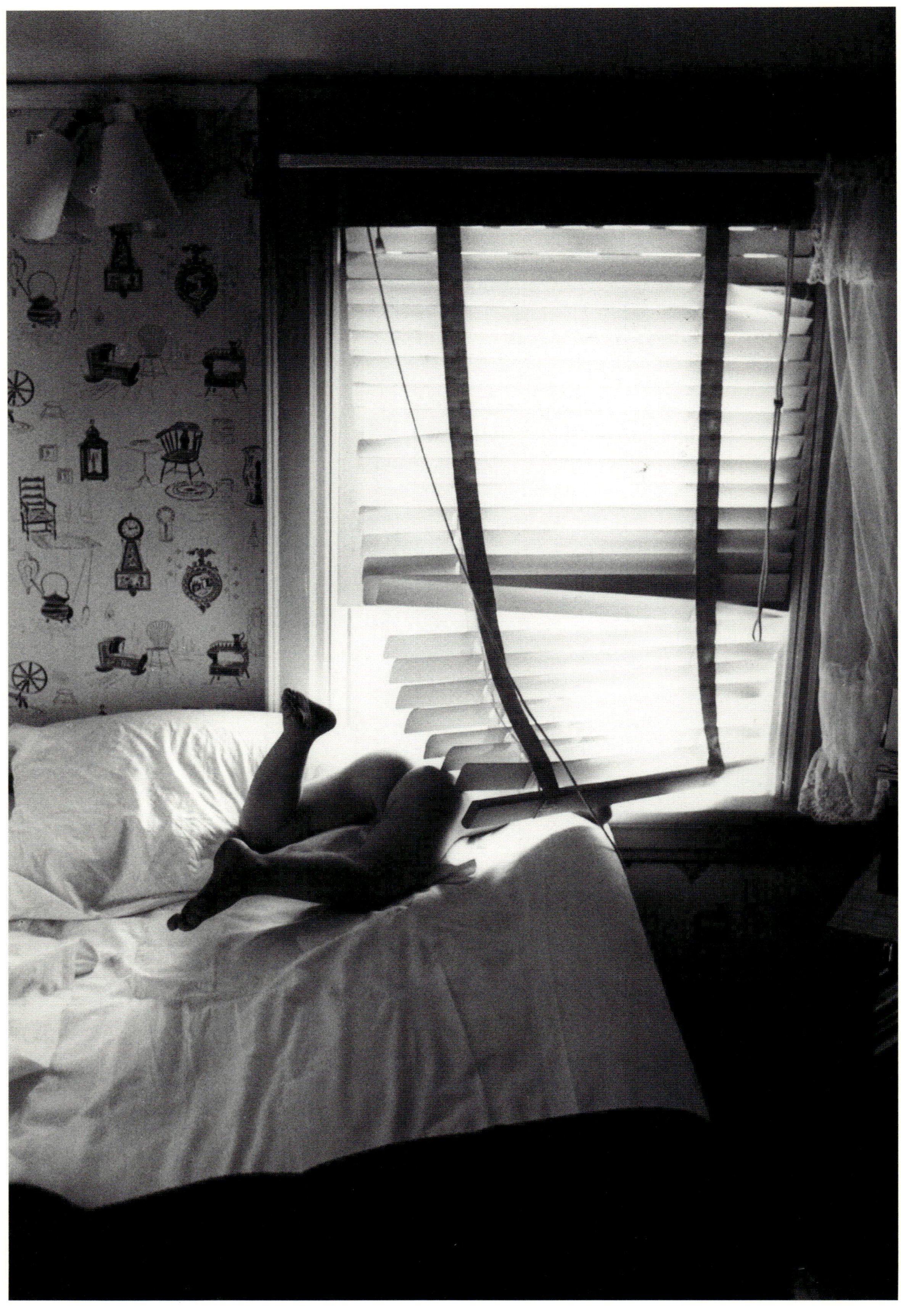

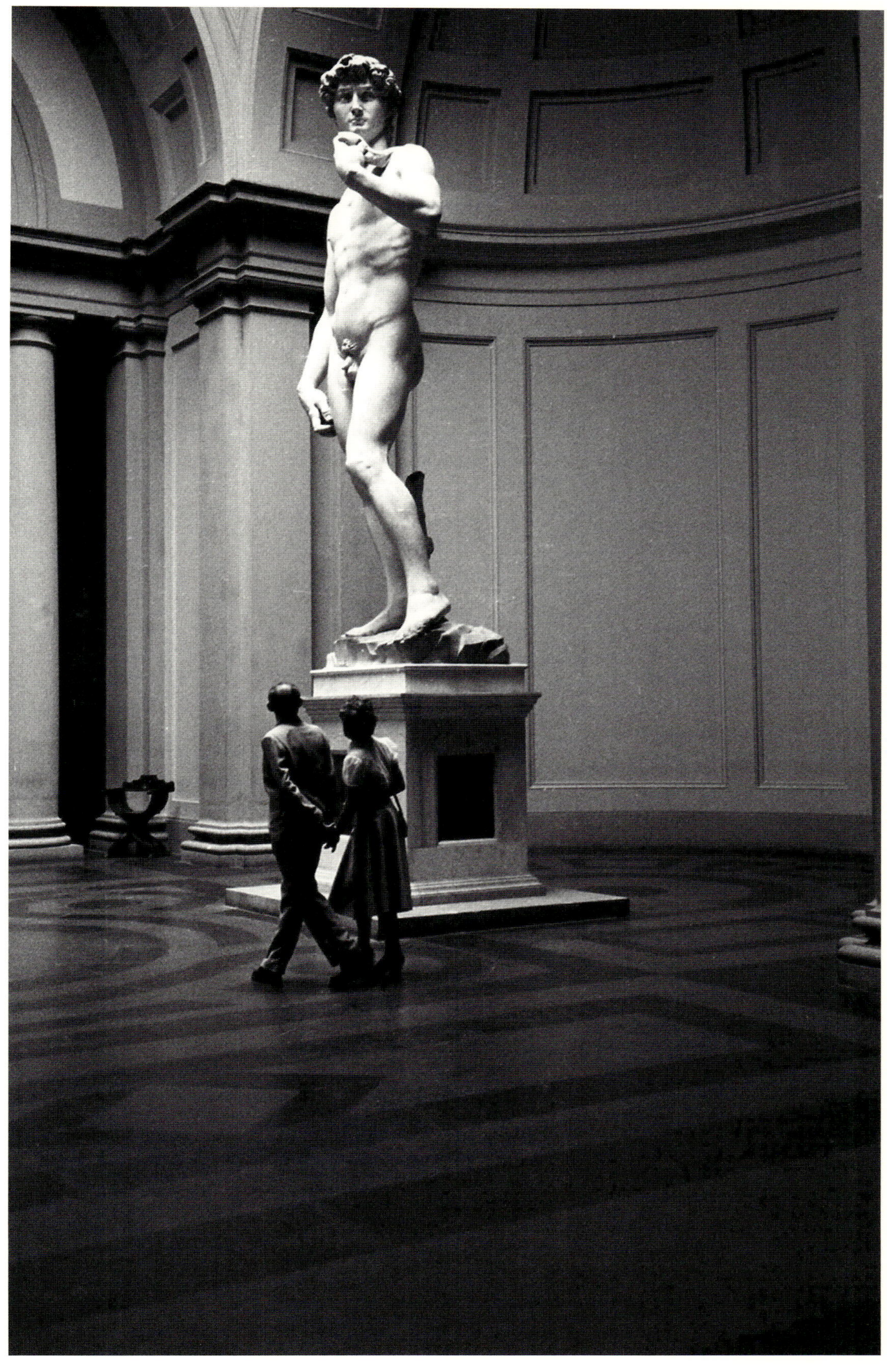

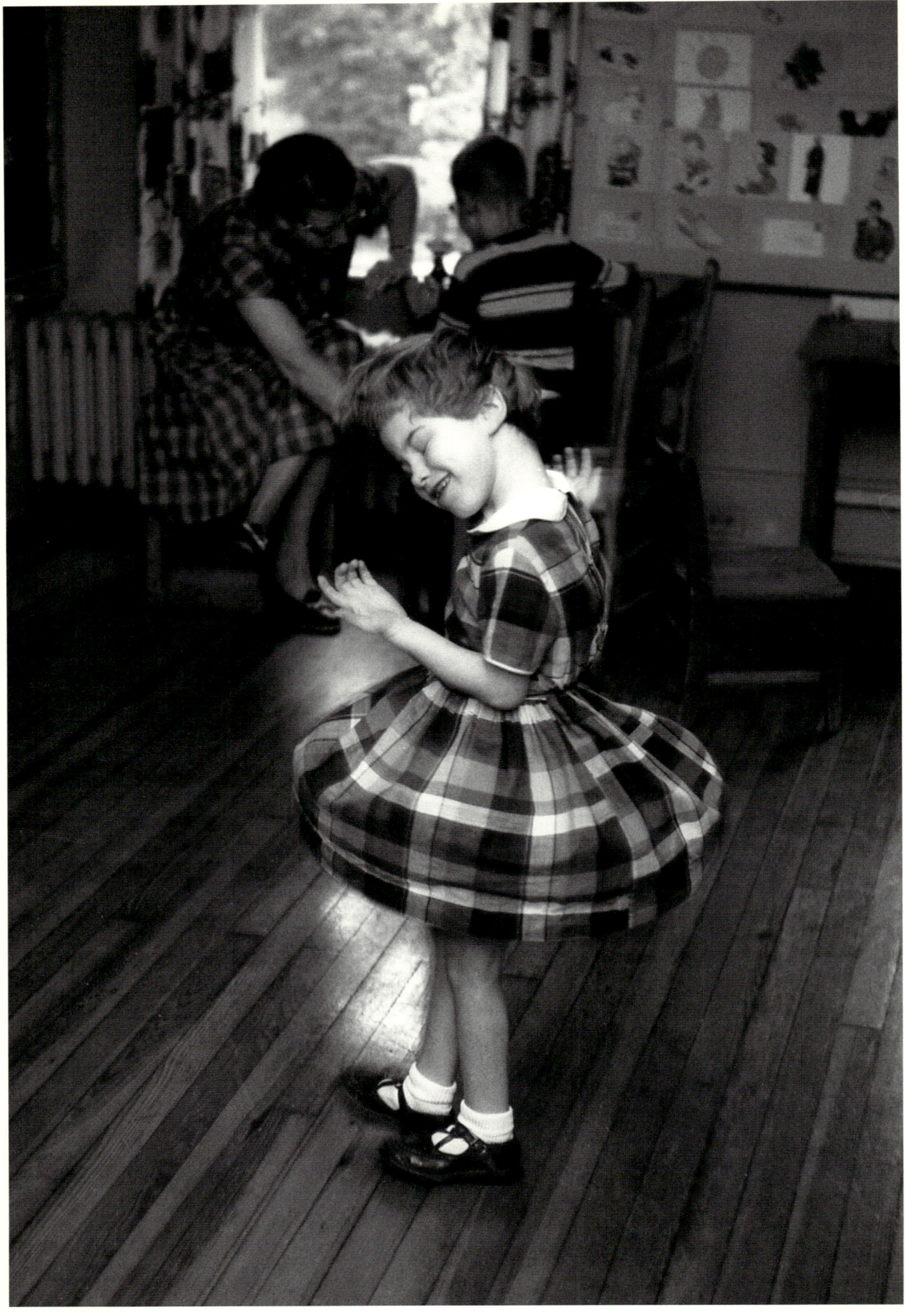

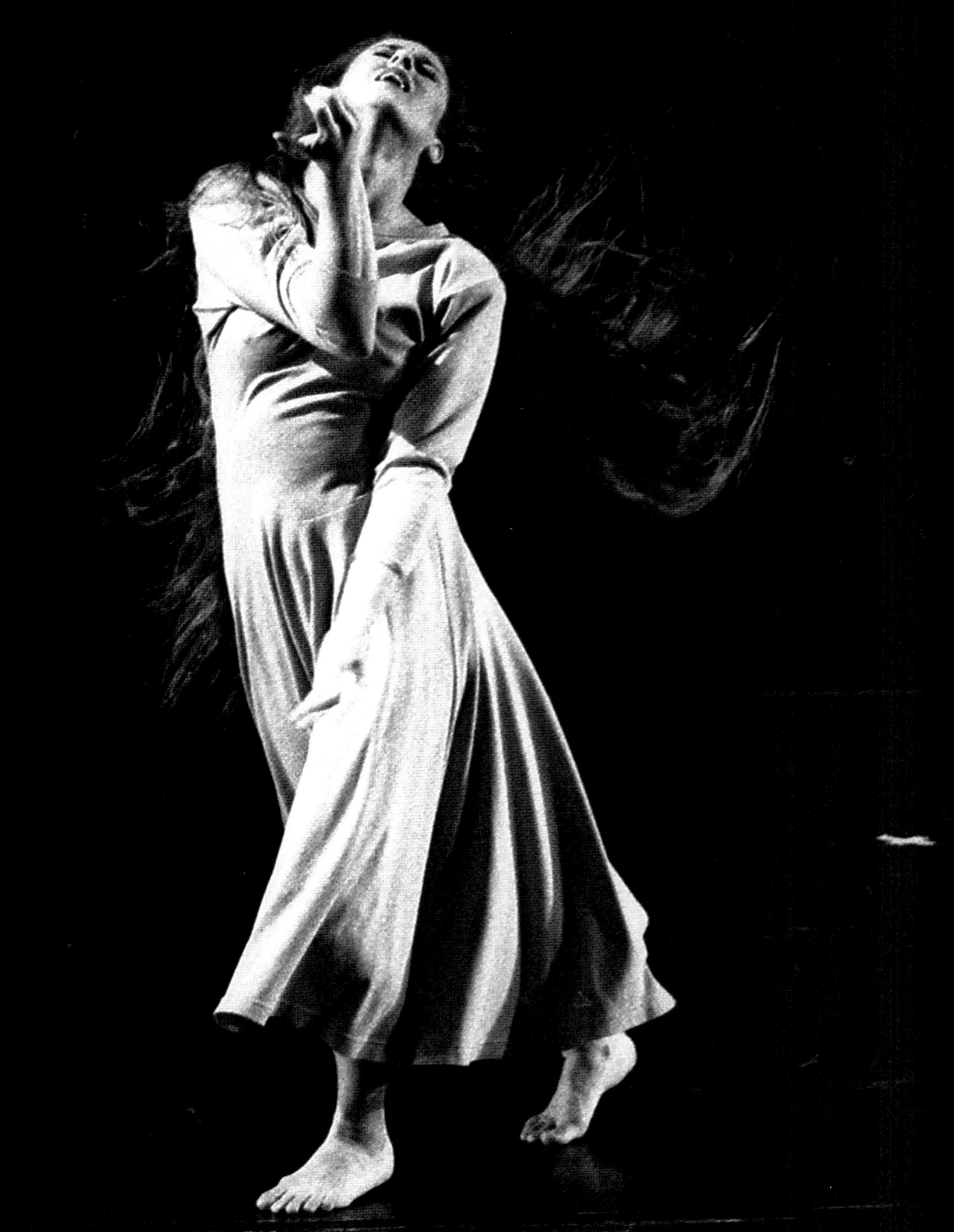

His approach is like that of an anthropologist, he searches to show the world what he sees and it is a very personal point of view. His work has an opinion.

Josep Monzo, Former Curator, Institut Valencia d'Art Moderne

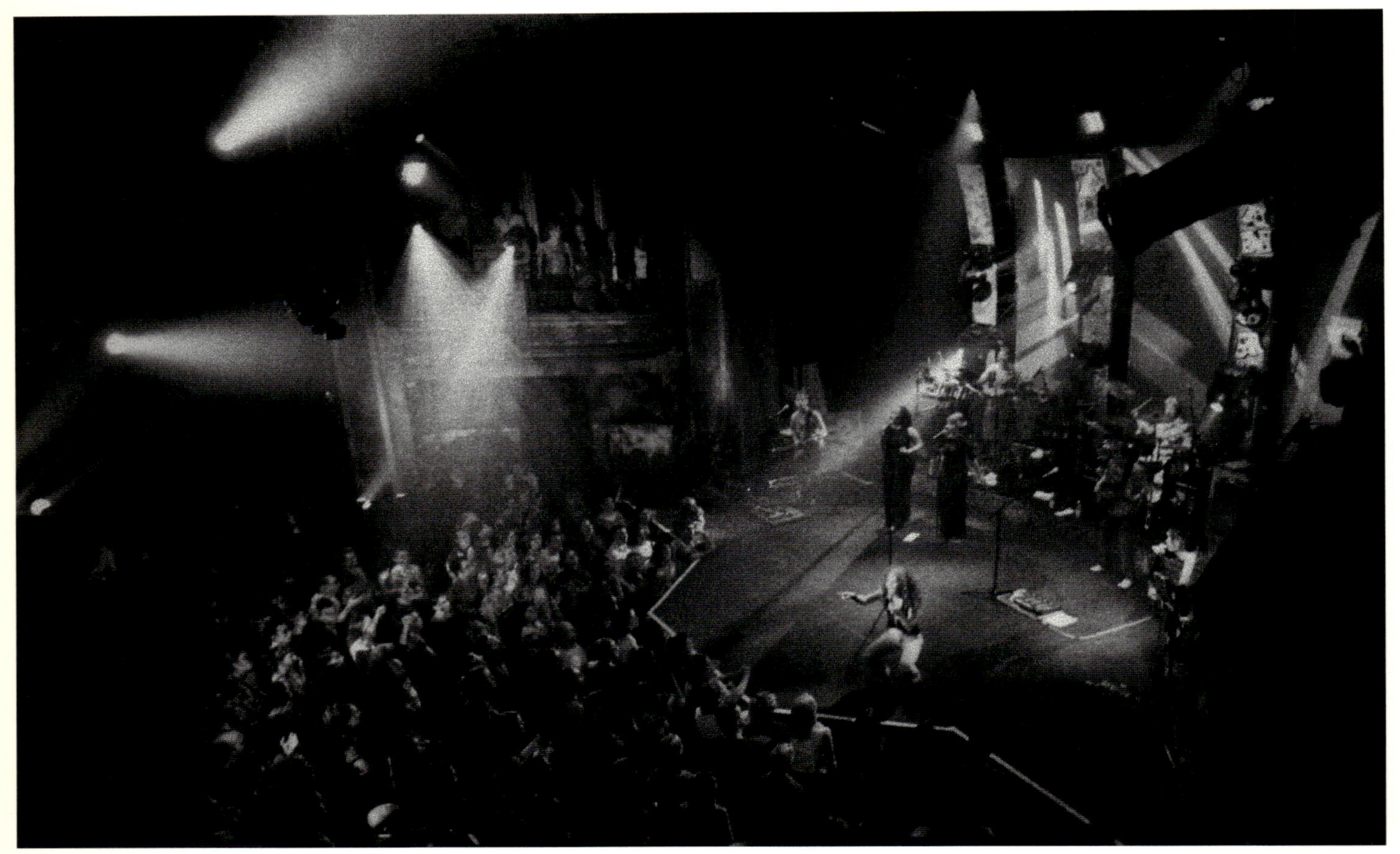

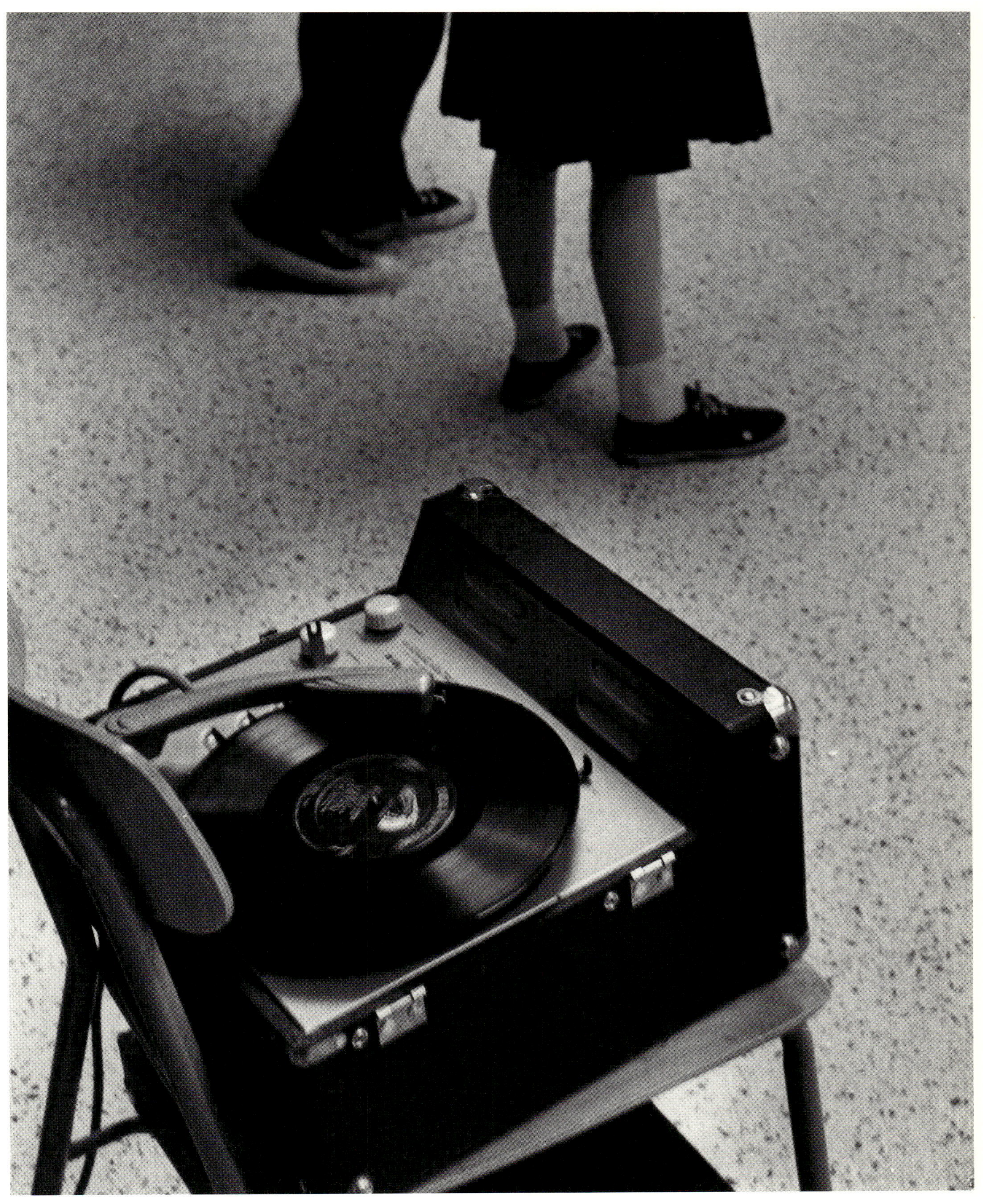

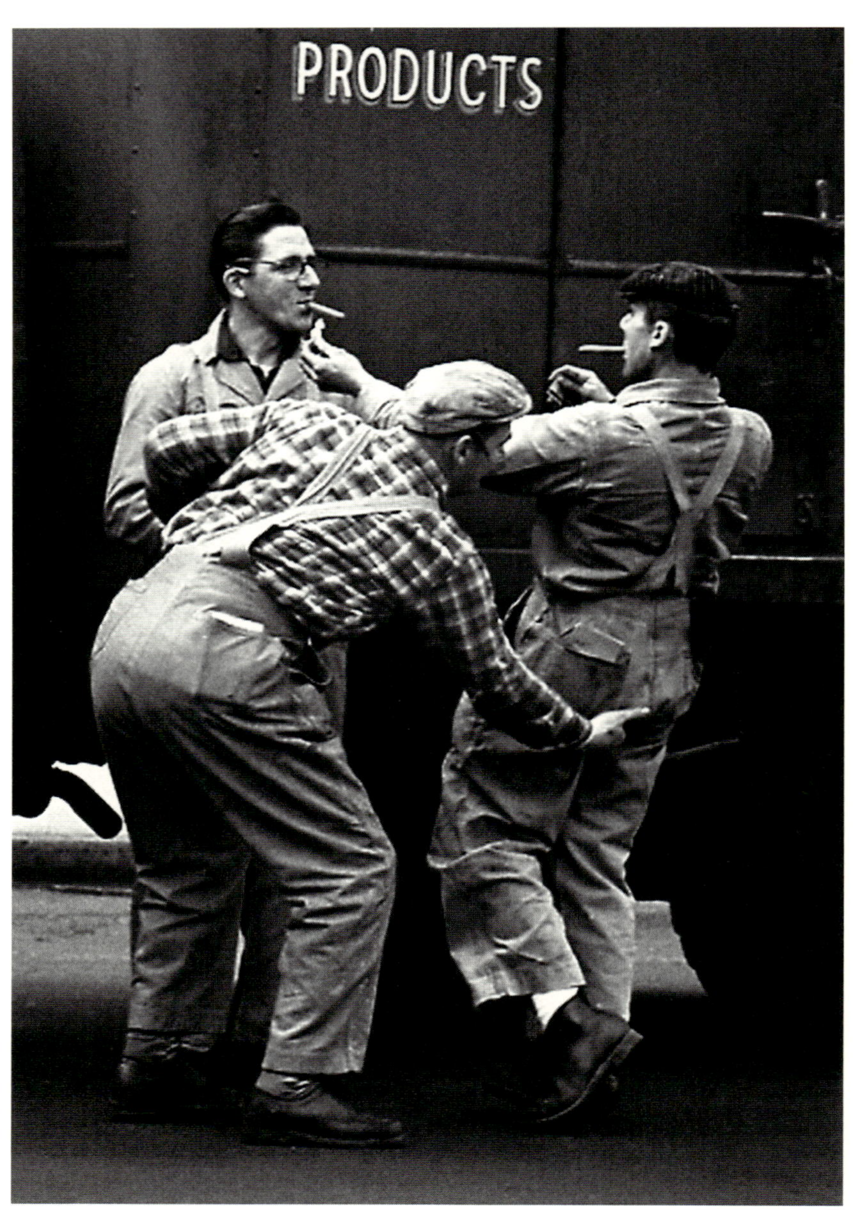
PRODUCTS

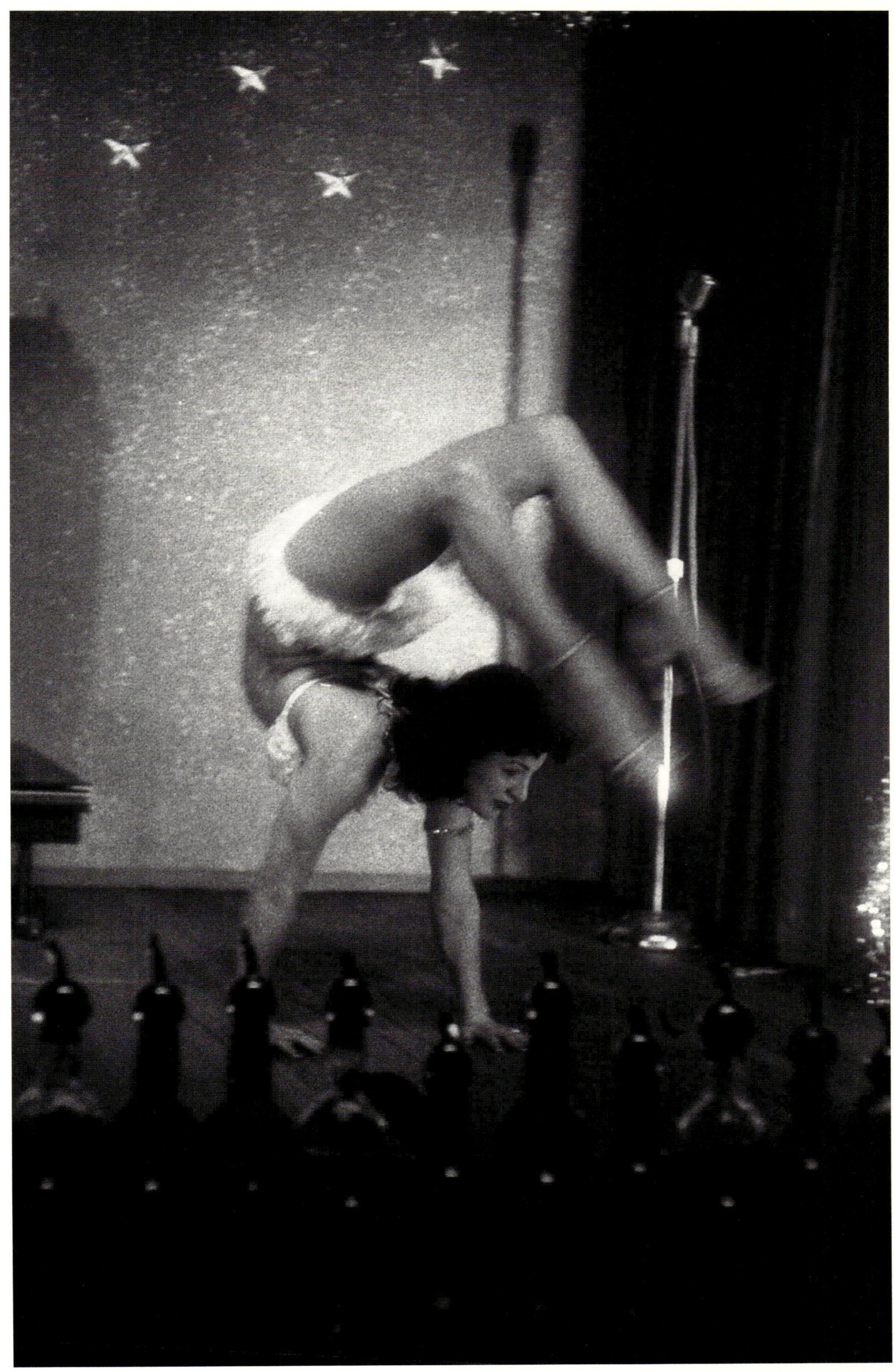

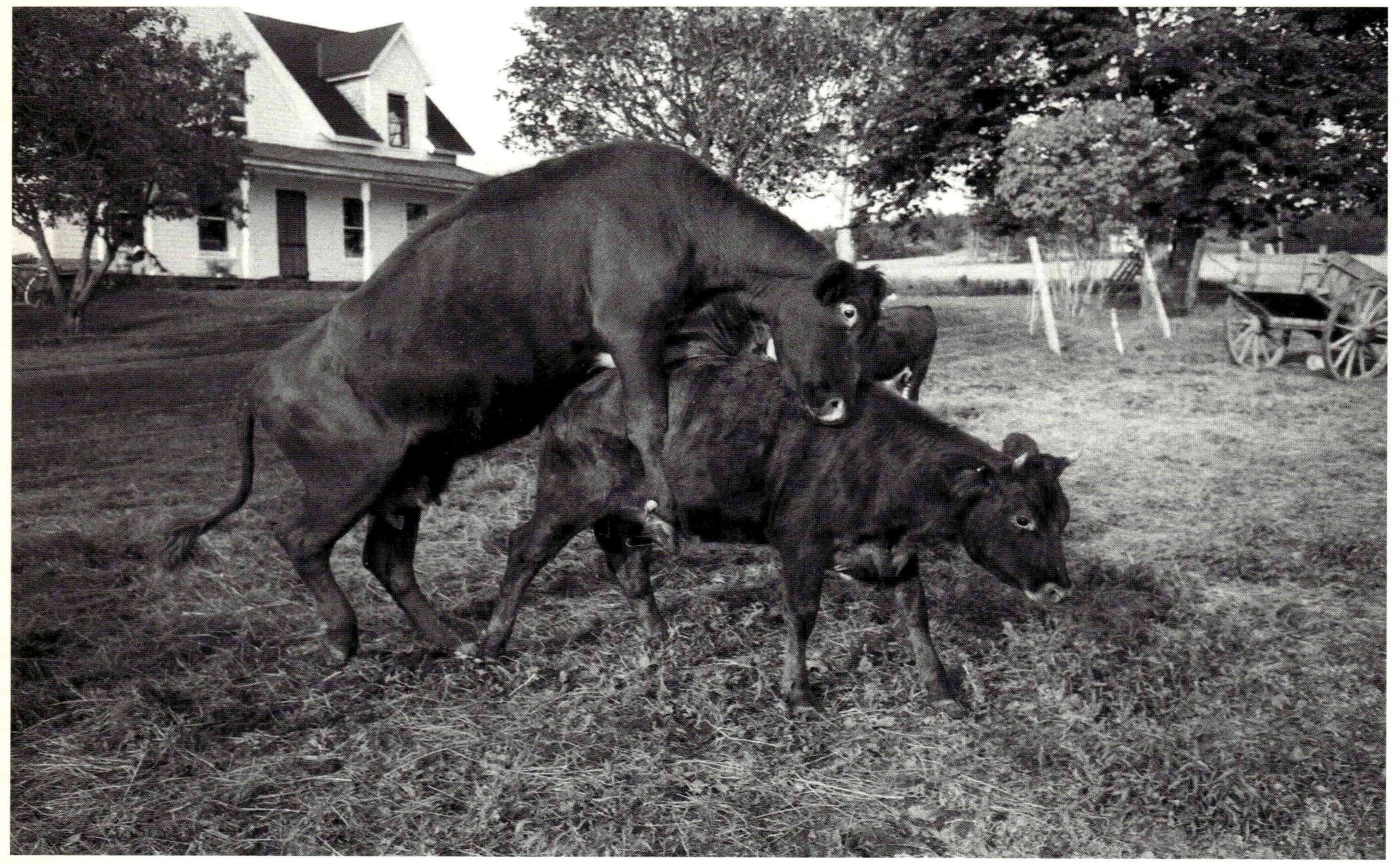

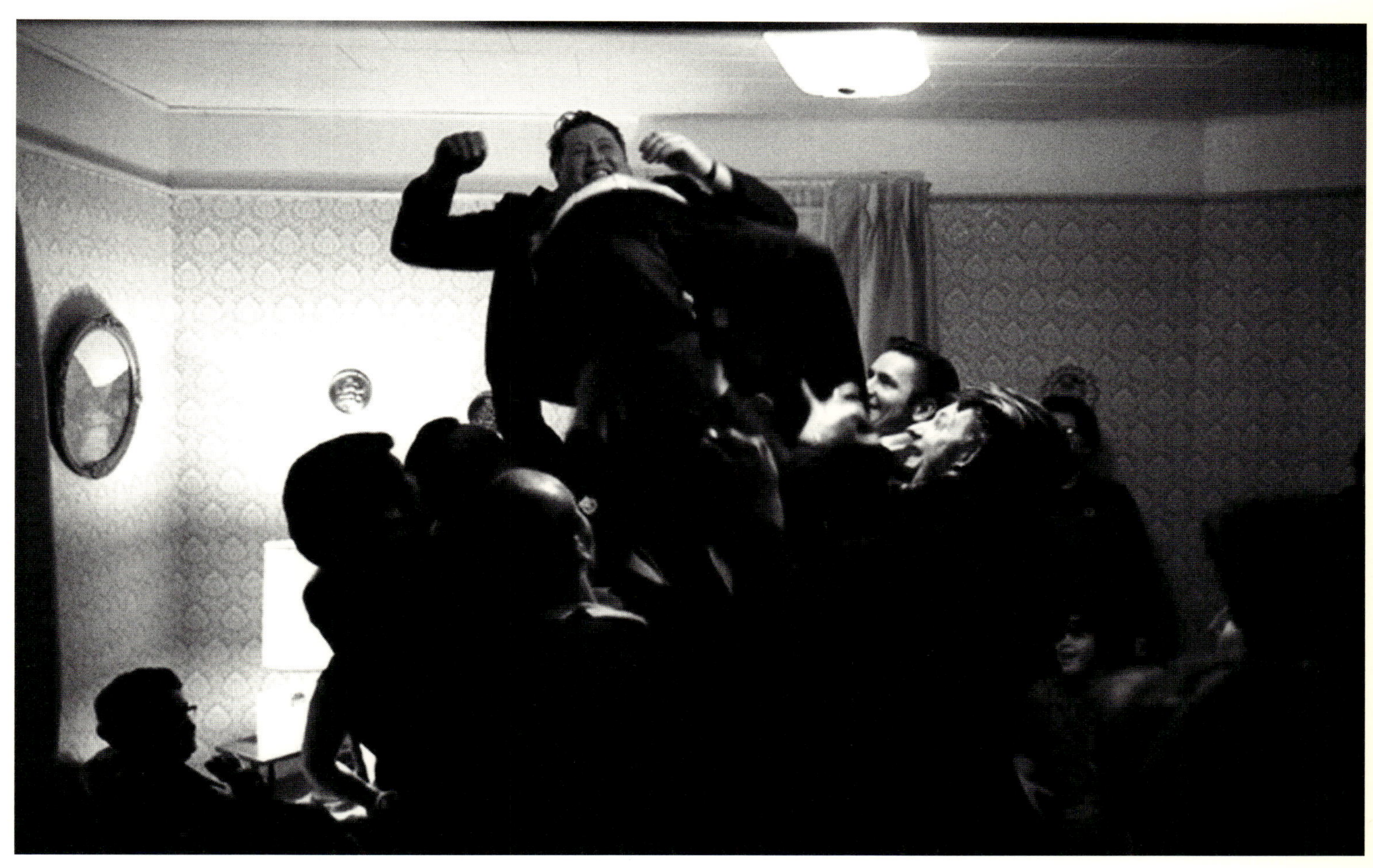

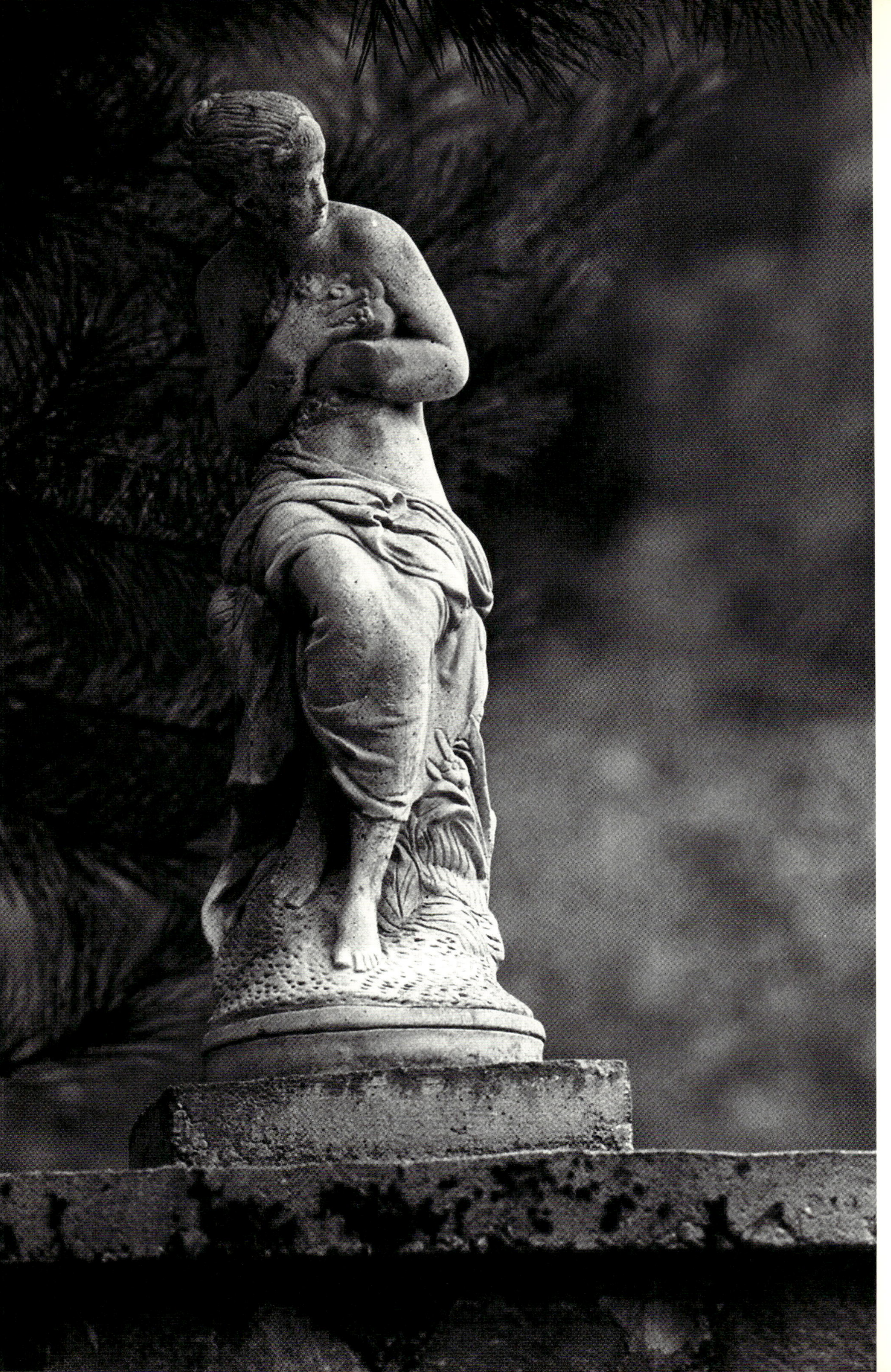

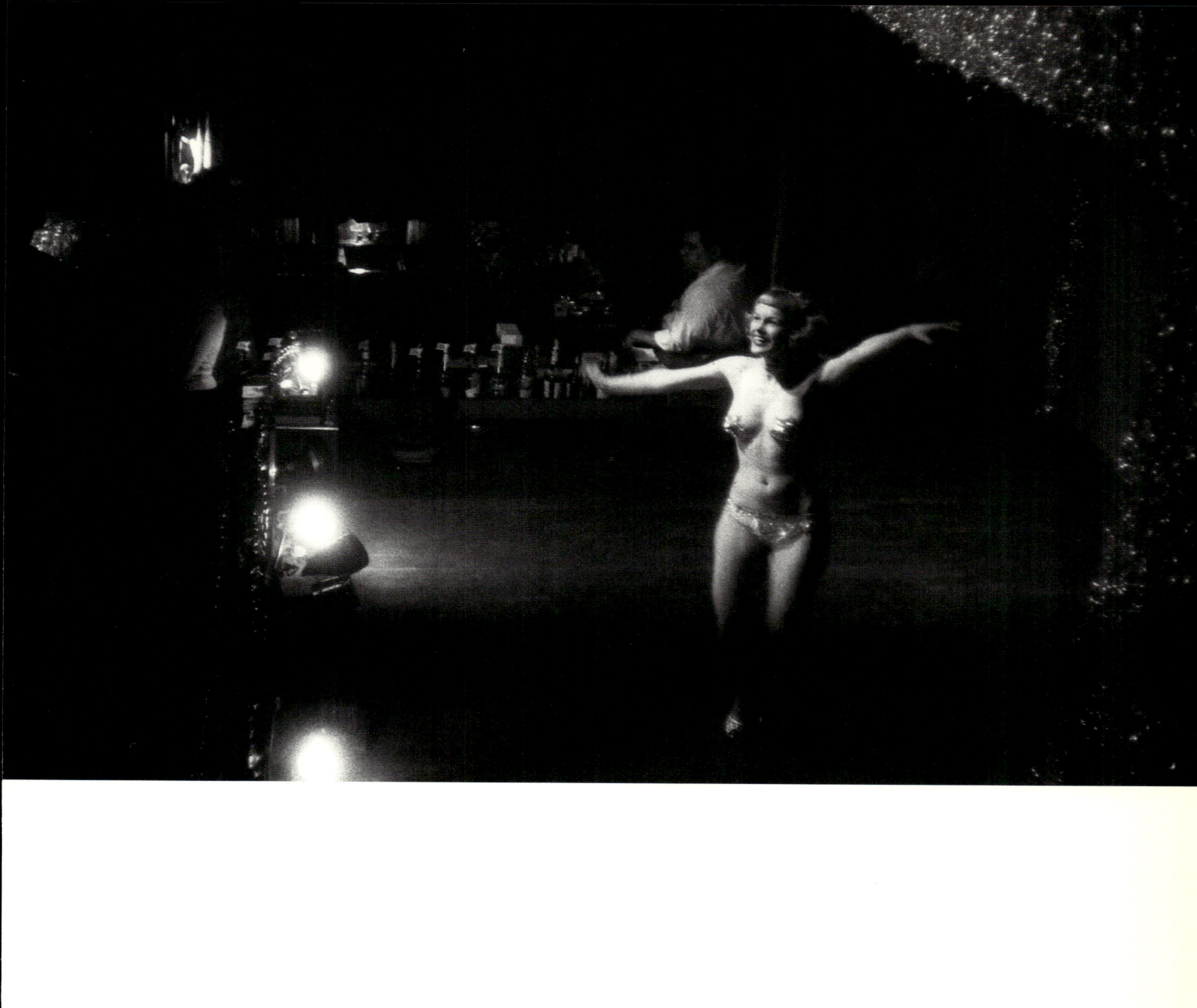

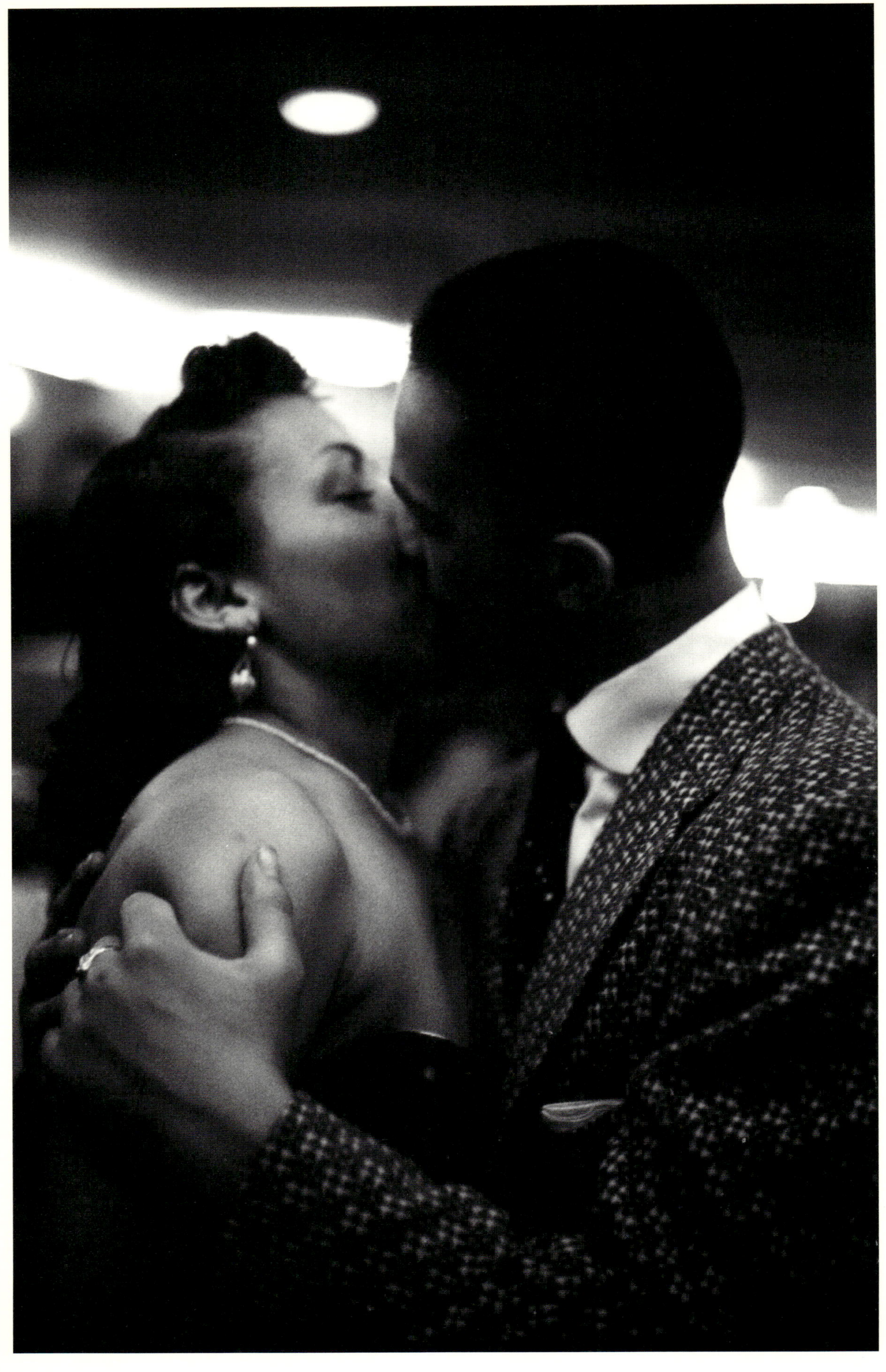

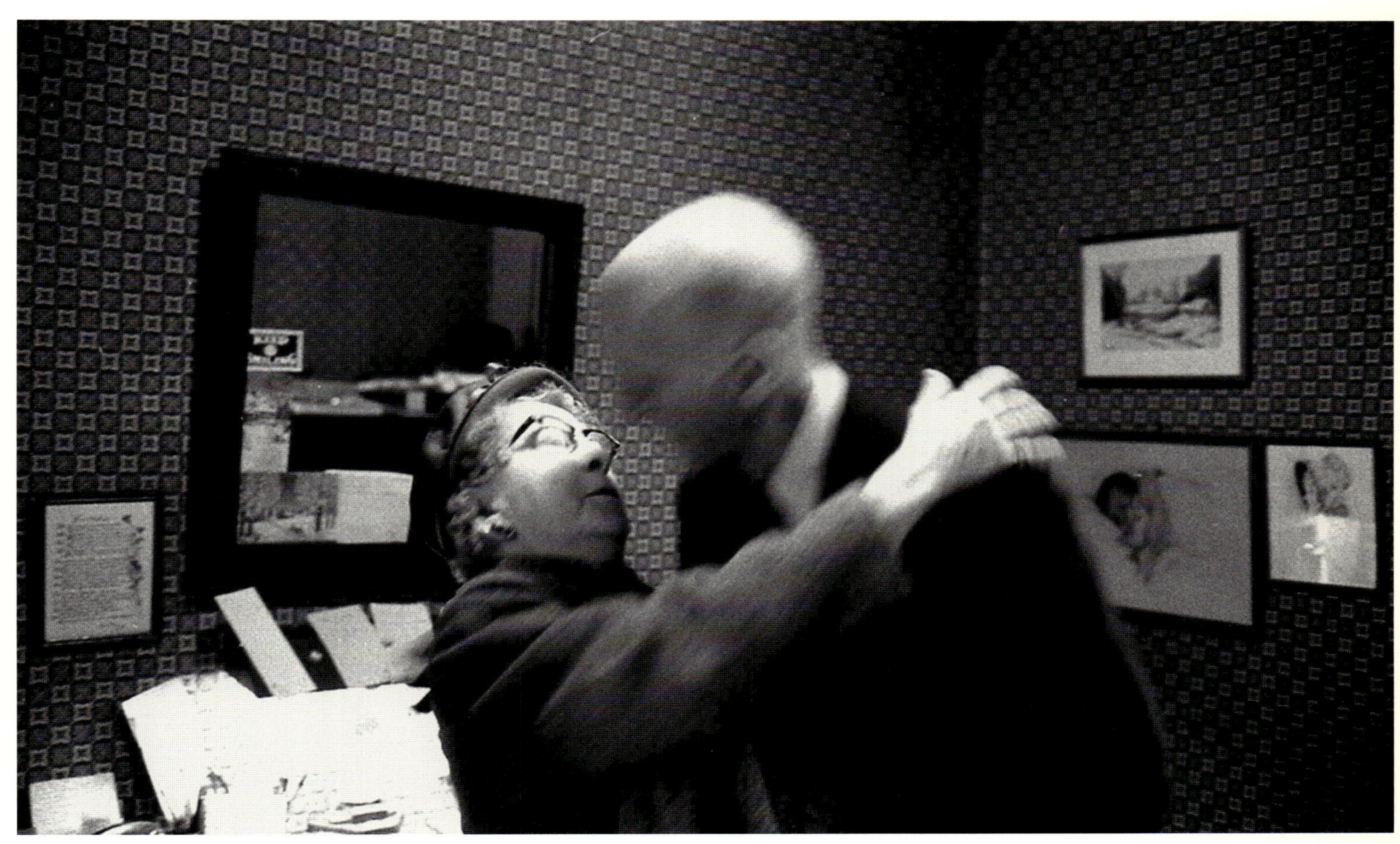

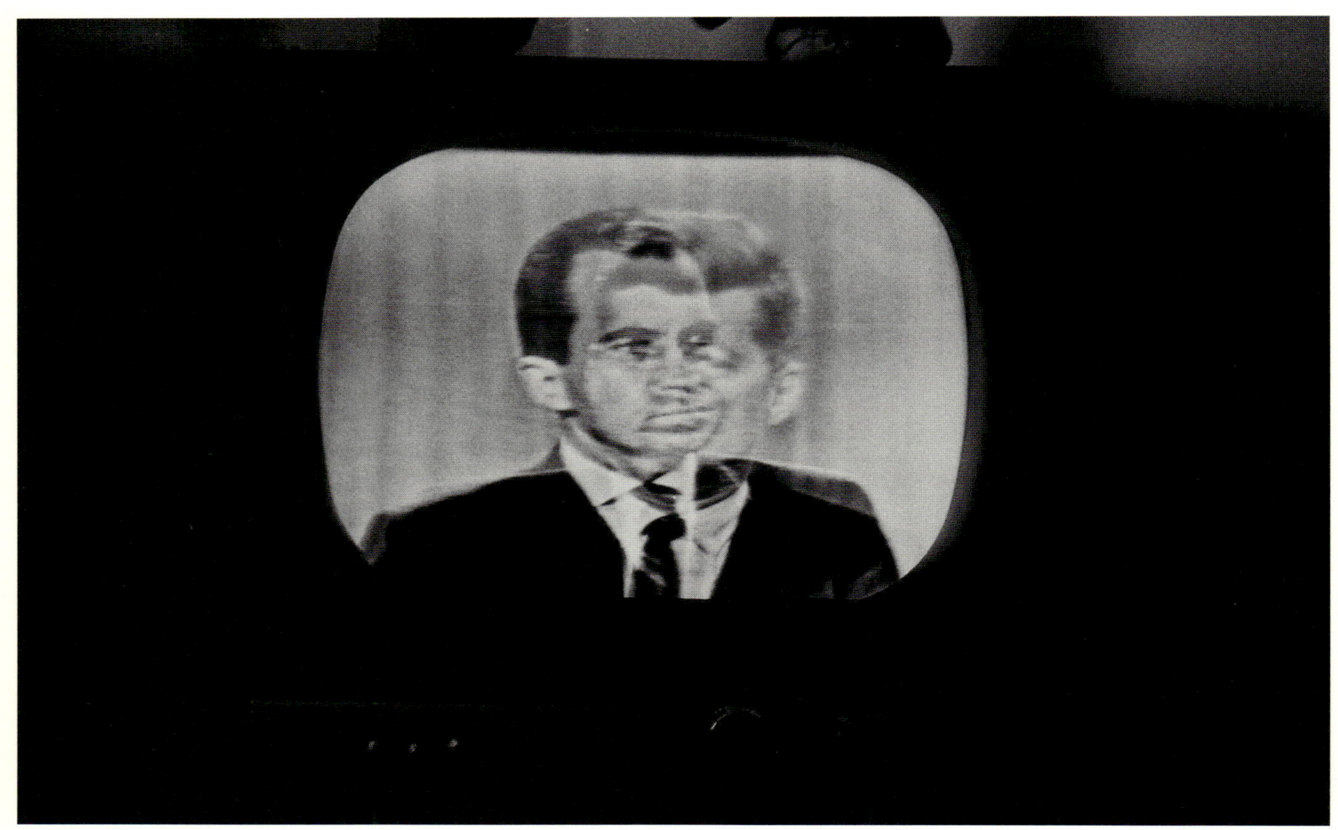

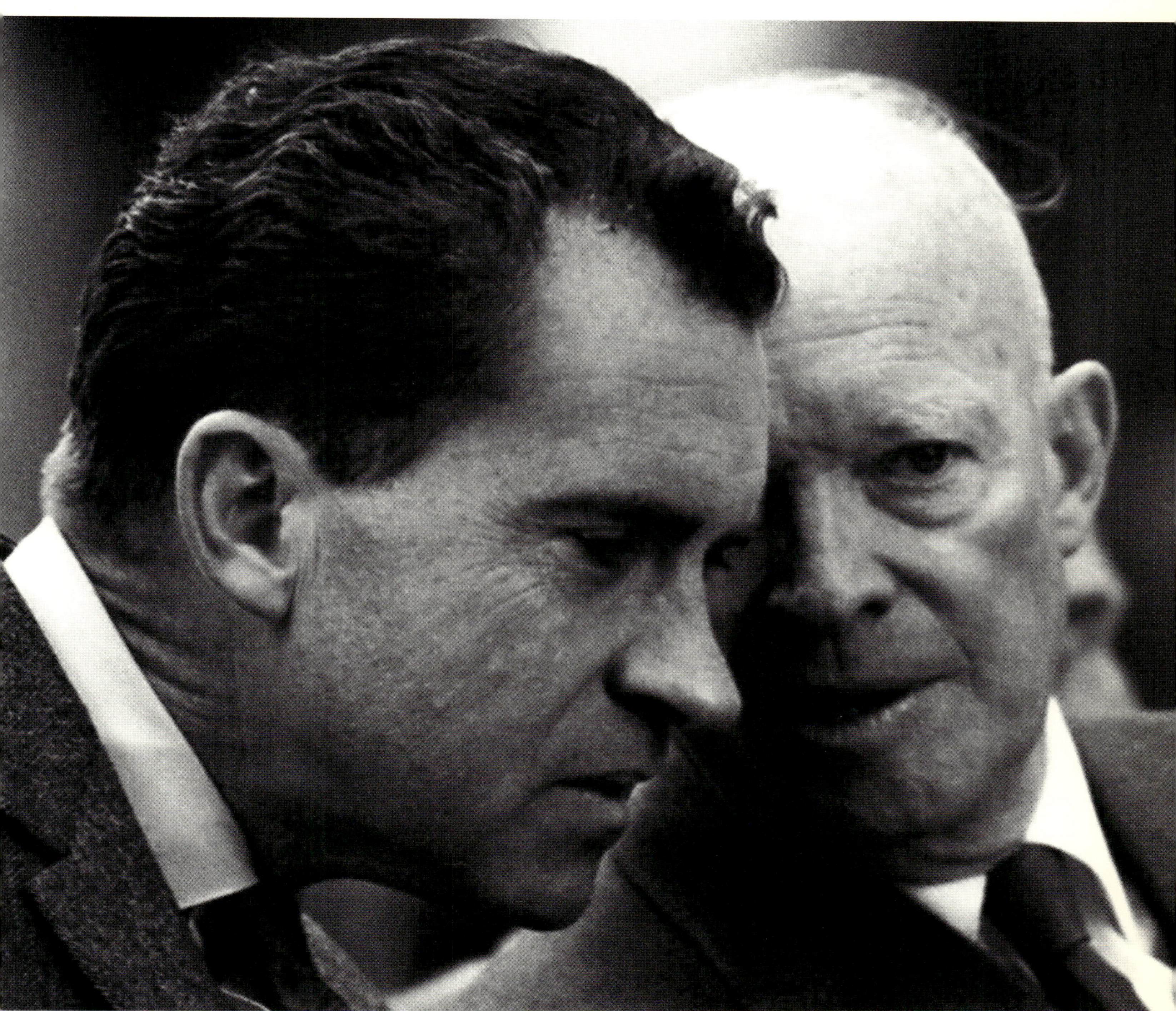

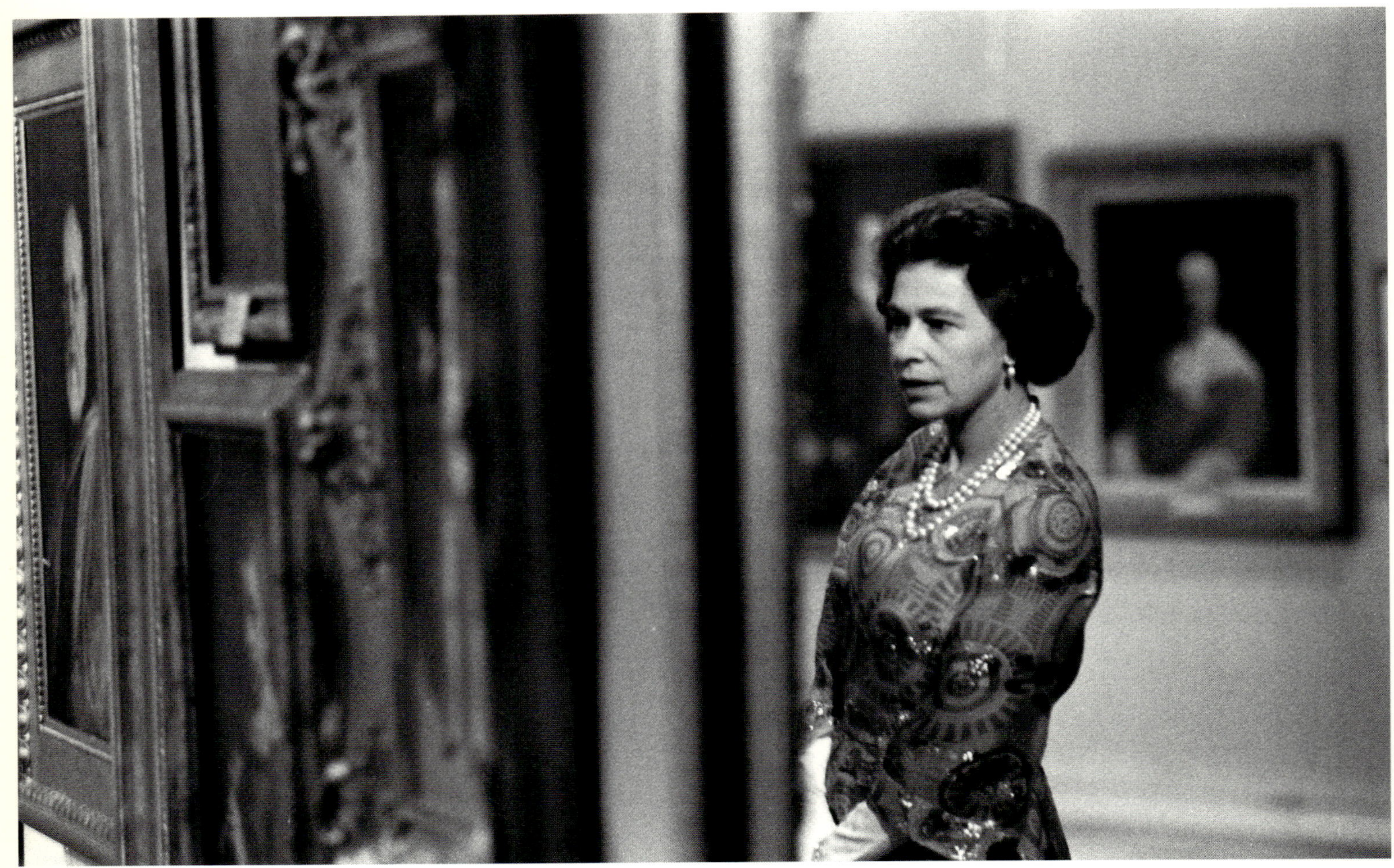

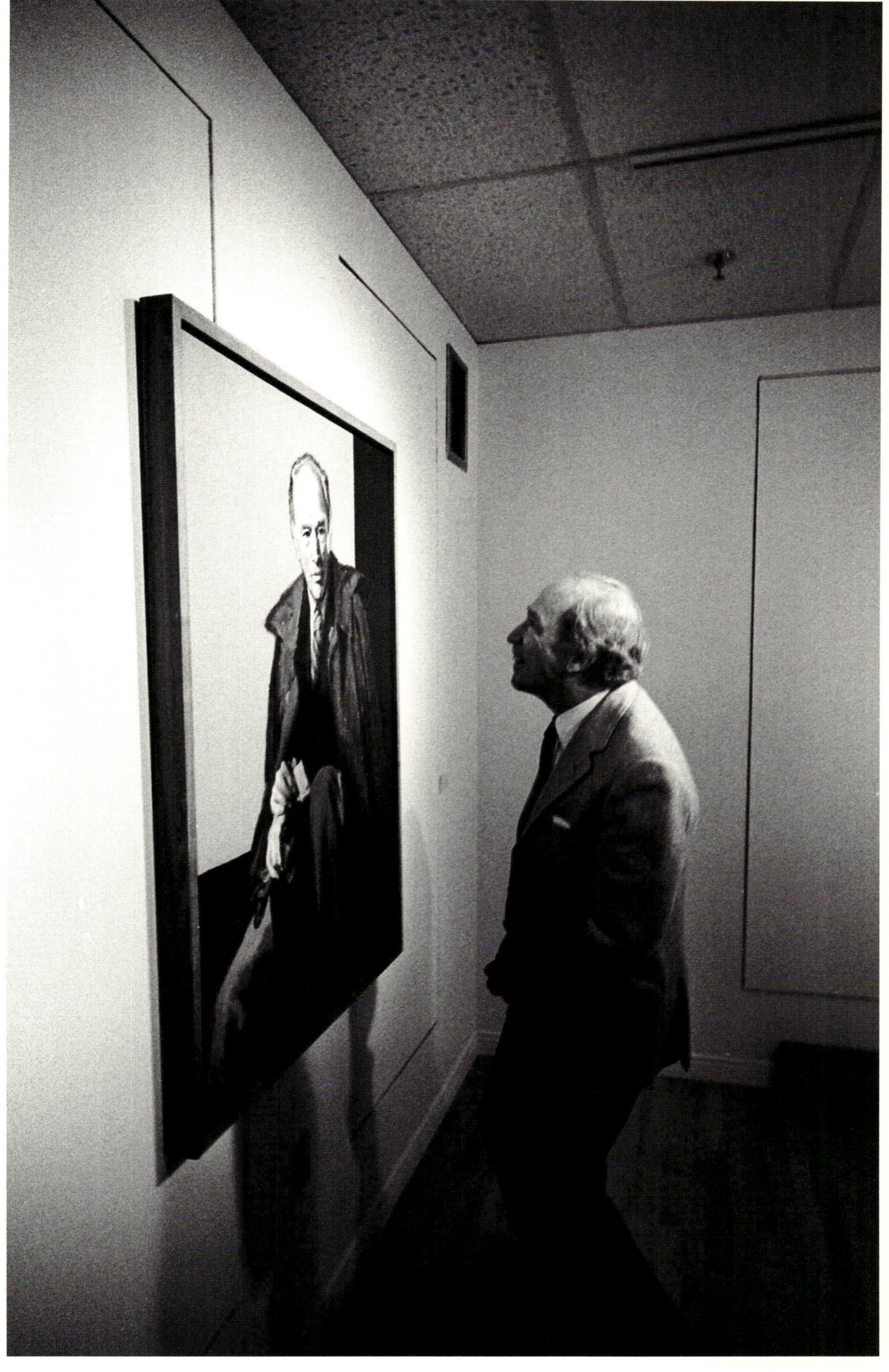

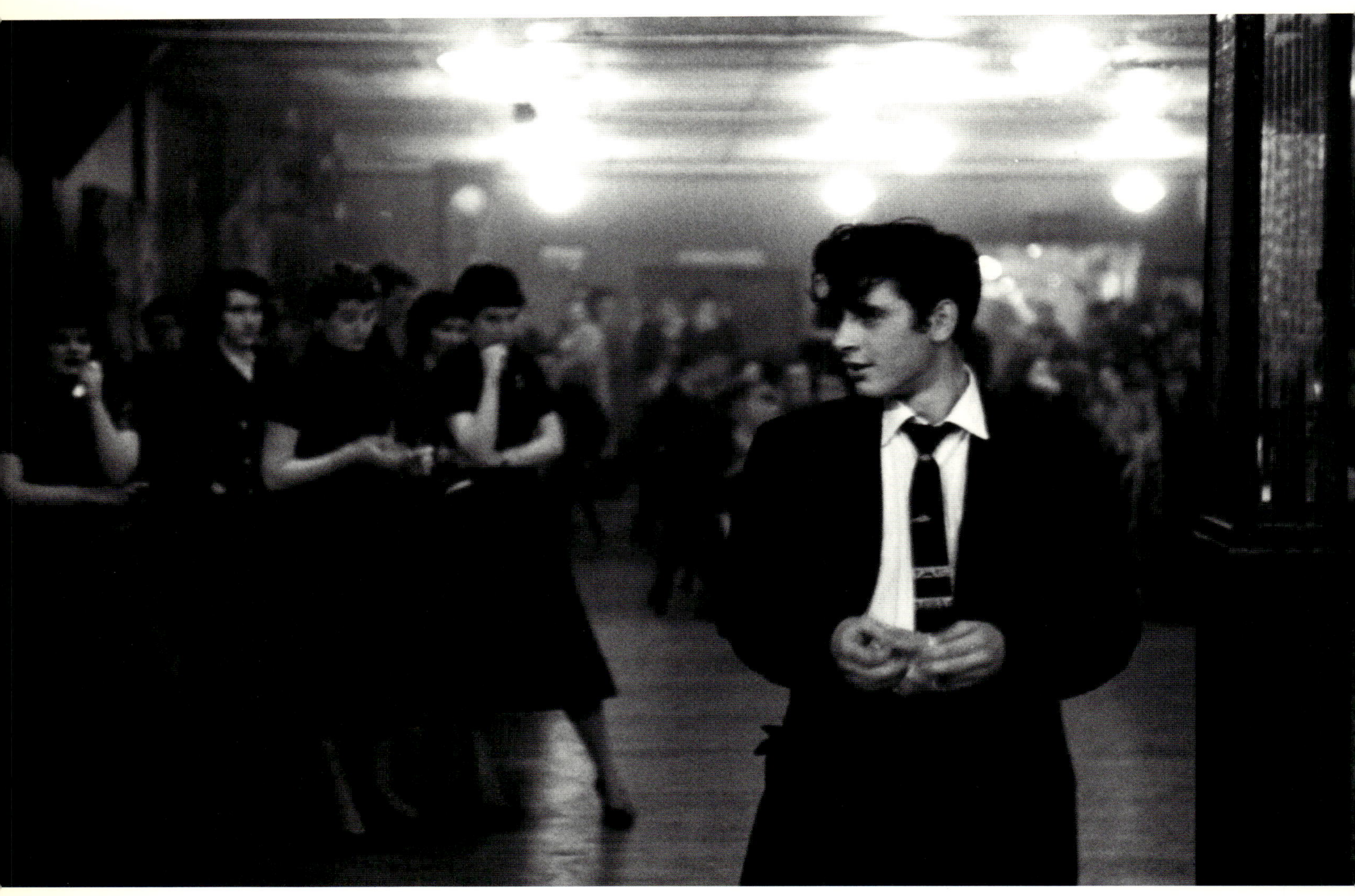

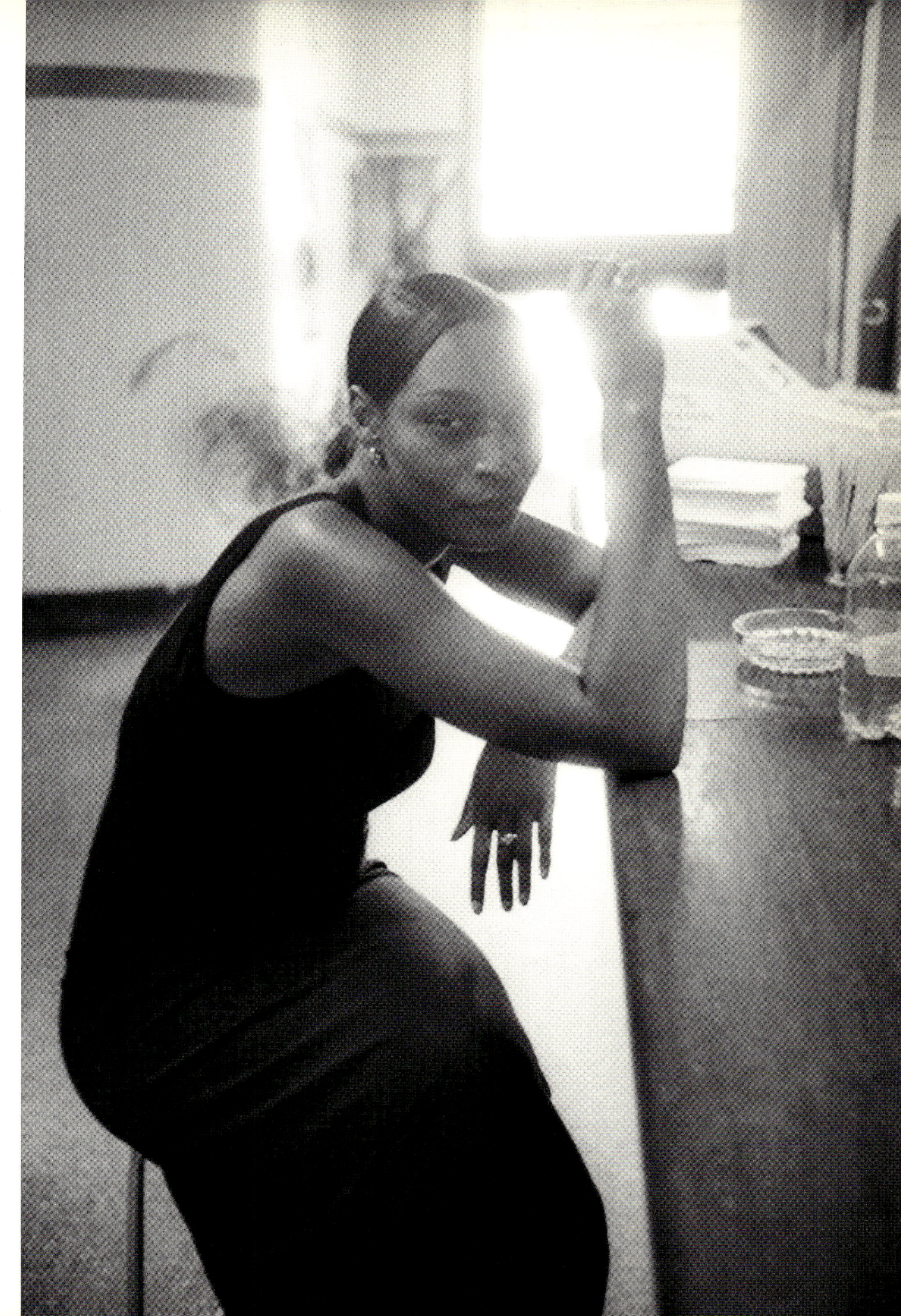

We talk about a photograph being a moment in a time that has passed, but his work lets you feel like you are living that moment again.

Diane Charbonneau, Curator of Photography, Montreal Museum of Fine Arts

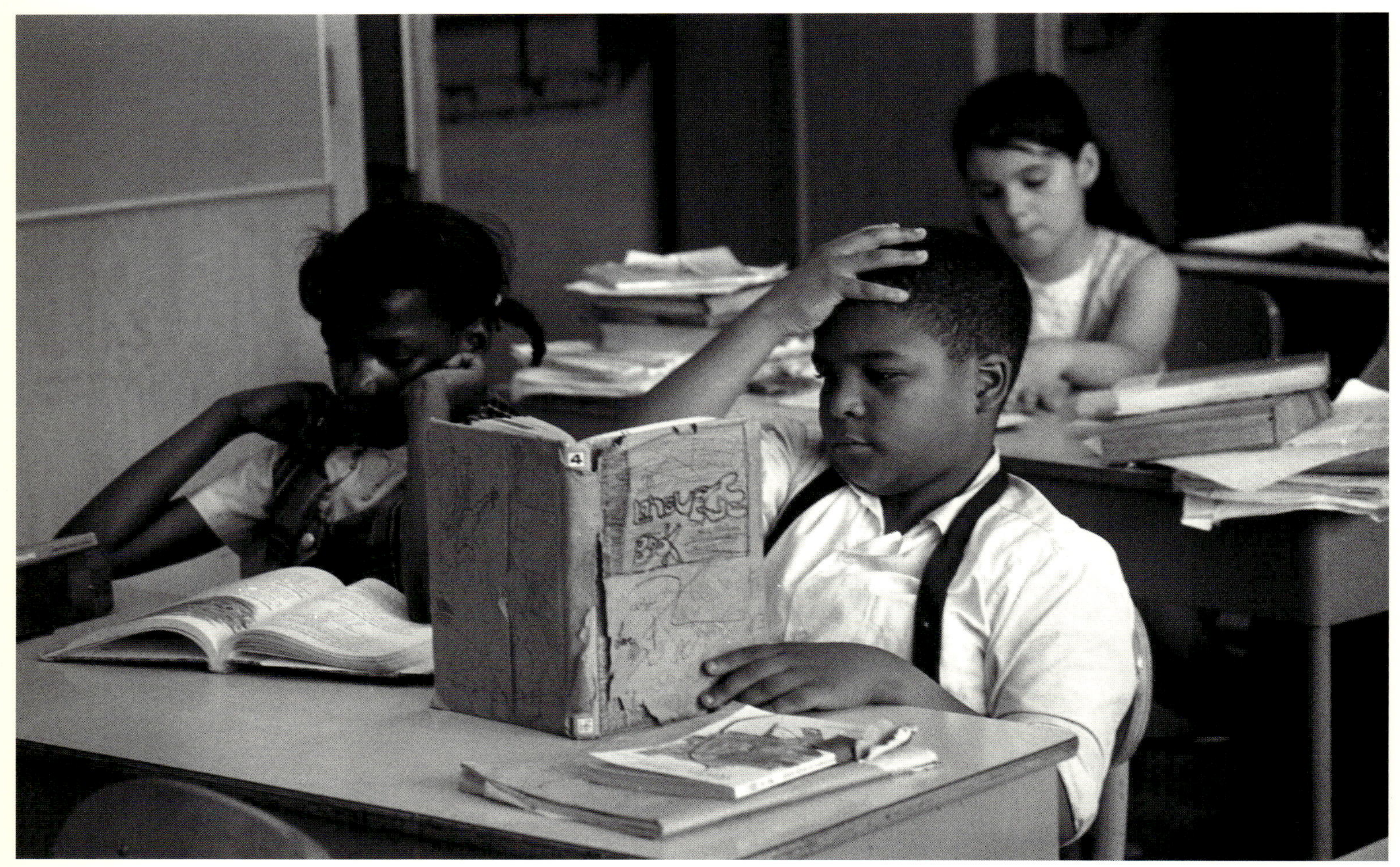

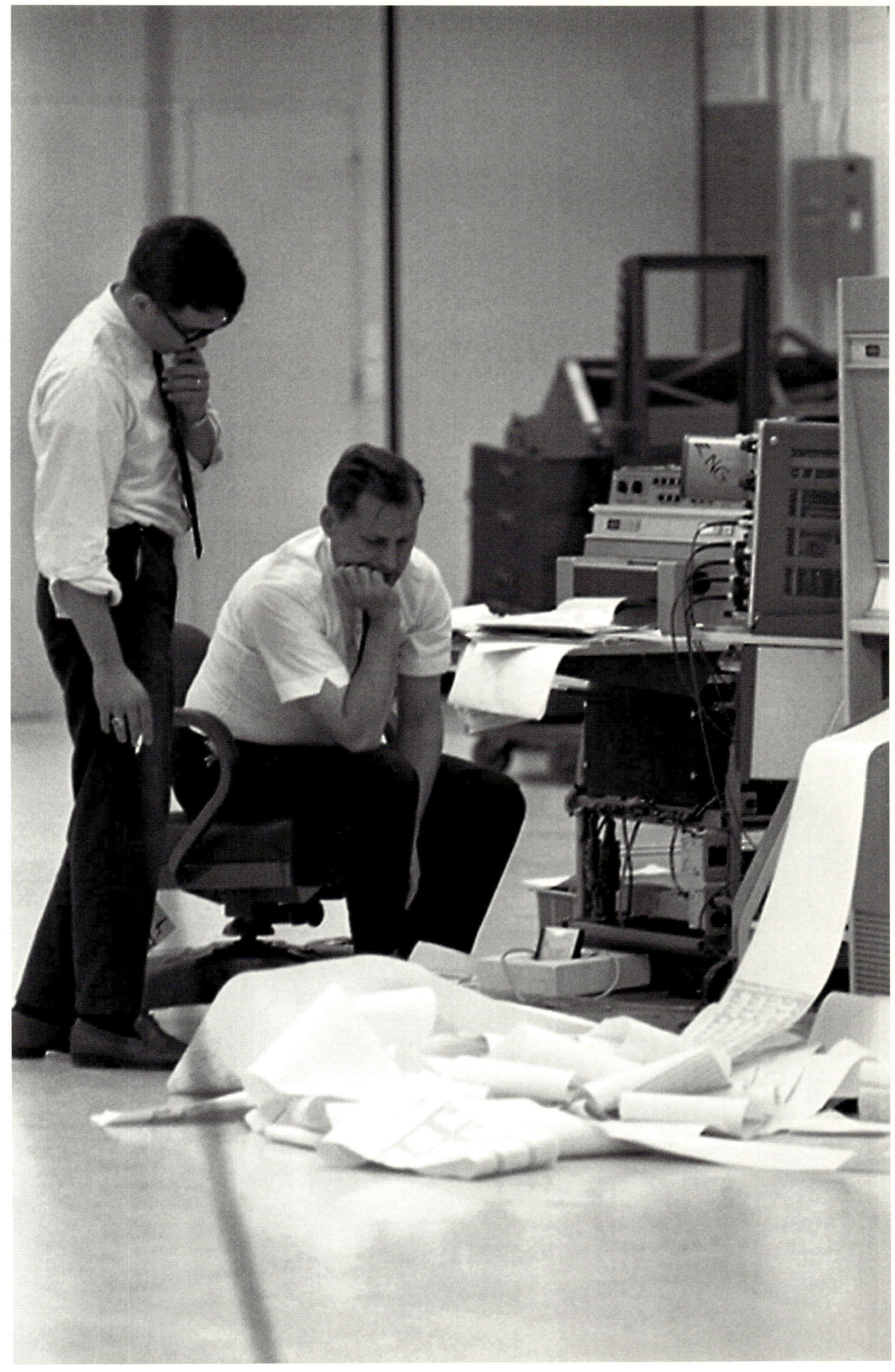

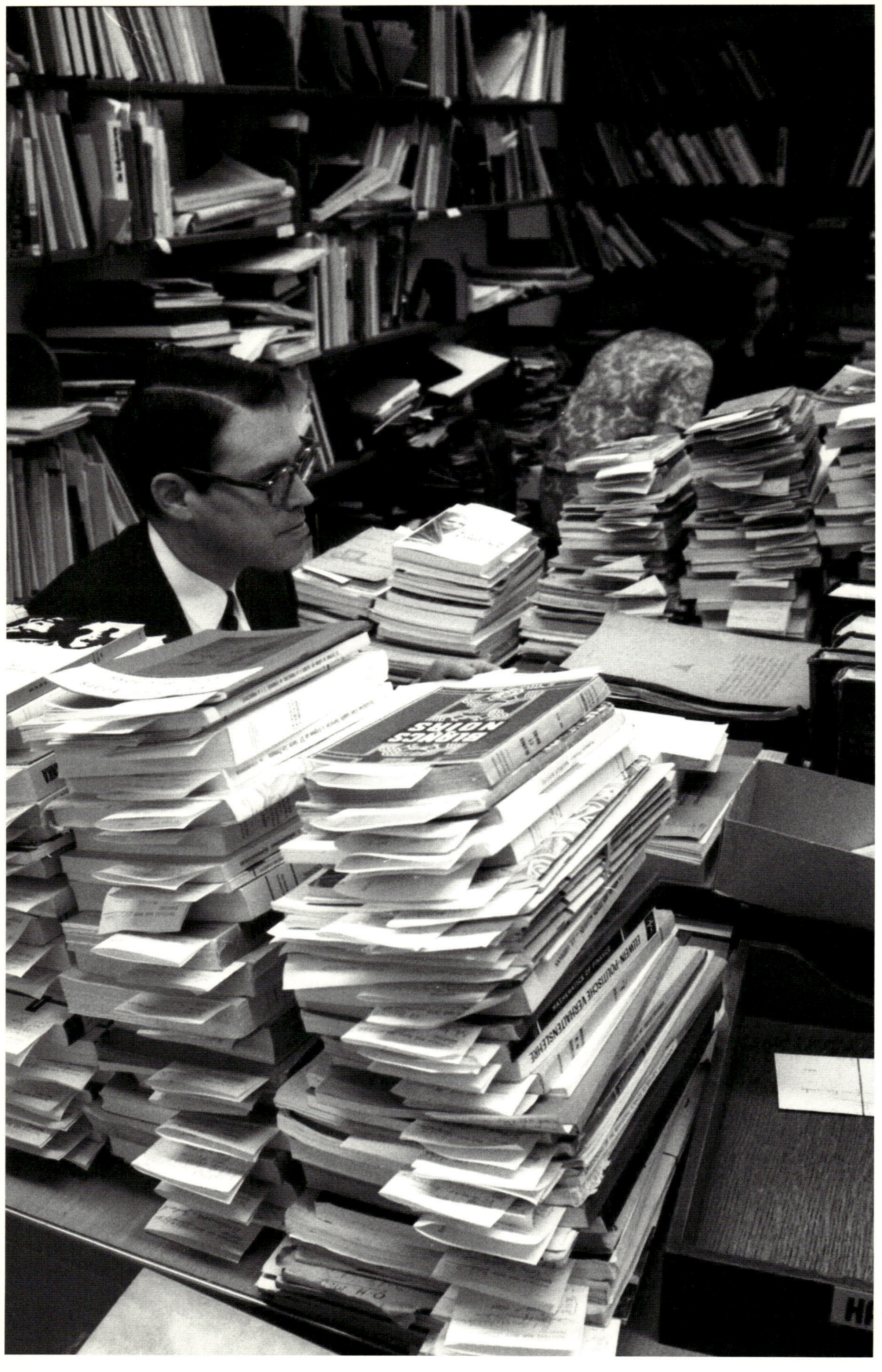

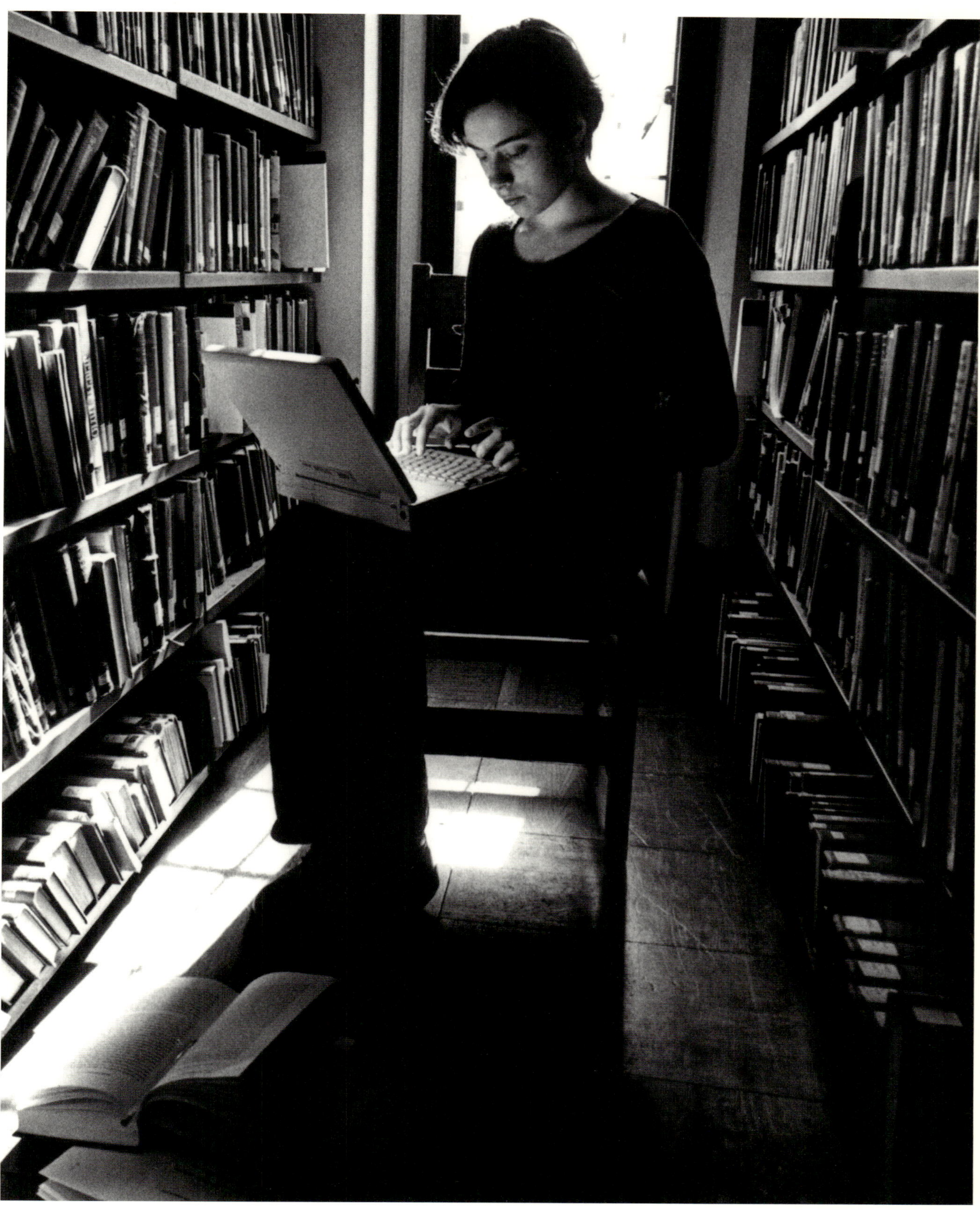

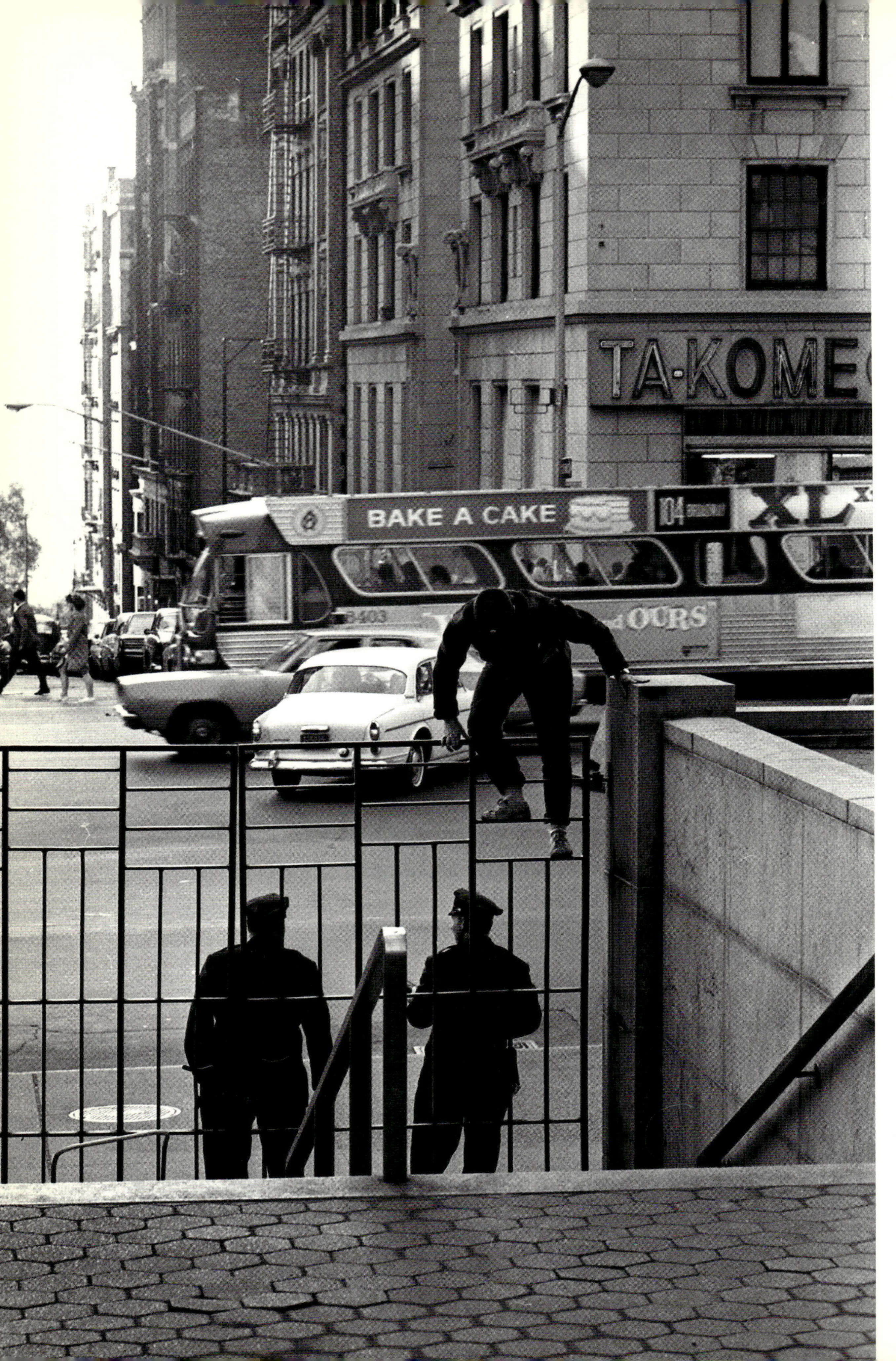
TA-KOME
BAKE A CAKE
104
XL
OURS

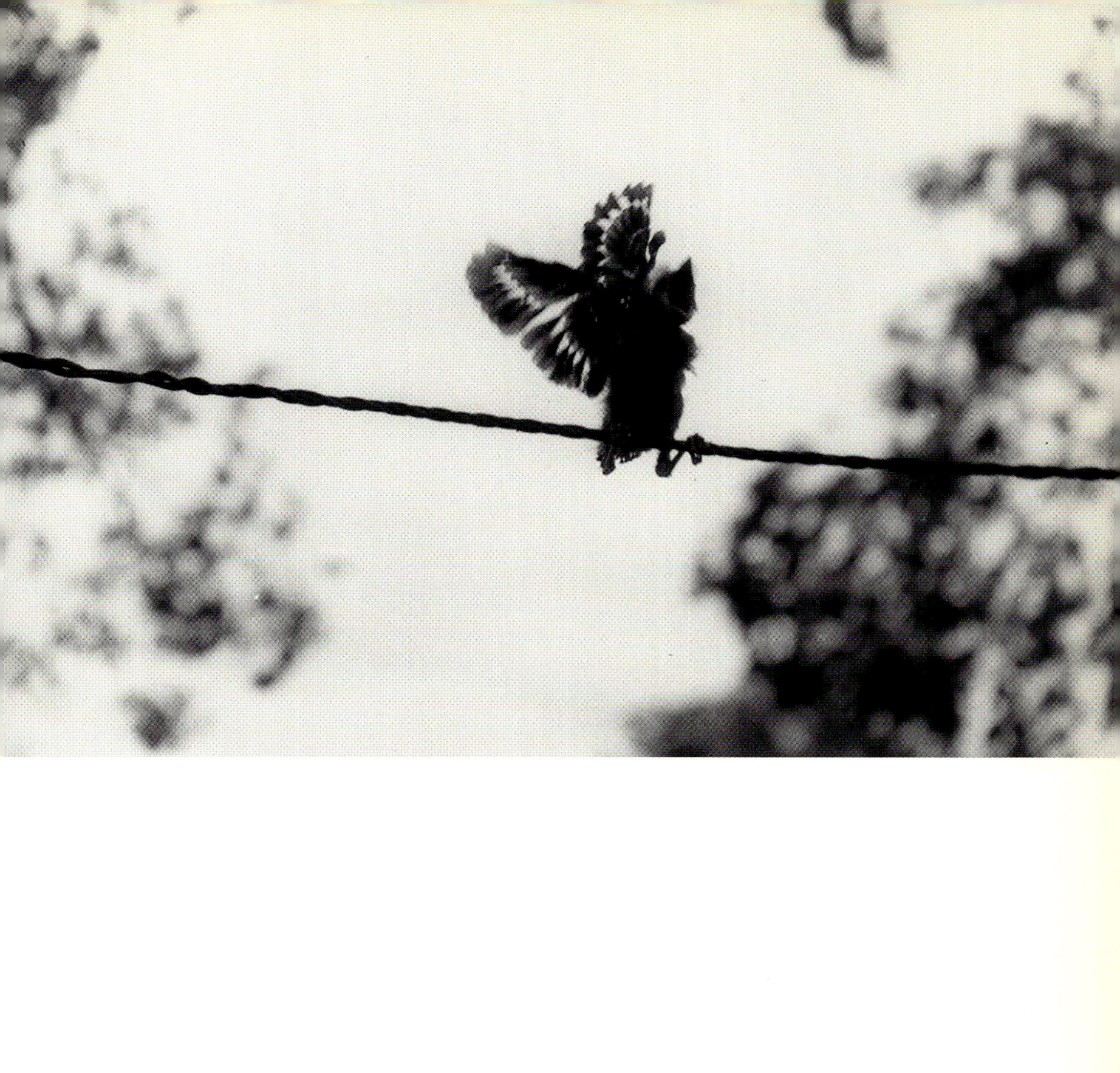

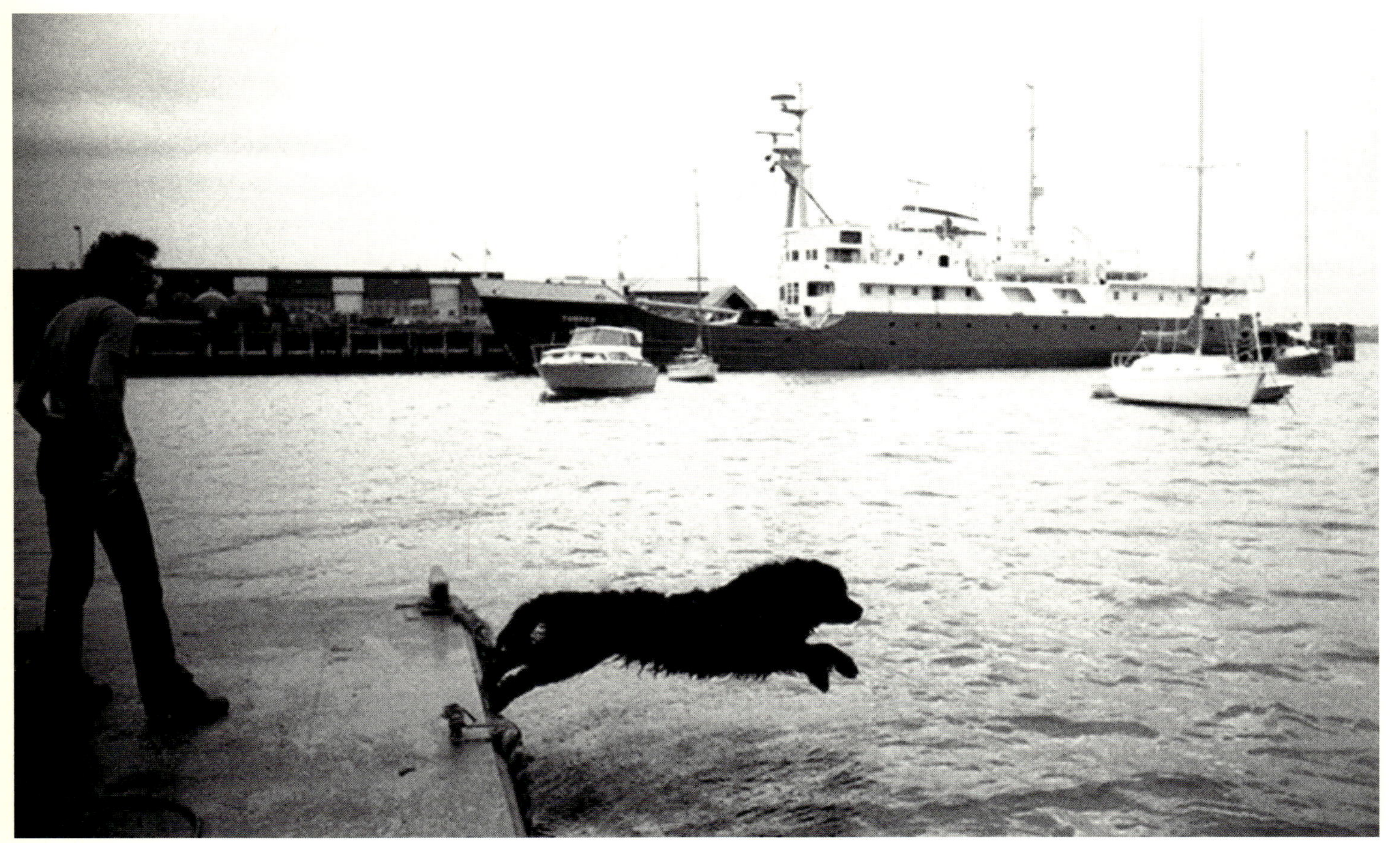

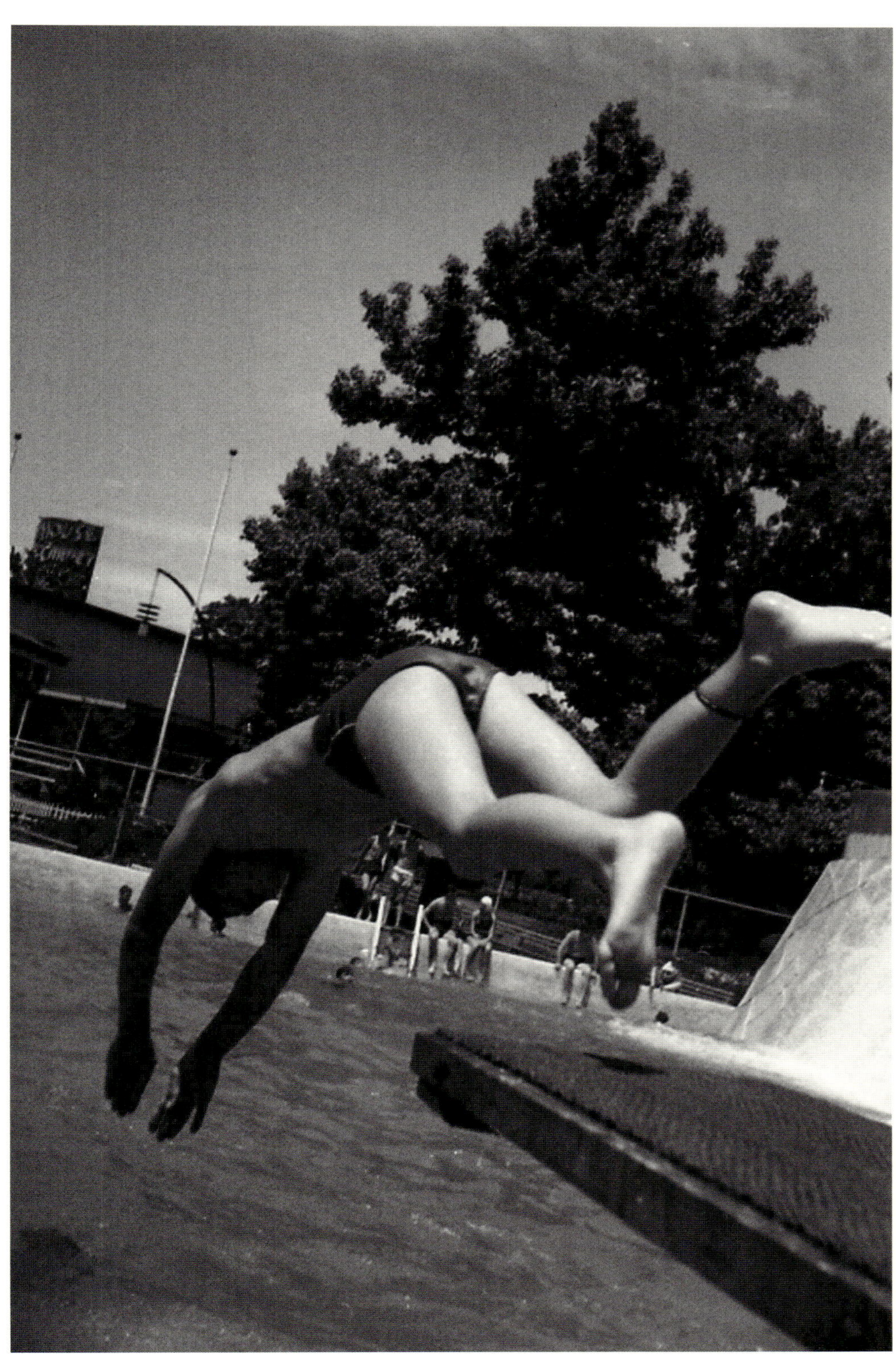

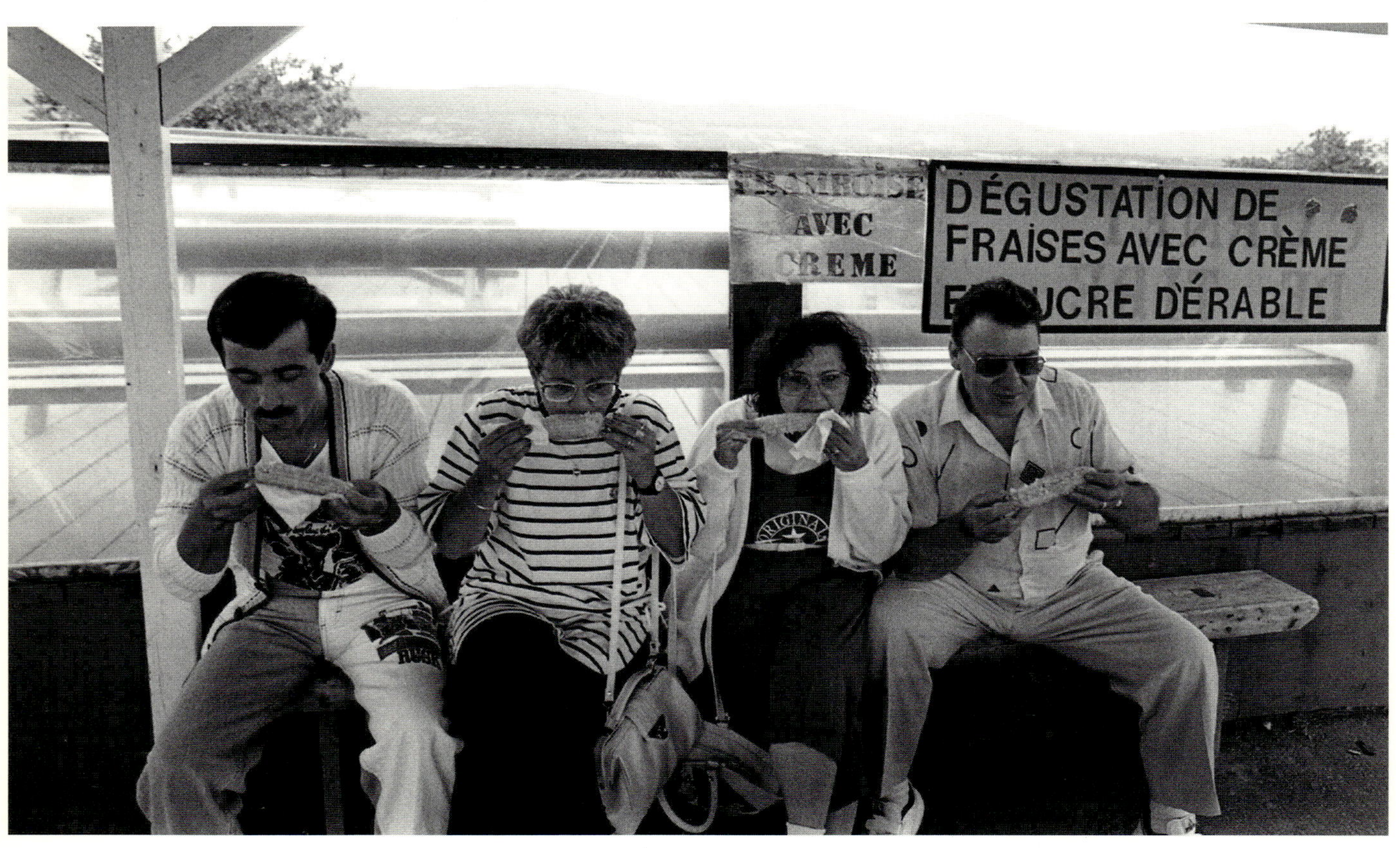
AVEC
DÉGUSTATION DE
FRAISES AVEC CRÈME
UCRE D'ÉRABLE

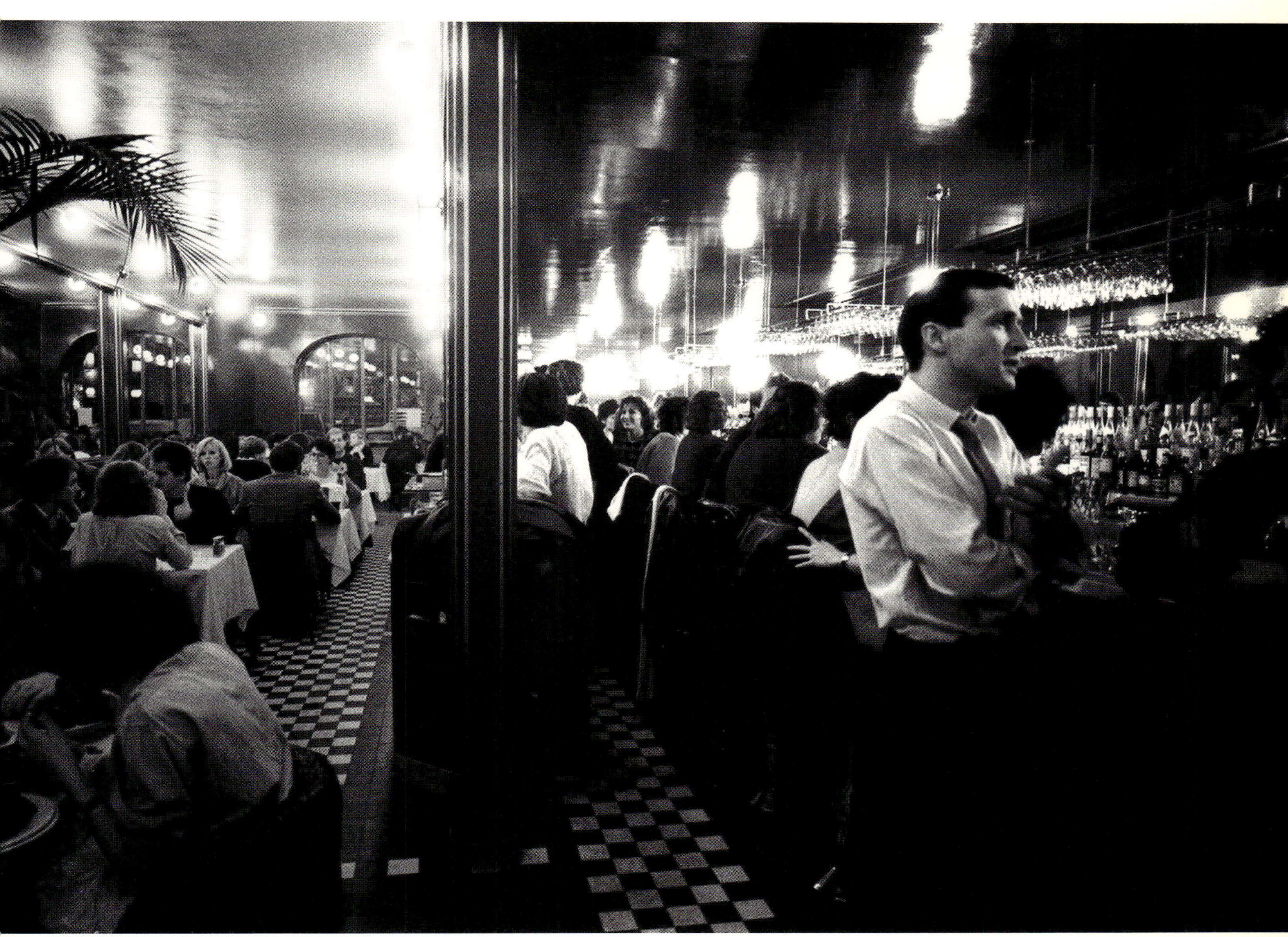

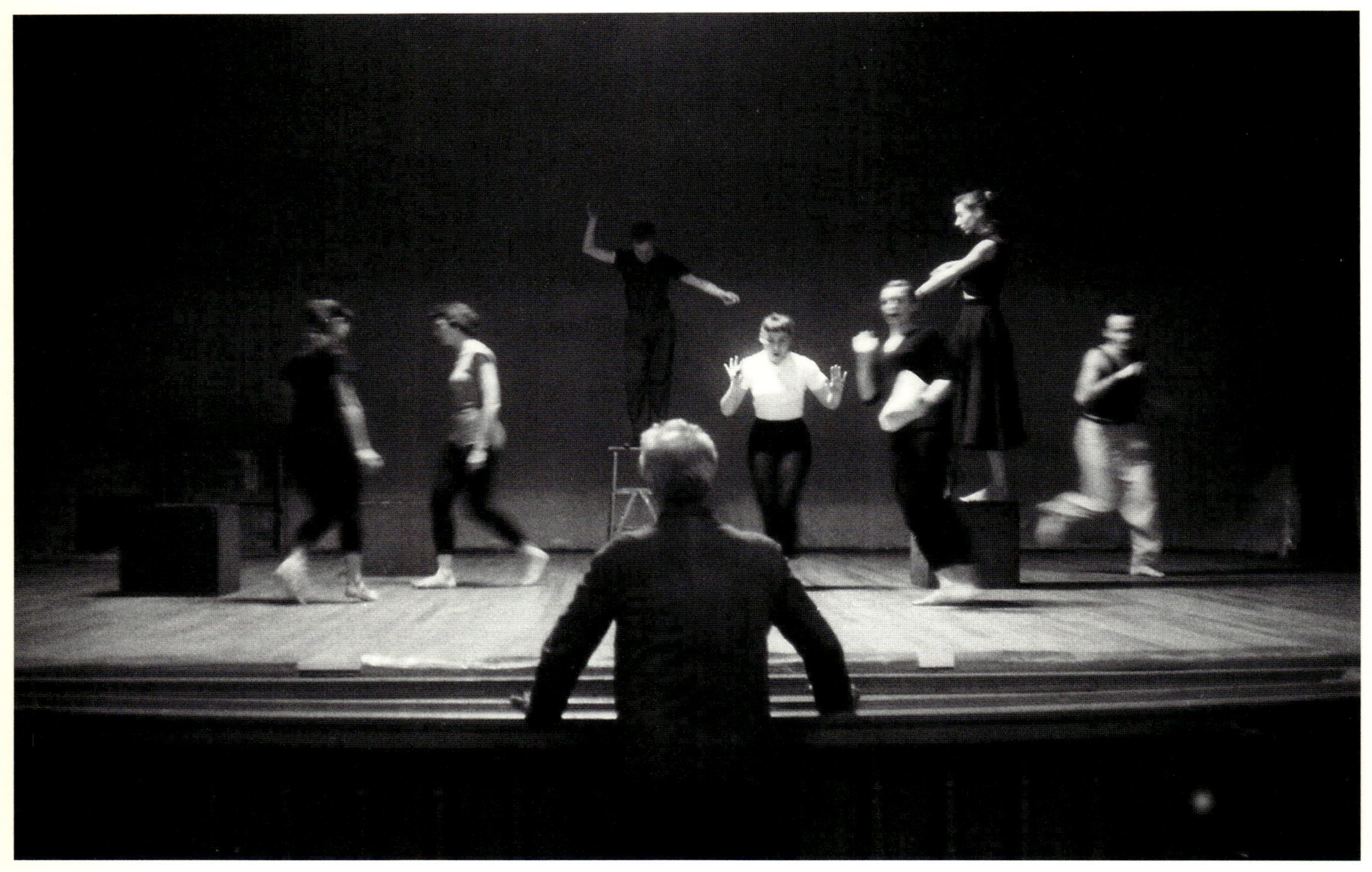

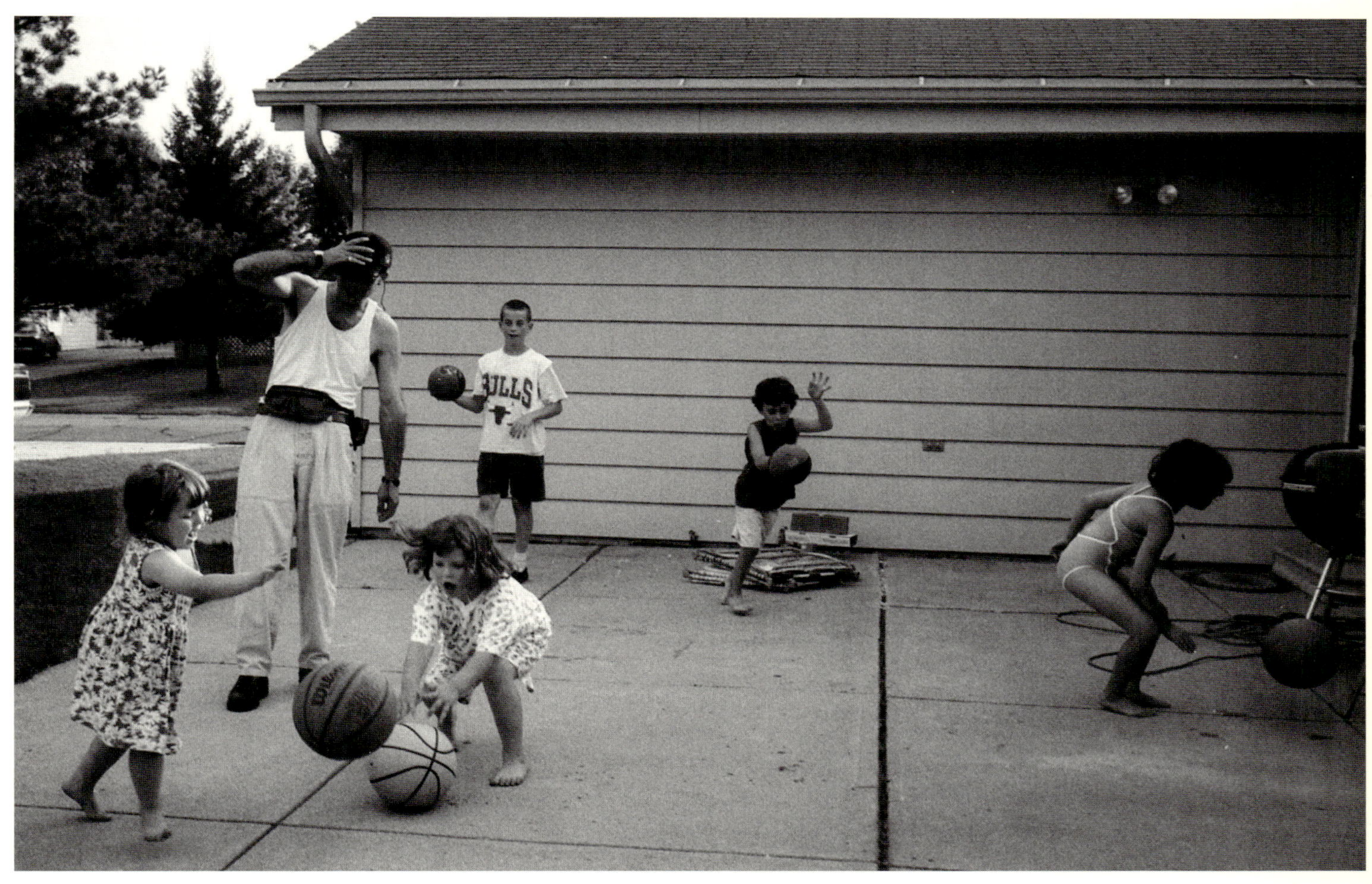
BULLS

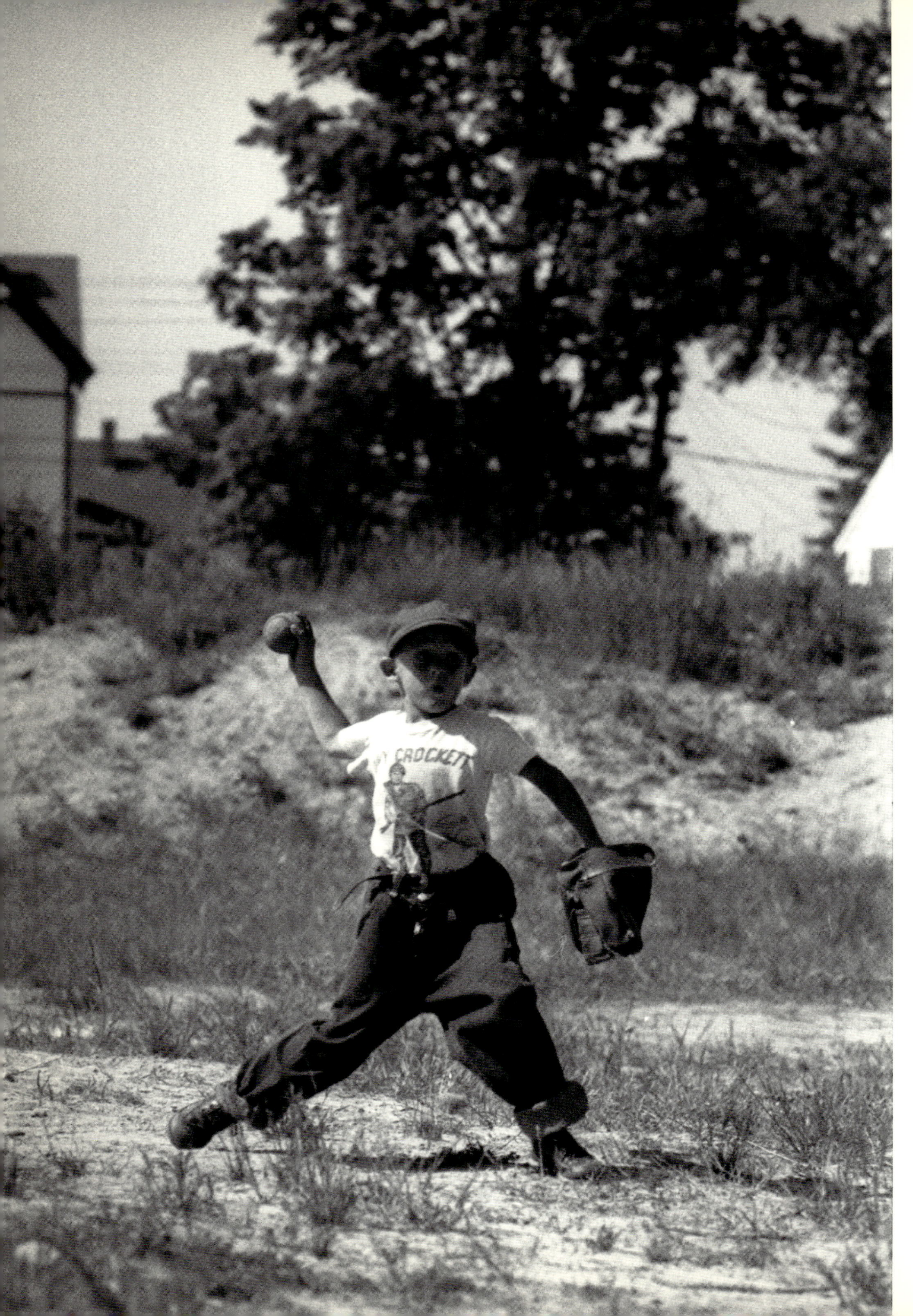

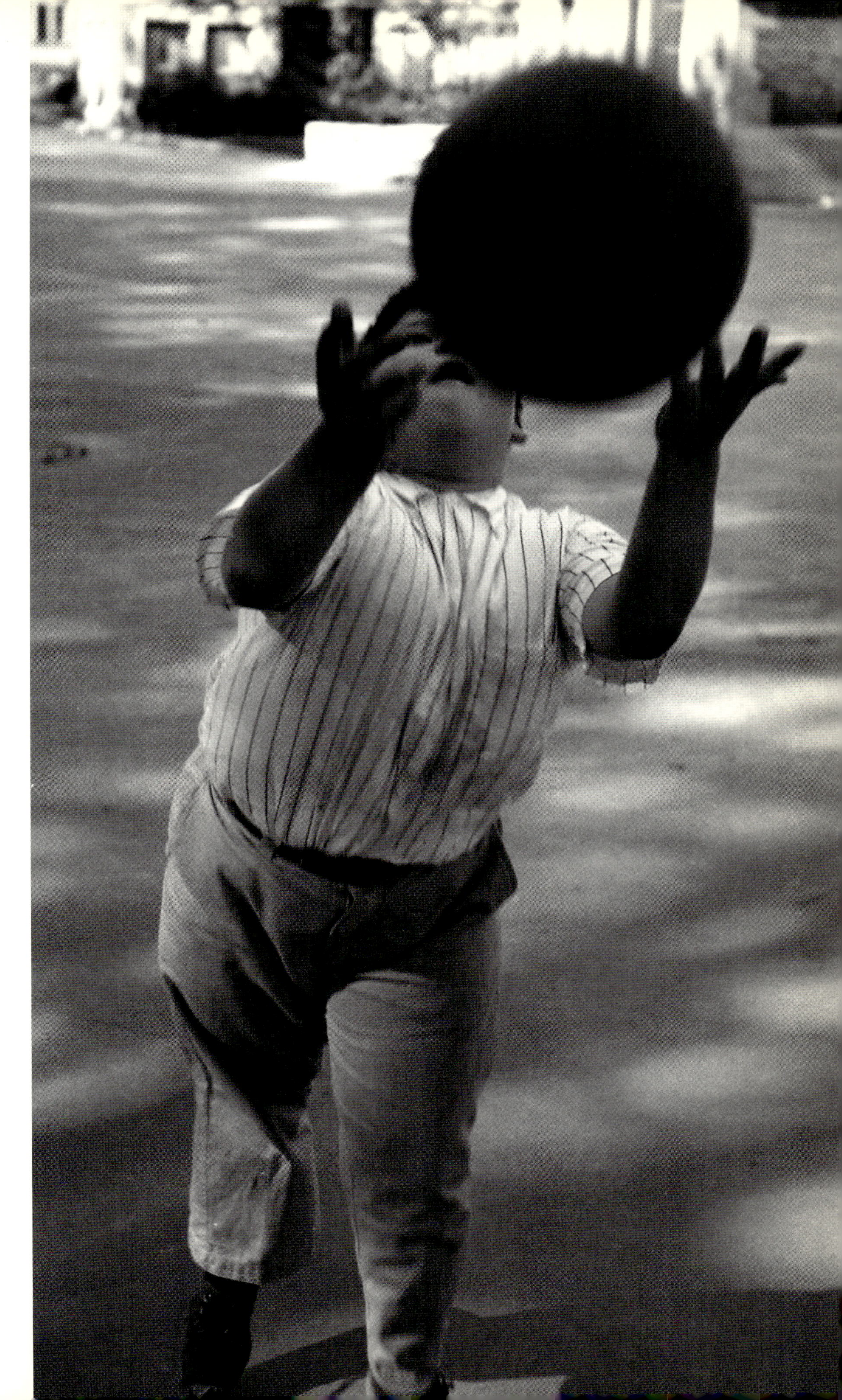

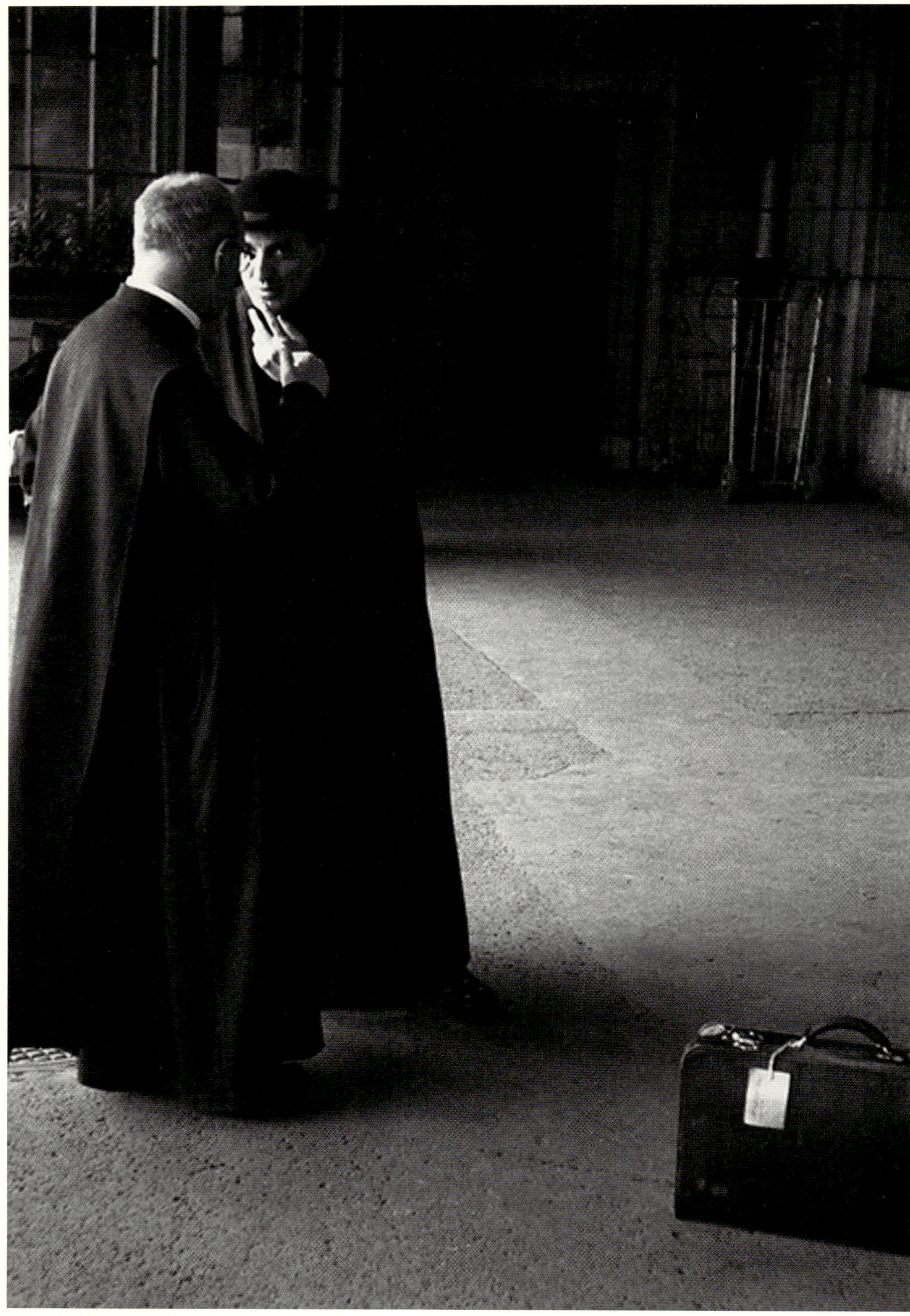

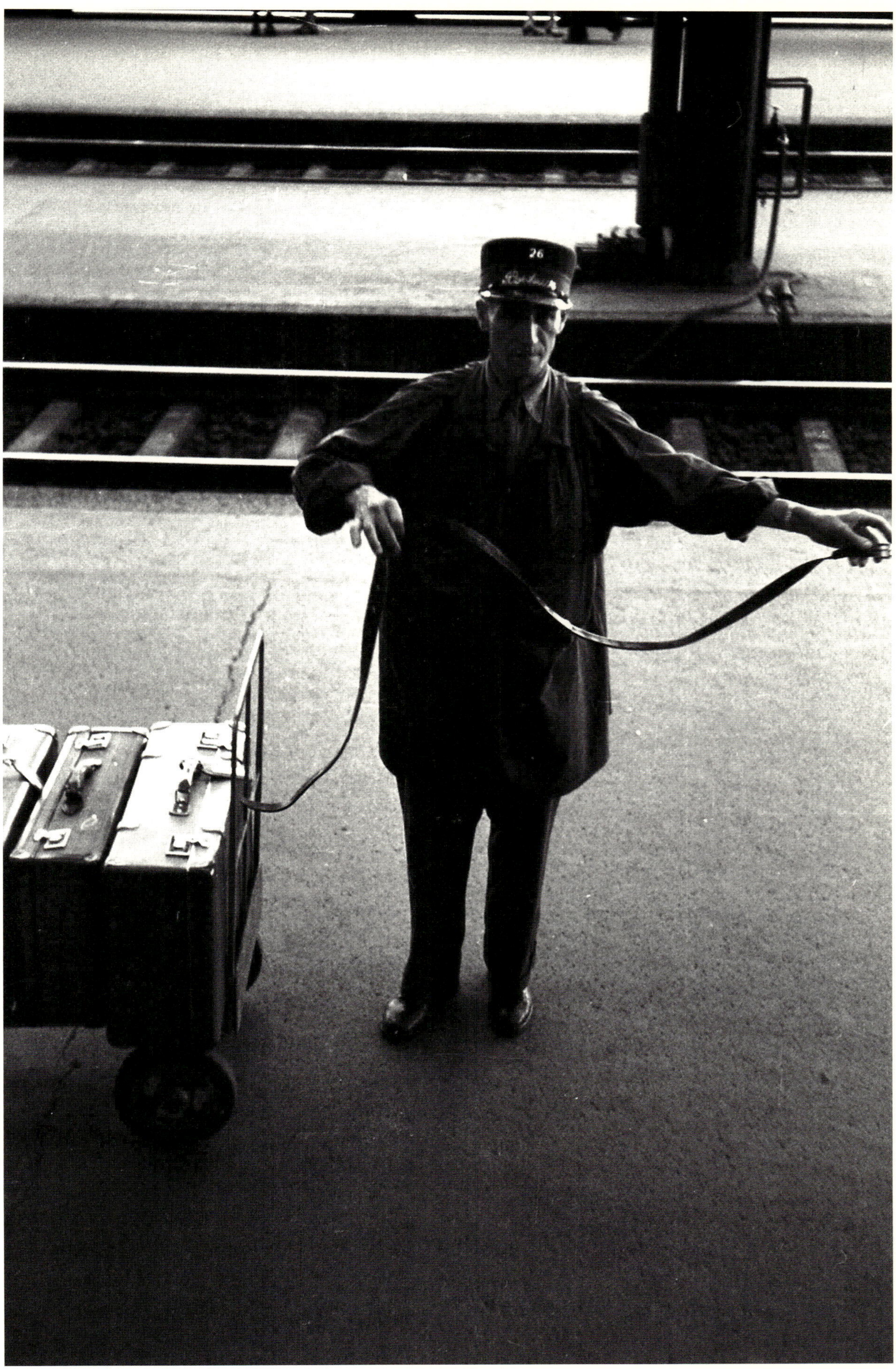

George comes from a line of humanist photographers.
He is interested in people and their stories, and
gives utmost respect to the people he is photographing.
His work is both fine art and documentary.

Stephen Bulger, President of Stephen Bulger Gallery, Toronto

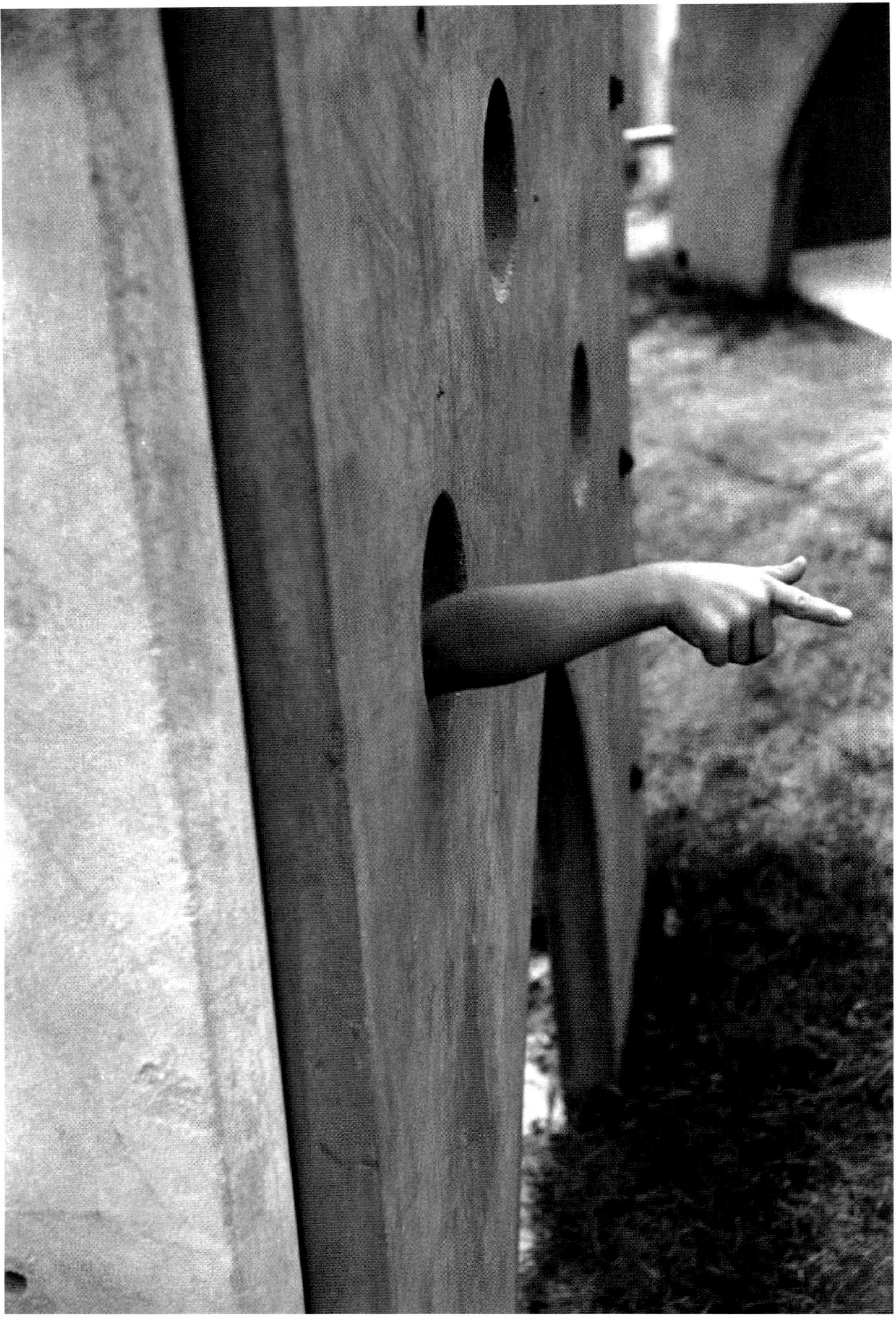

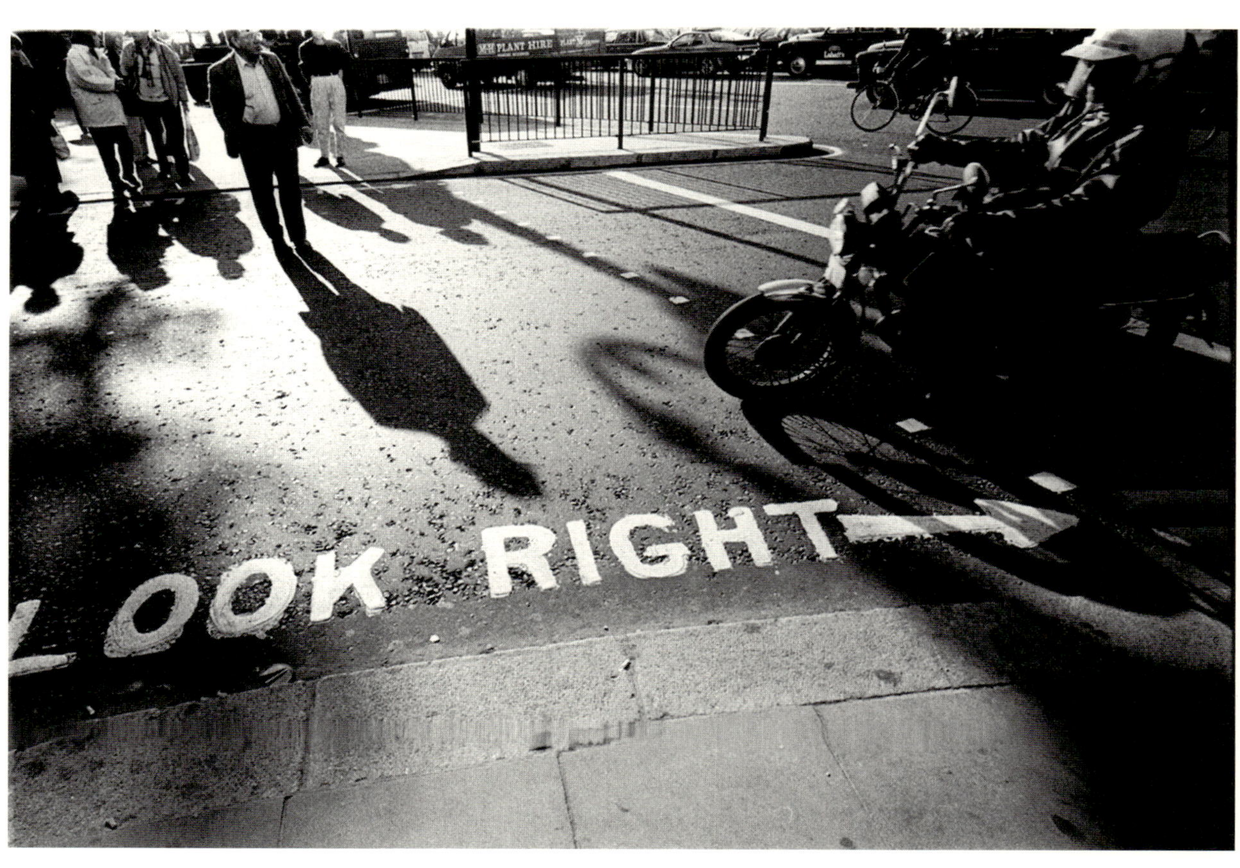
PLANT HIRE
LOOK RIGHT

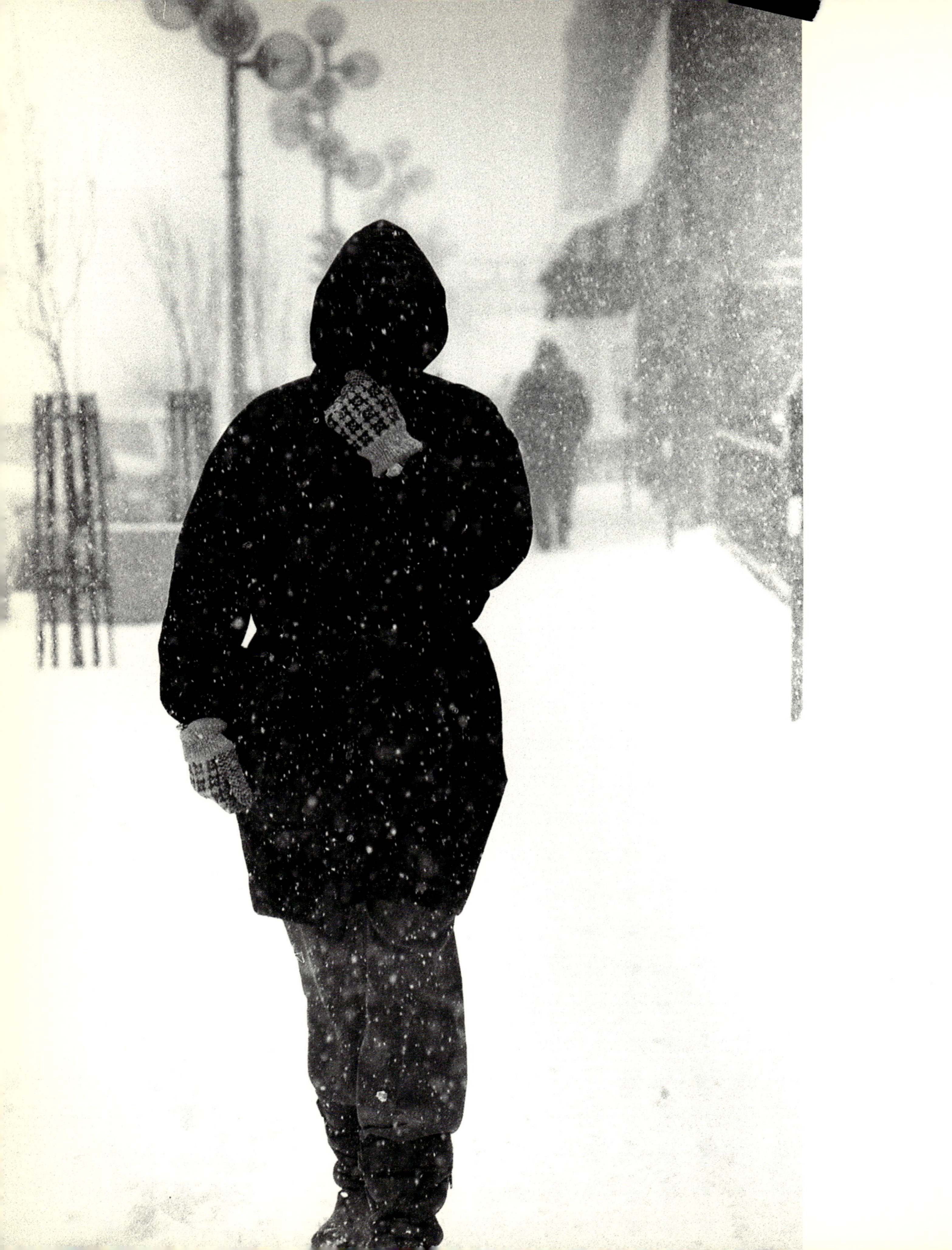

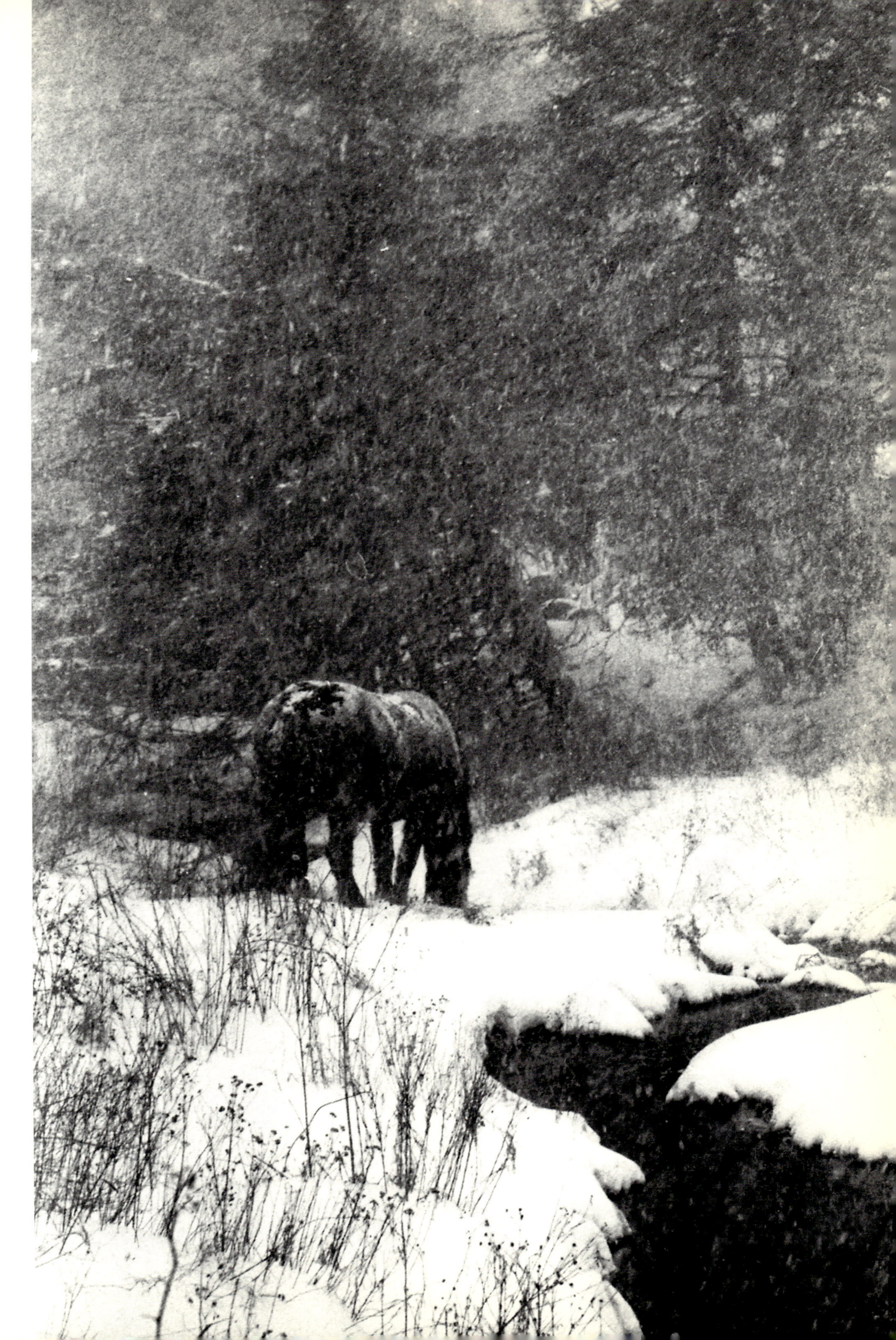

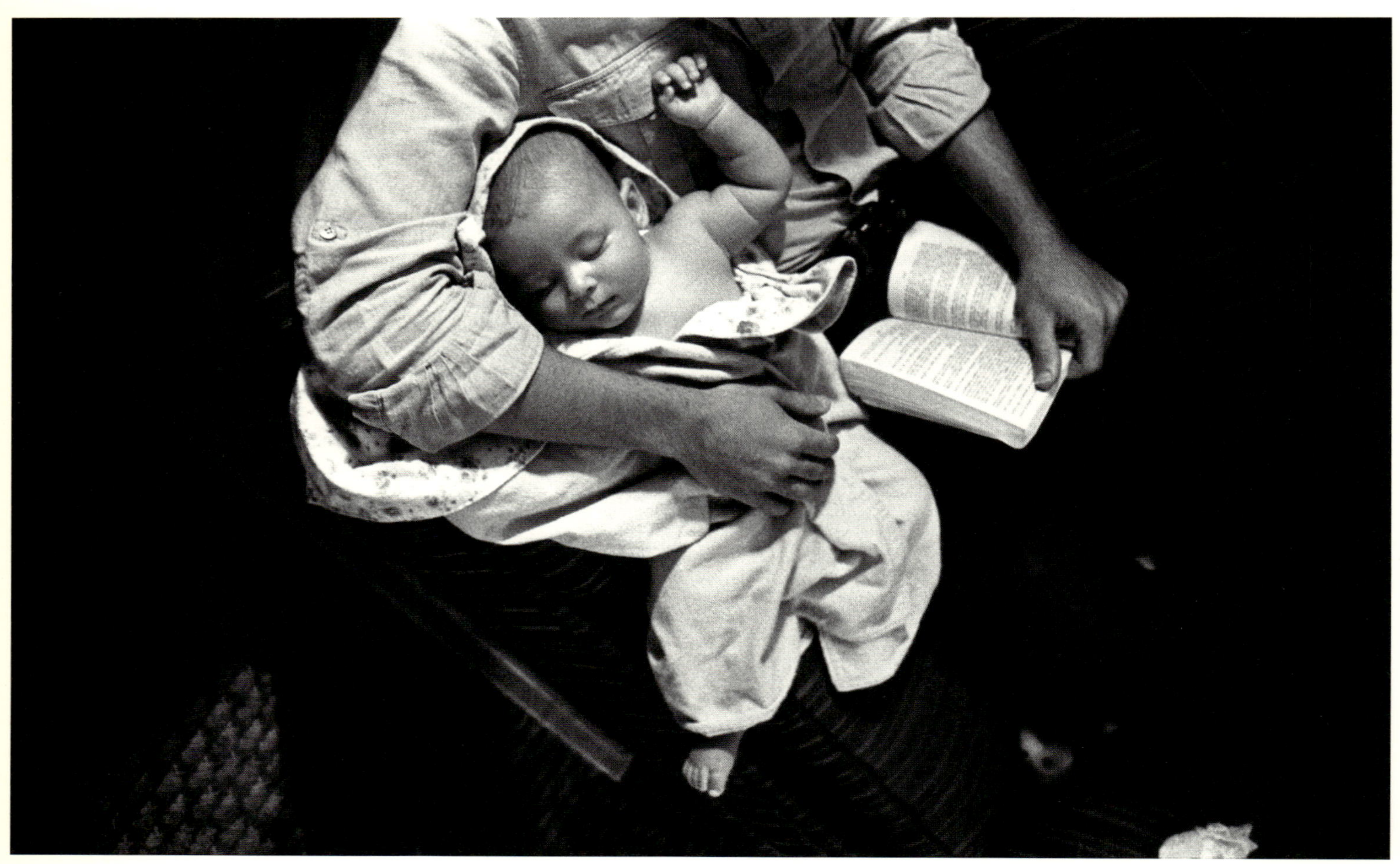

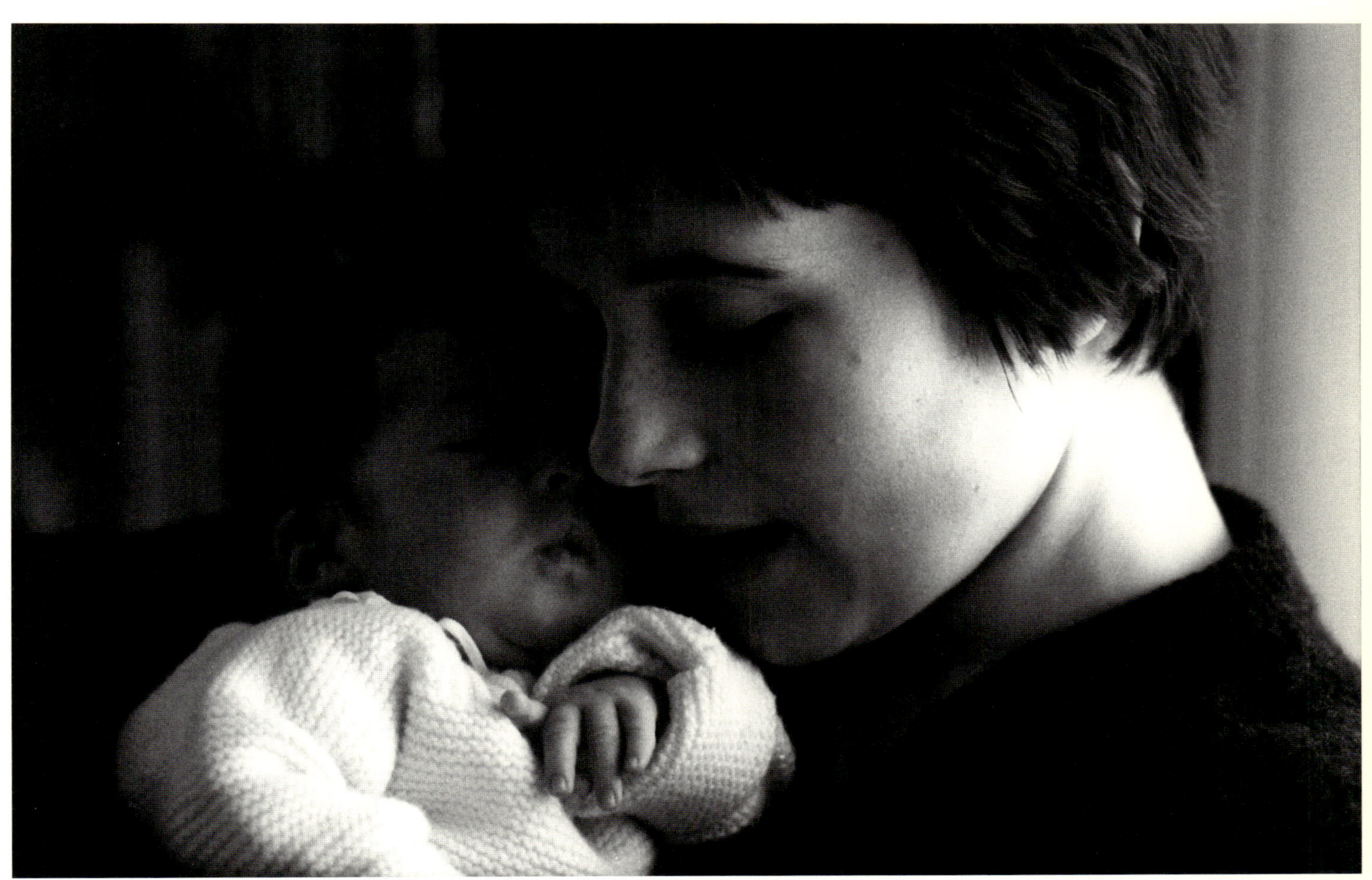

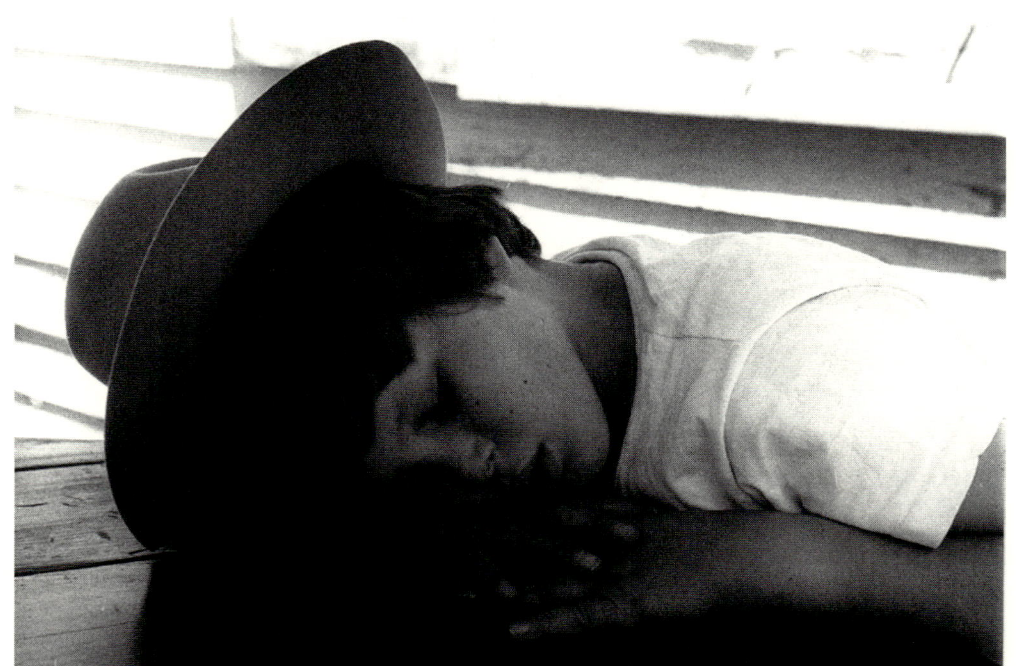

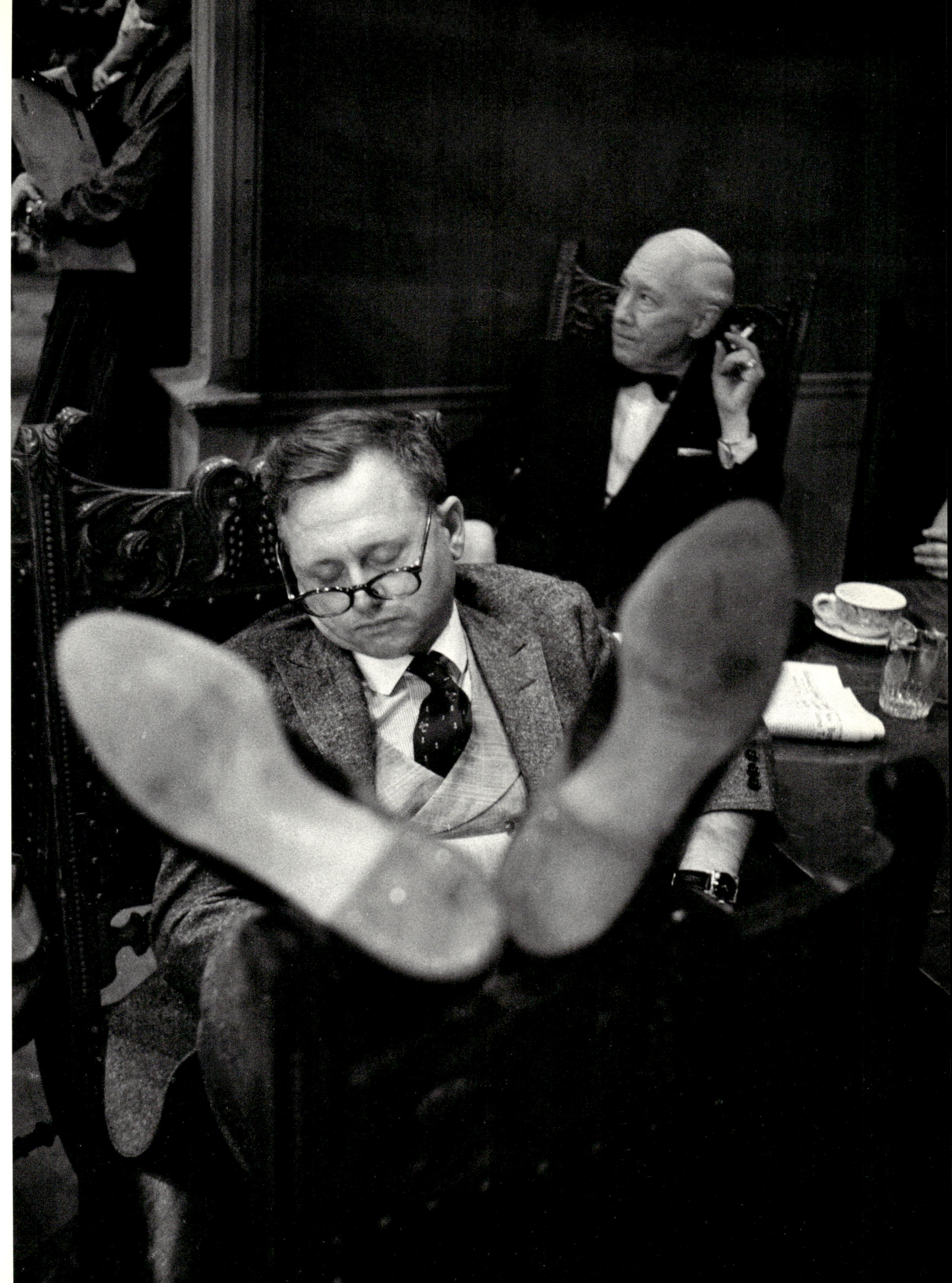

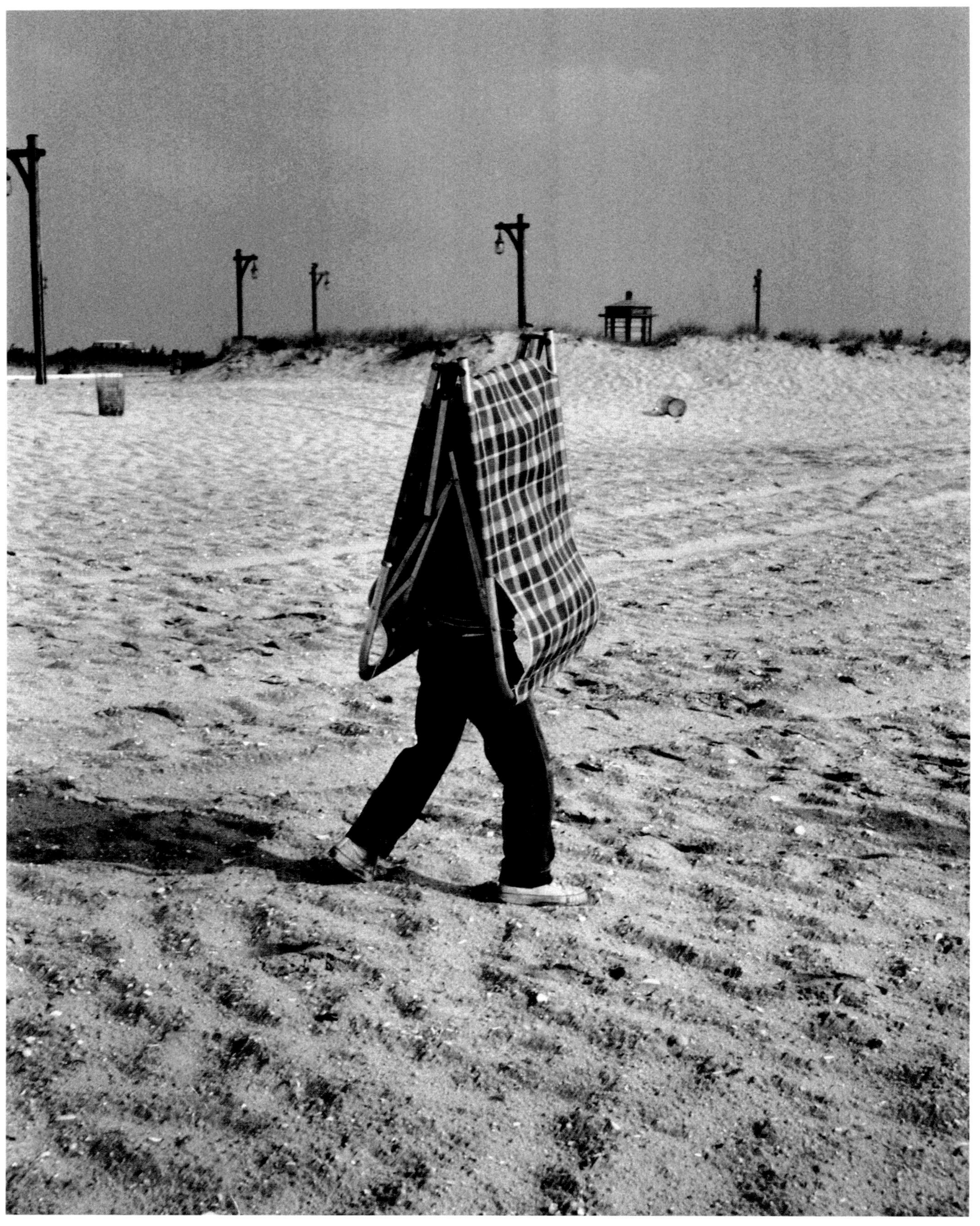

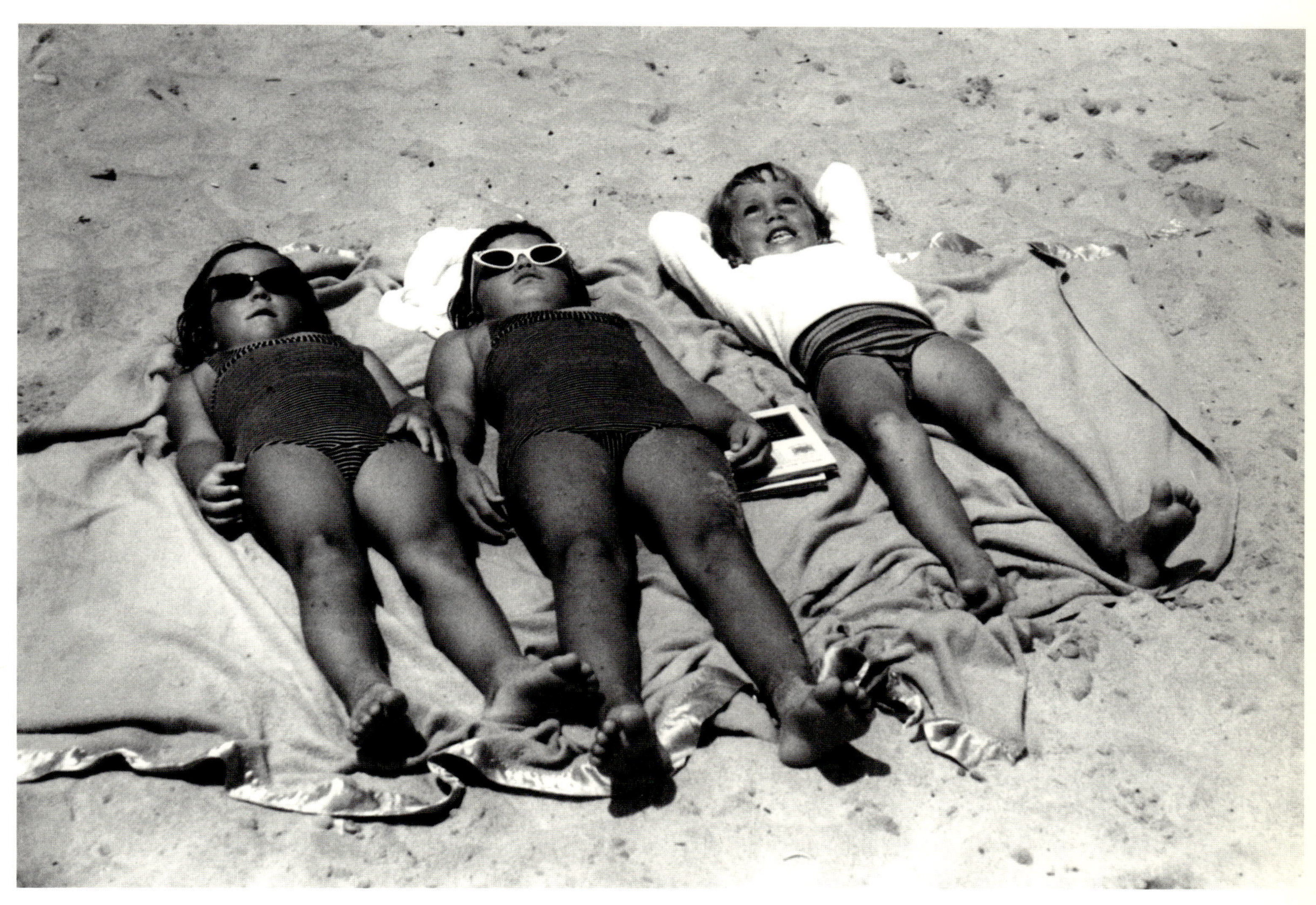

I tend to think he is more like some of the French street photographers of his time. I once said to him something about his being an optimistic photographer and he said 'I'm not a jolly person', well maybe not but he's got a jolly eye.

Vicki Goldberg, photography critic, author and photo historian

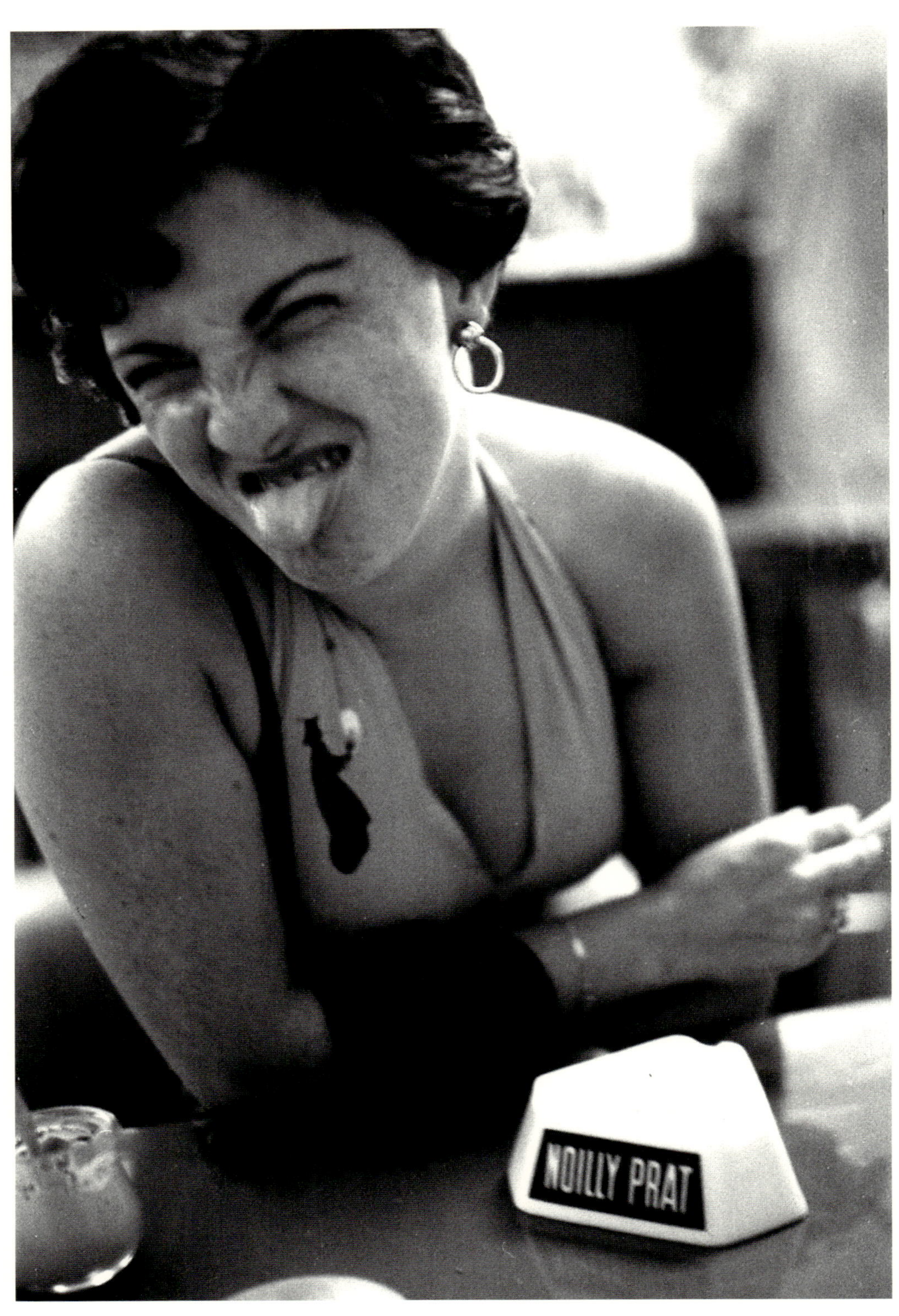
NOILLY PRAT

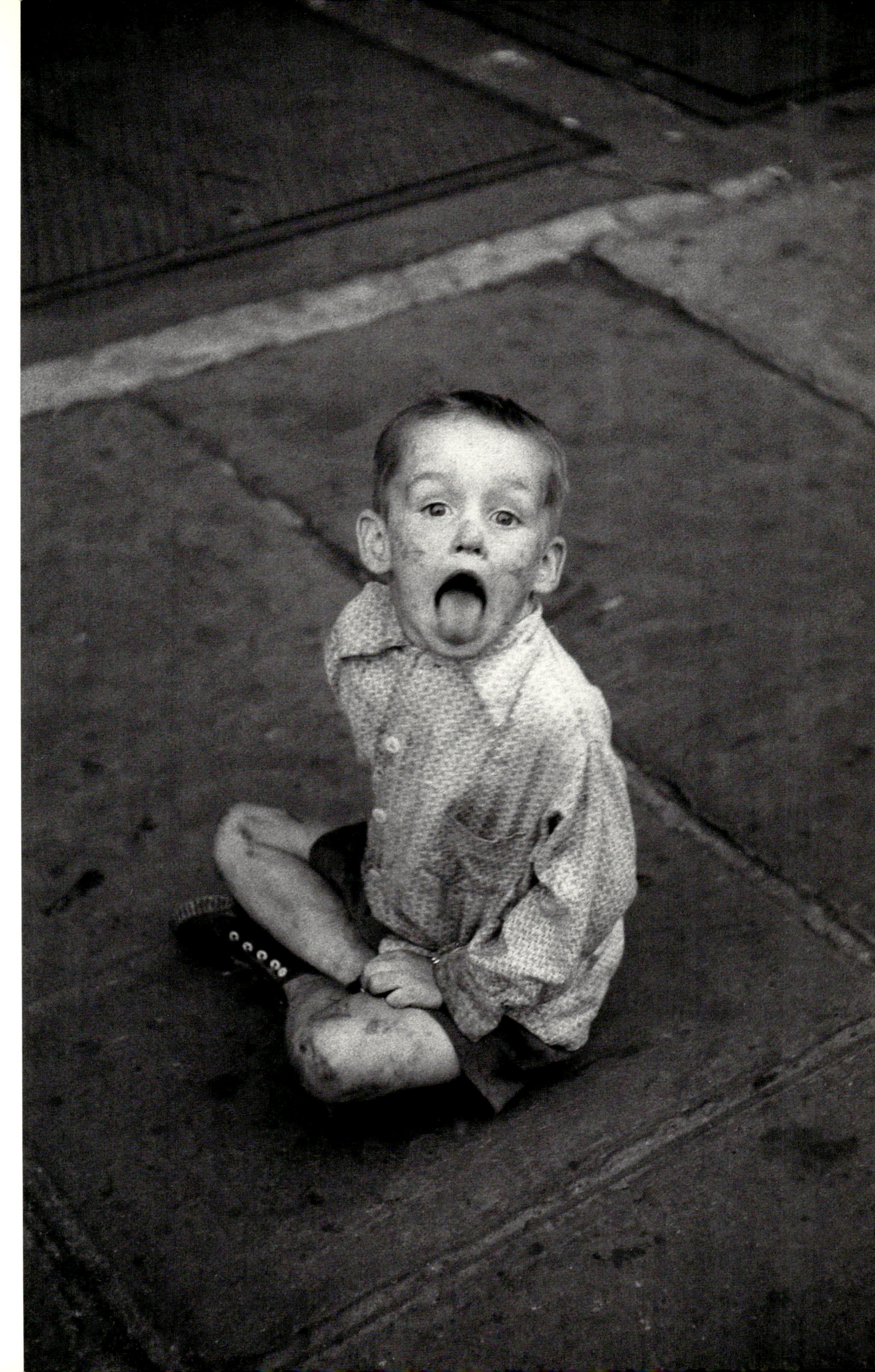

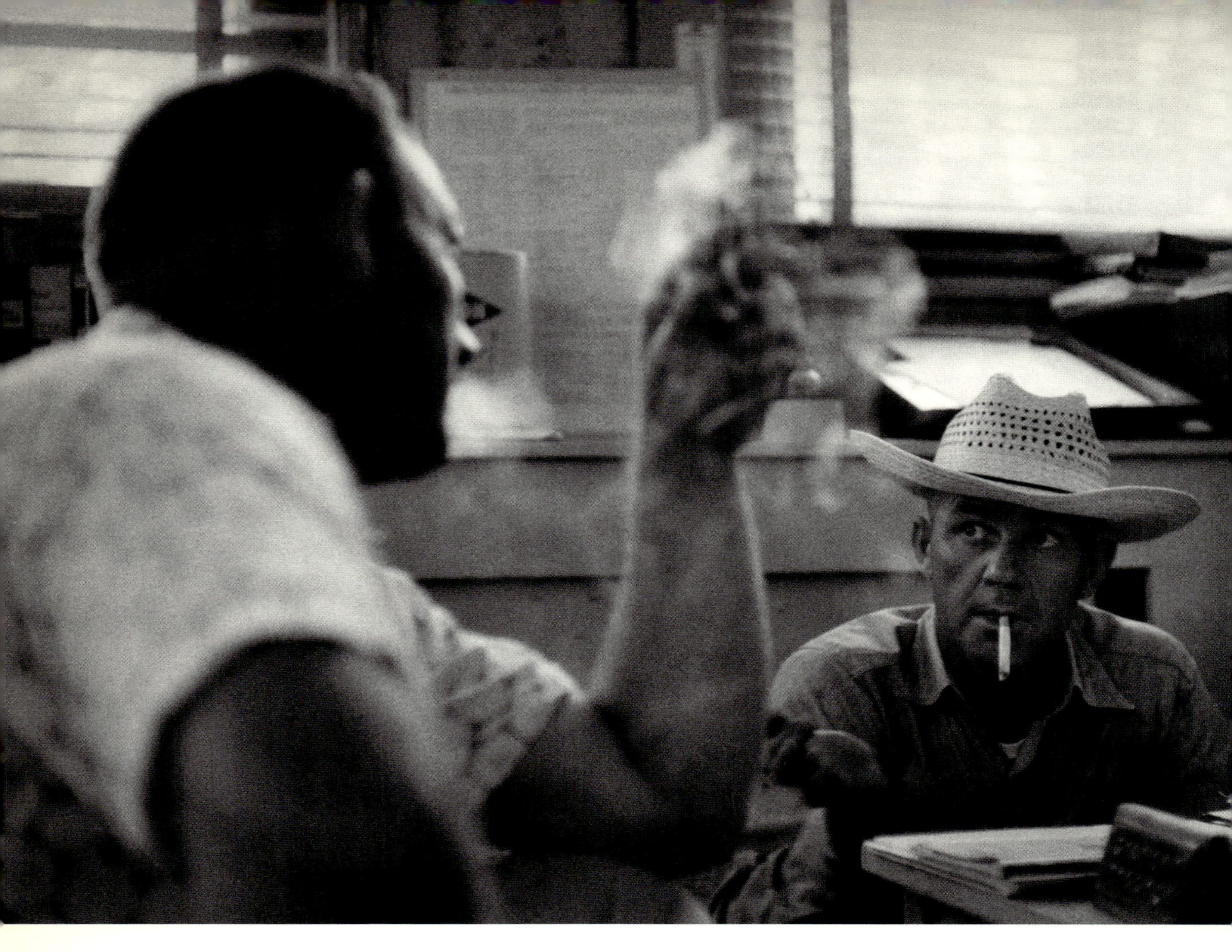

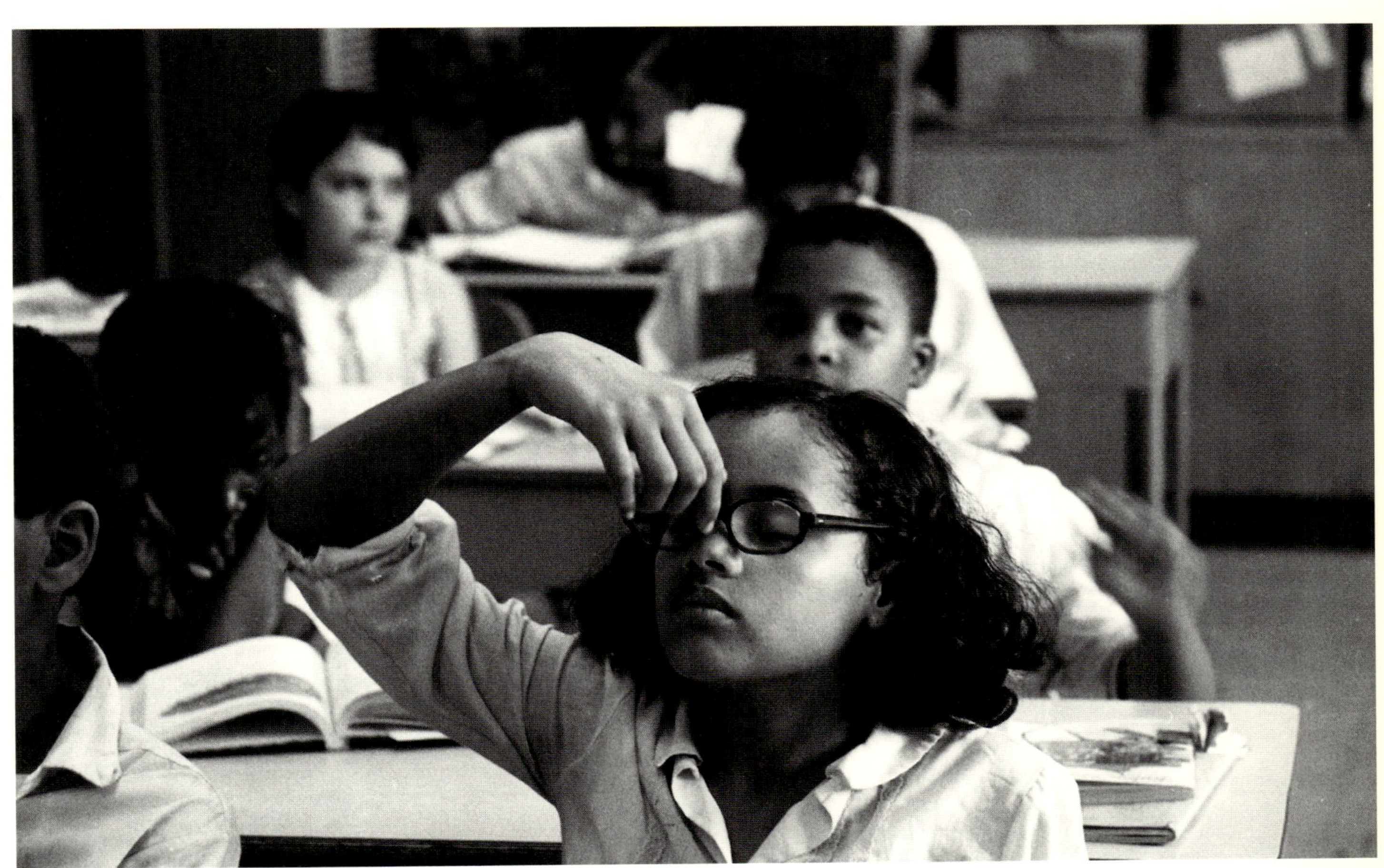

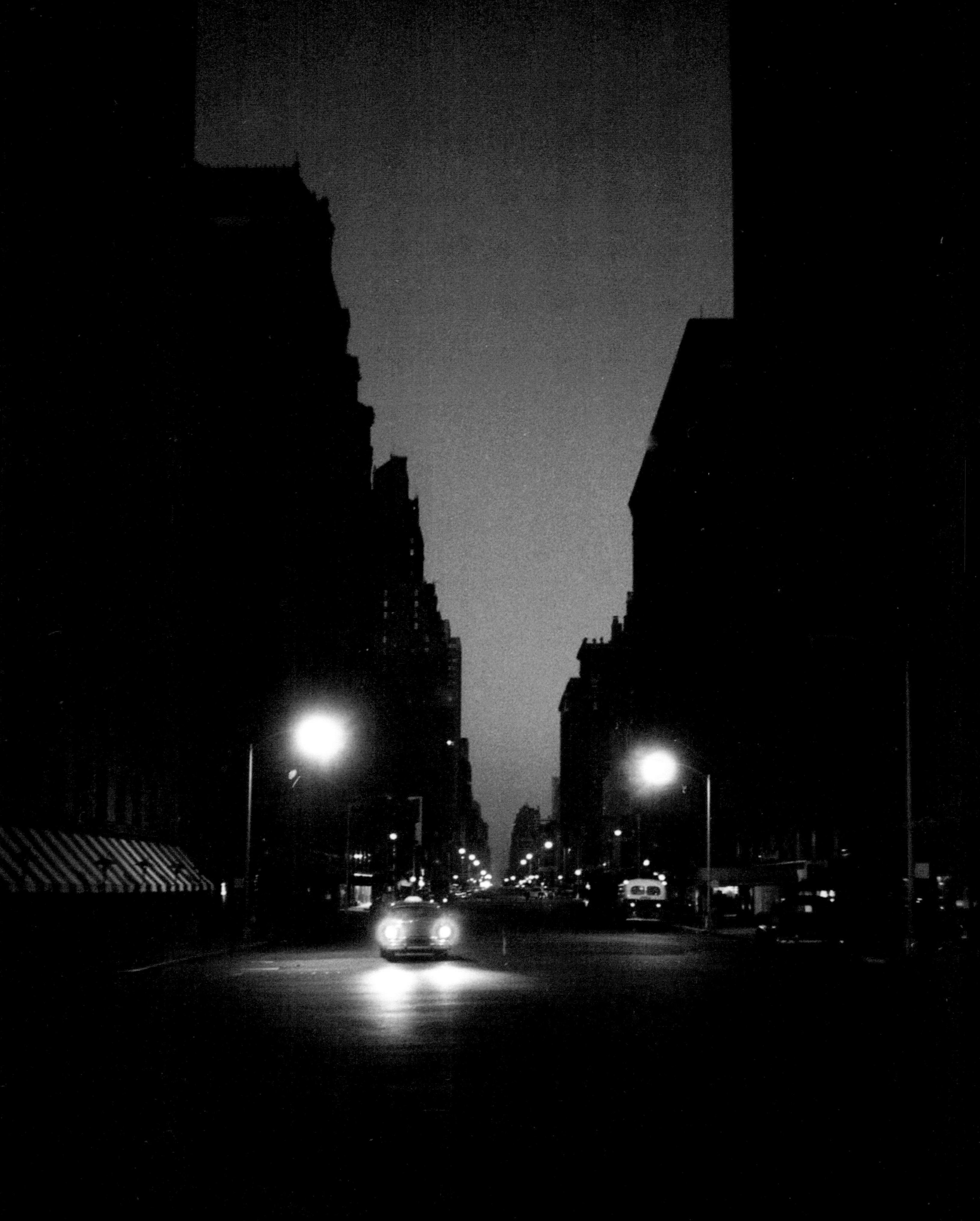

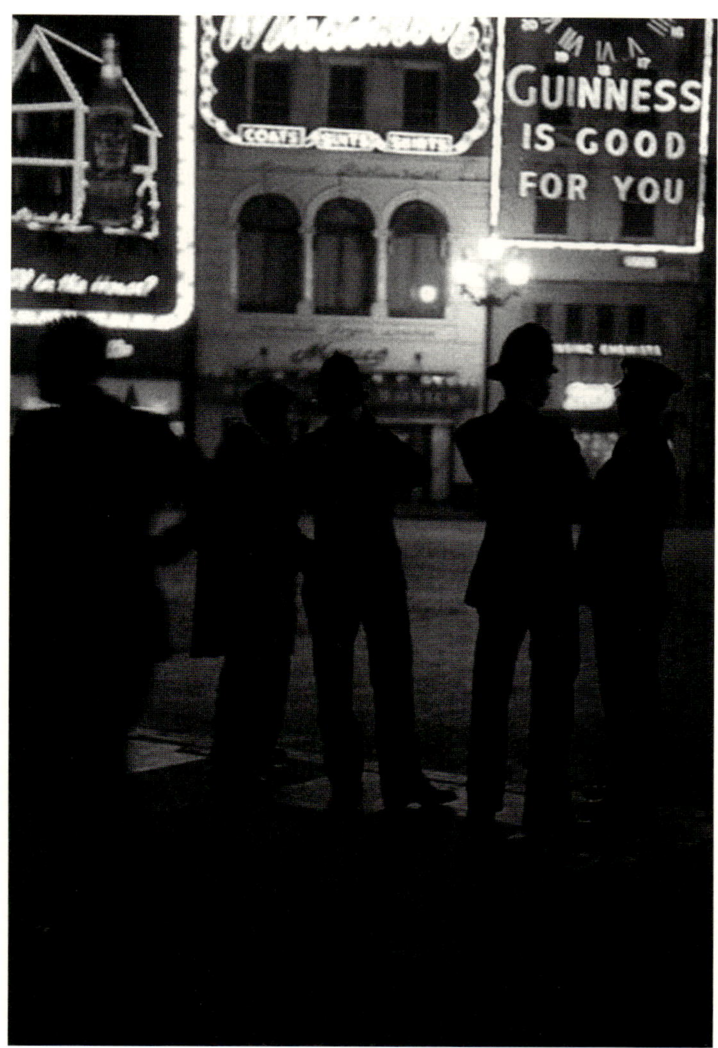
GUINNESS
IS GOOD
FOR YOU
COATS

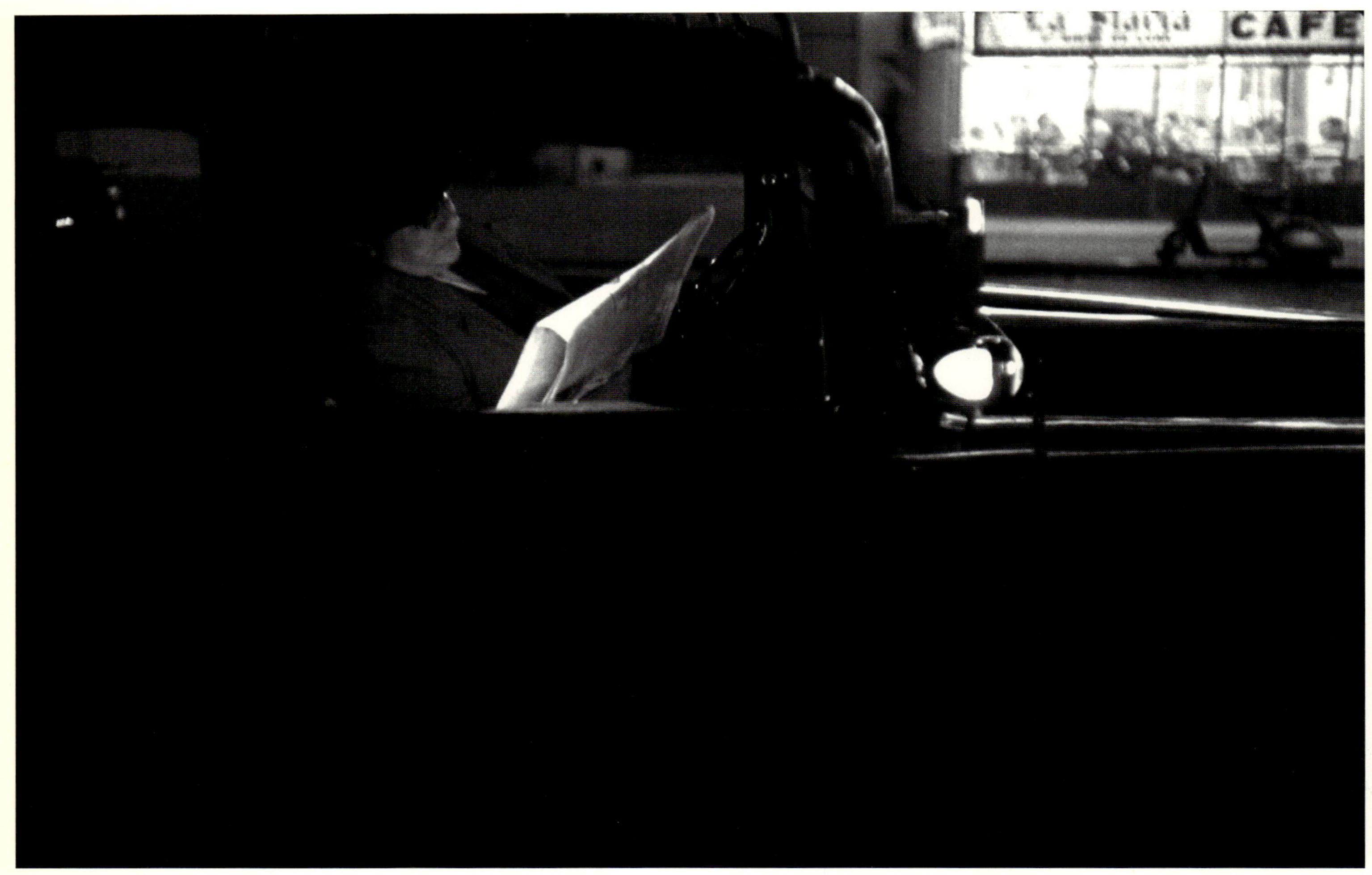
CAFE

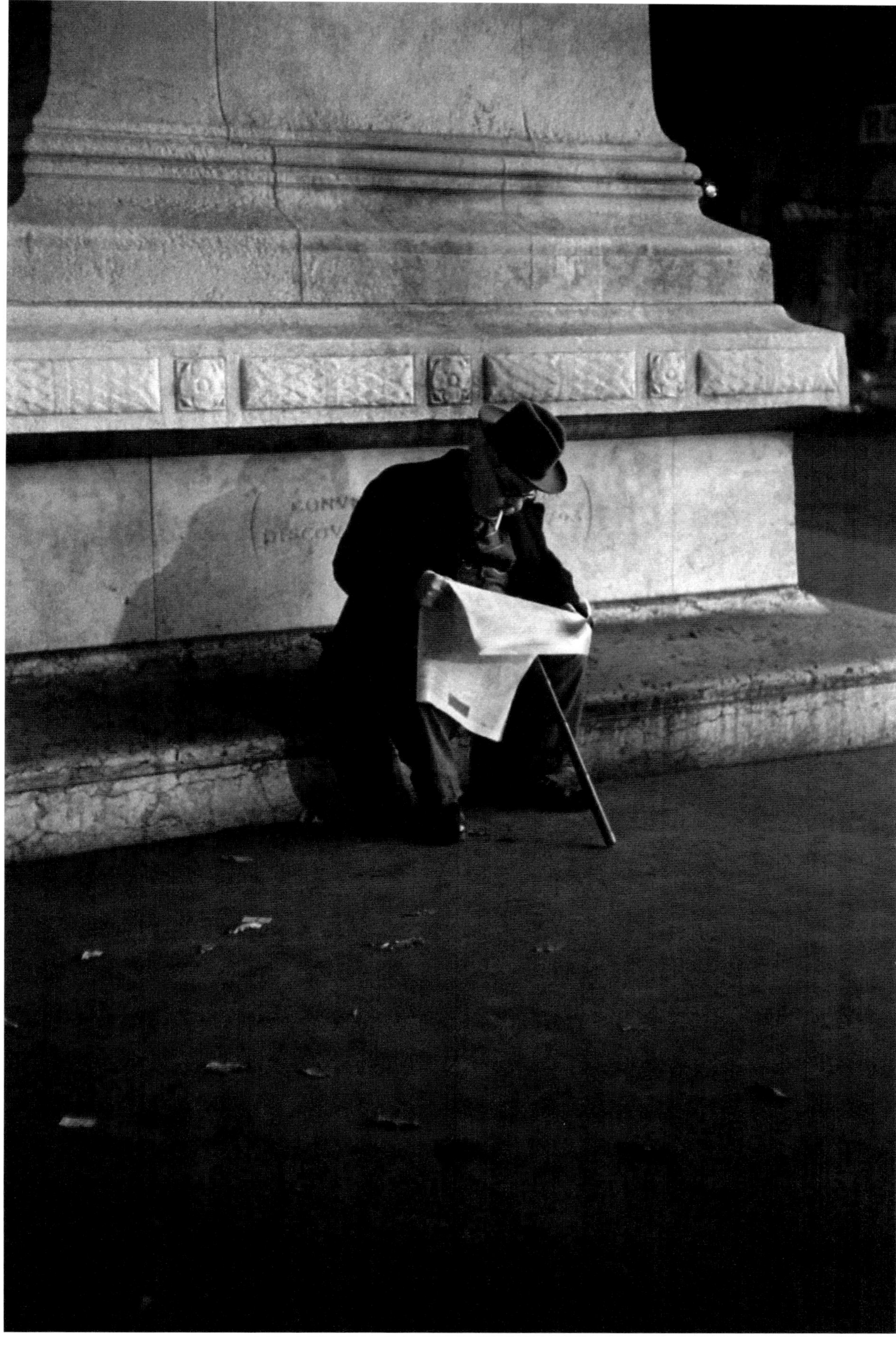

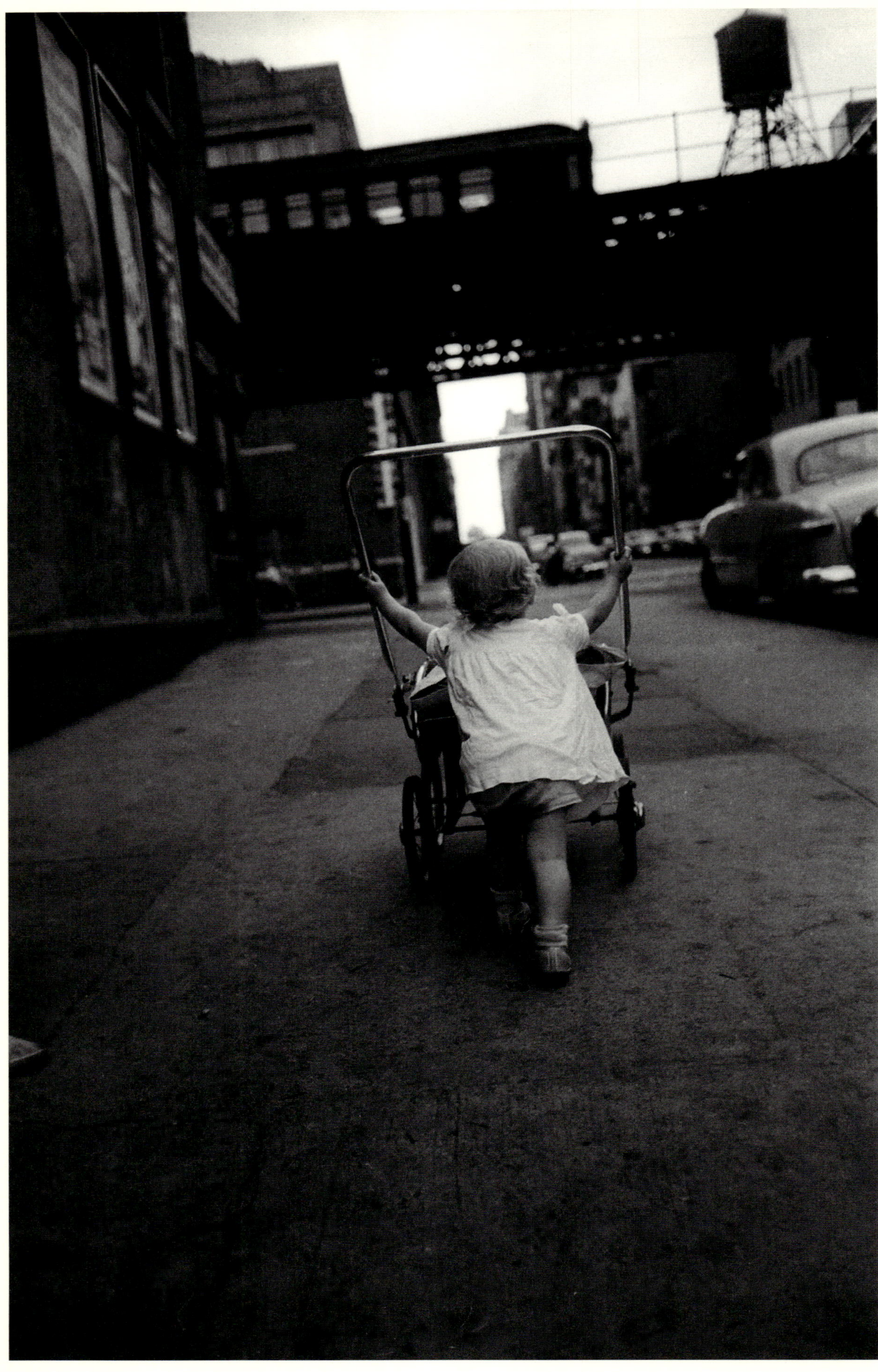

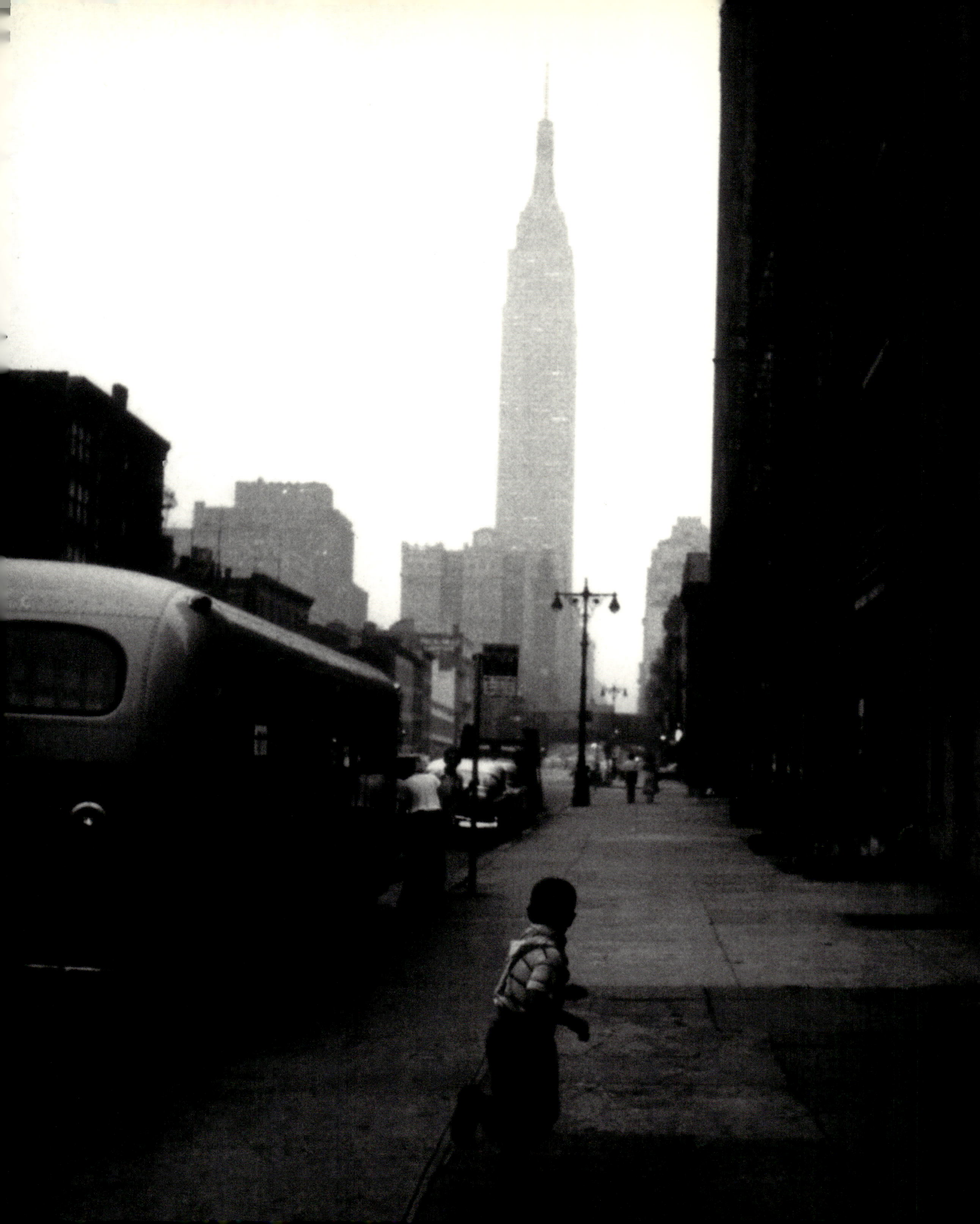

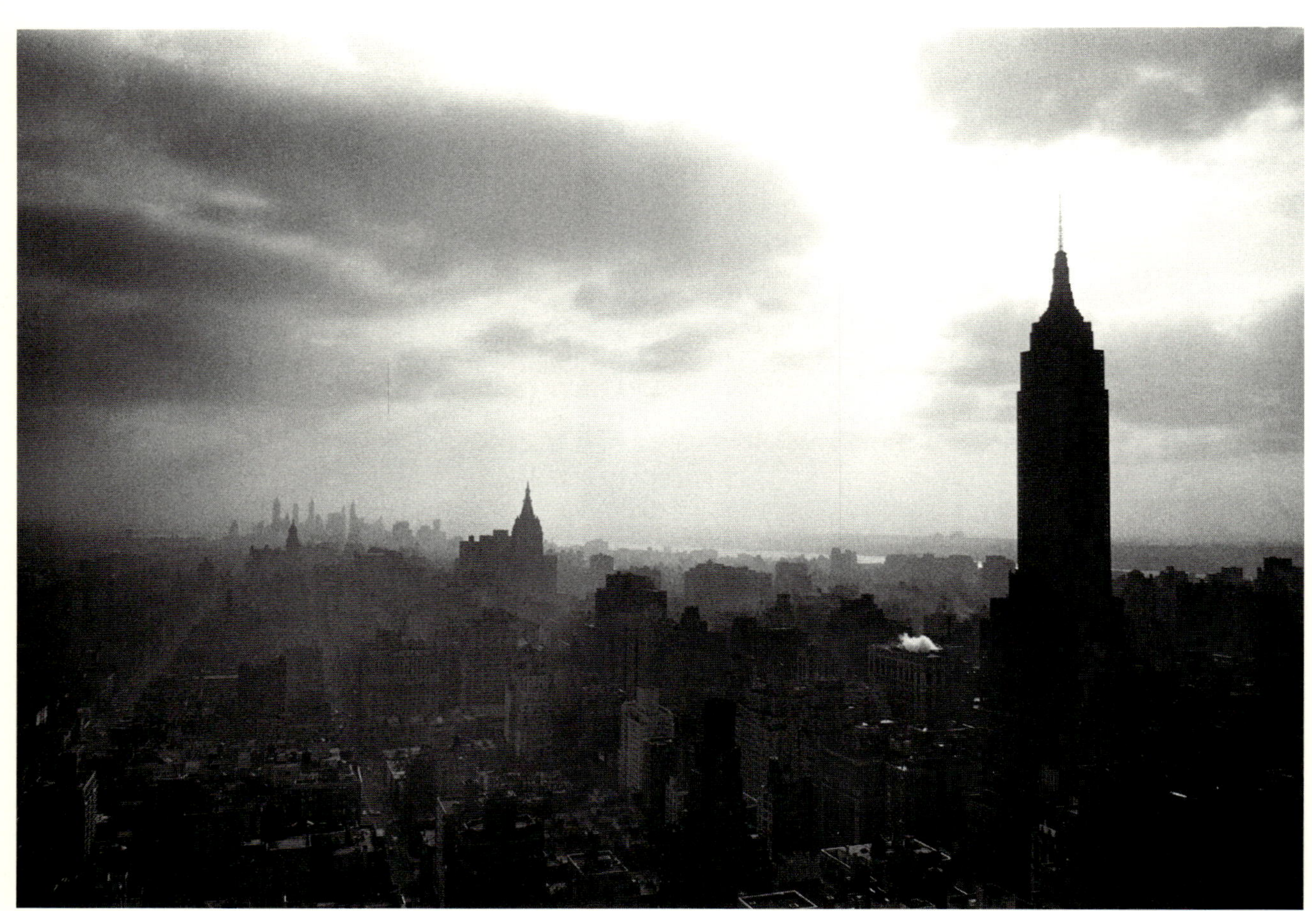

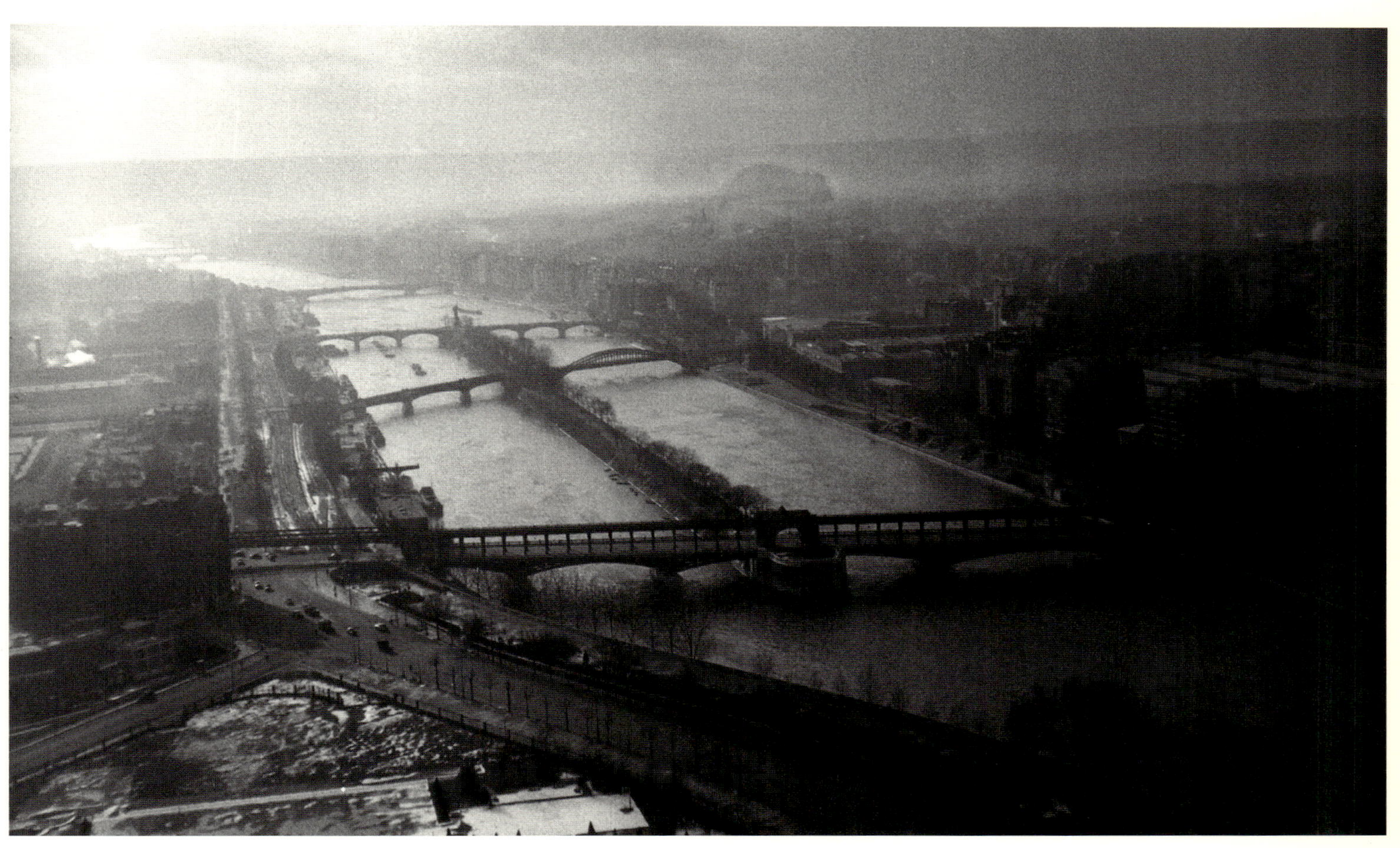

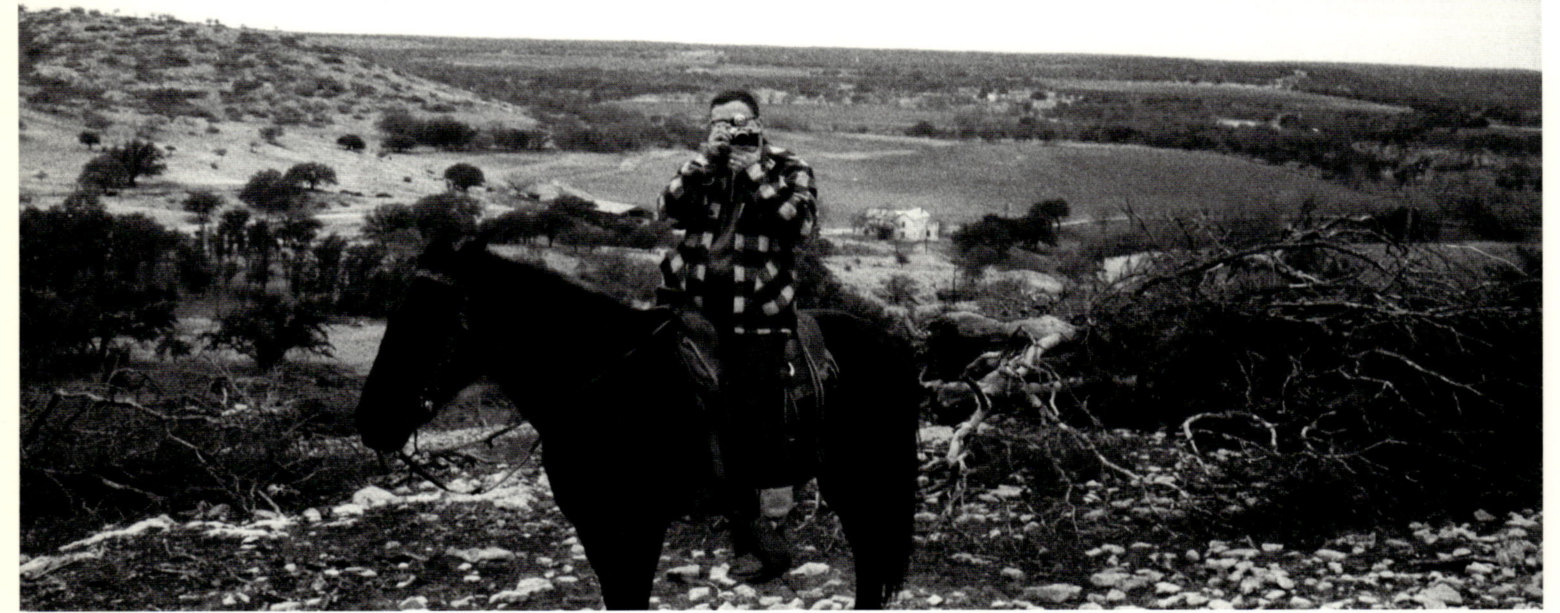

LIST OF PHOTOGRAPHS

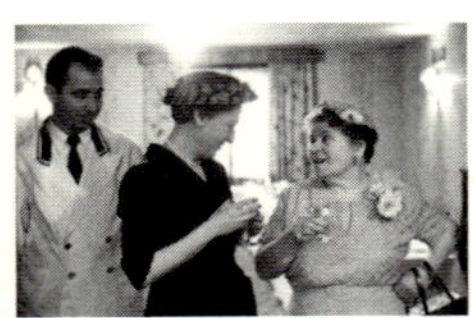

P 29 Libby at a Wedding
Milwaukee
1957

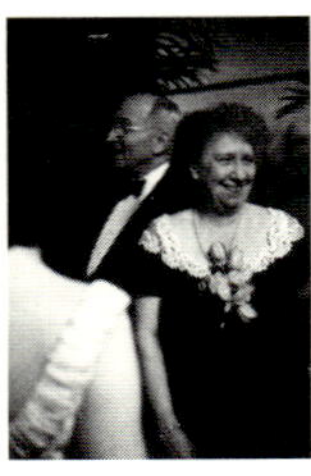

P 30 Harry & Bess Truman
NYC
1954

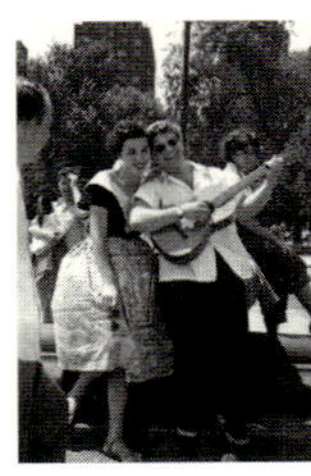

P 31 Joy of Music
Washington Square NYC
1951

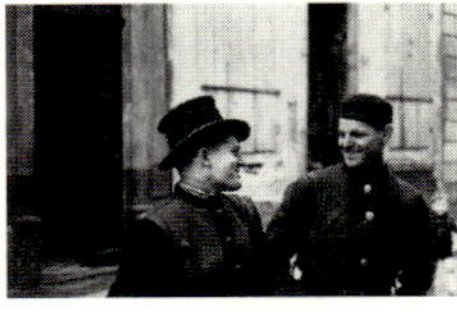

P 32 Chimney Sweeps
Karlsruhe Germany
1952

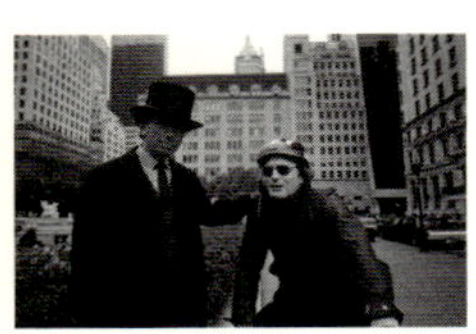

P 33 Friends
NYC
1990s

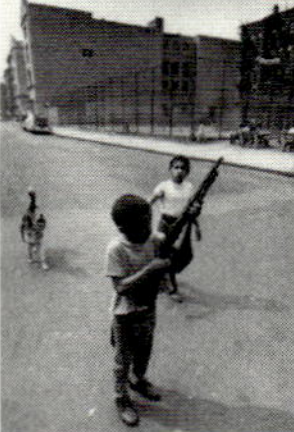

P 34 Boy & Gun
Bronx NY
1969

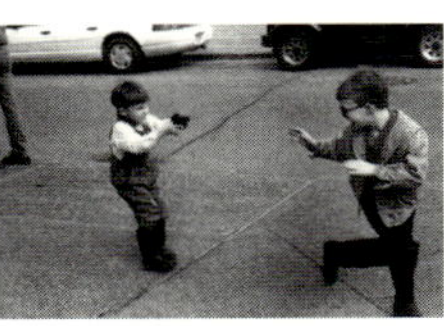

P 35 Incident on Rue Roy
Montreal
1996

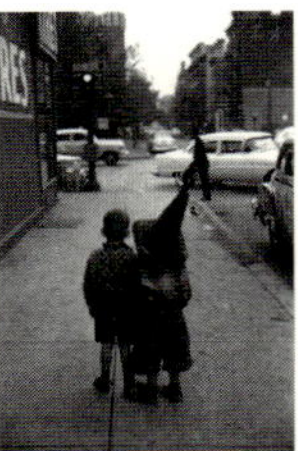

P 36 Boys with Hat
NYC
1955

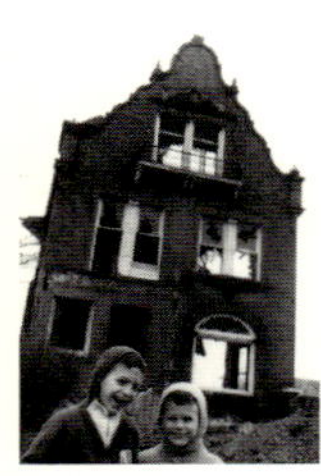

P 37 Boys with House
Milwaukee
1963

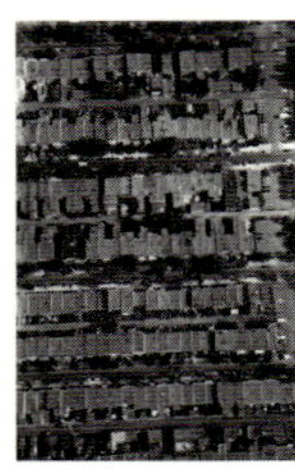

P 38 Rooftops
Montreal
1990s

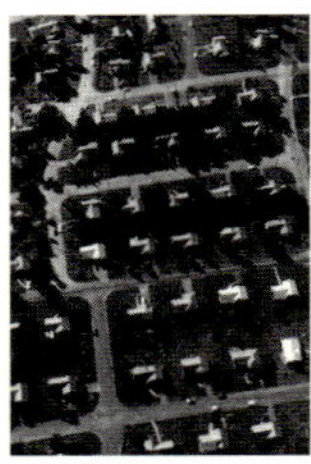

P 39 Rooftops
Westchester NY
1962

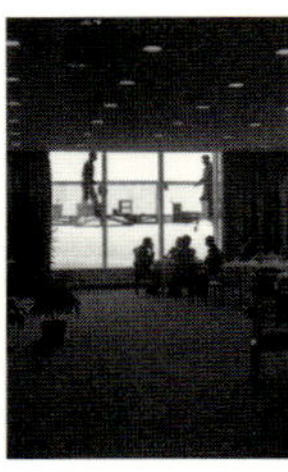

P 40 Washing Windows
Chase Manhattan Bank NYC
1964

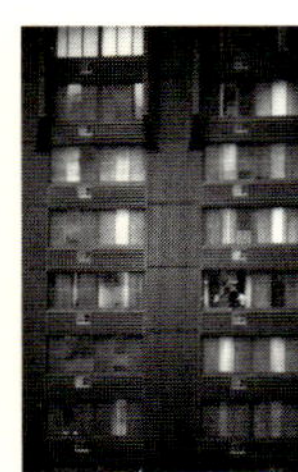

P 41 Washing Windows
Montreal
1986

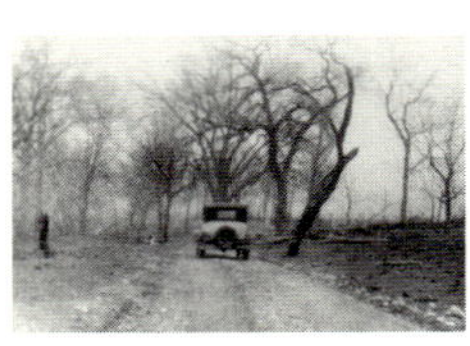

P 42 Car
Fredericksburg Texas
1955

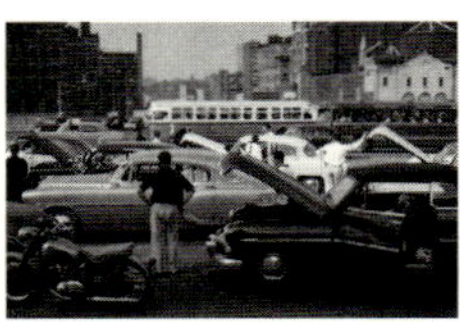

P 43 Hoods Up
NYC
1954

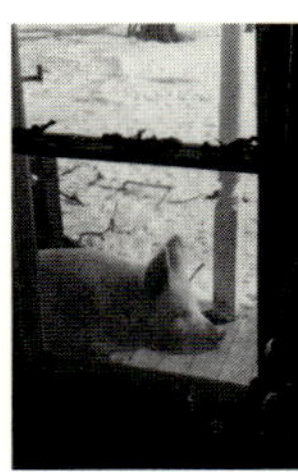

P 44 Sow at the Window
Bona Fide Farm
Prince Edward Island
1976

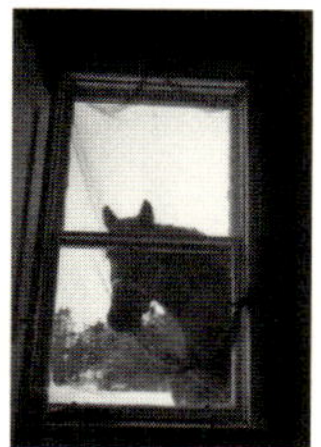

P 45 Dolly at the Window
Bona Fide Farm
Prince Edward Island
1976

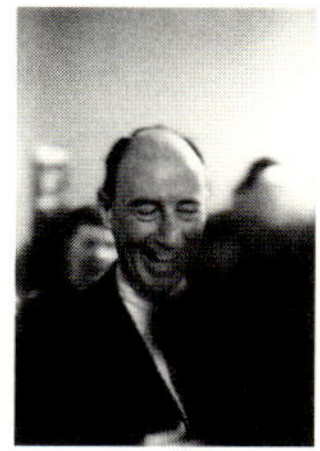

P 46 The Egghead (Adlai Stevenson)
NYC
1956

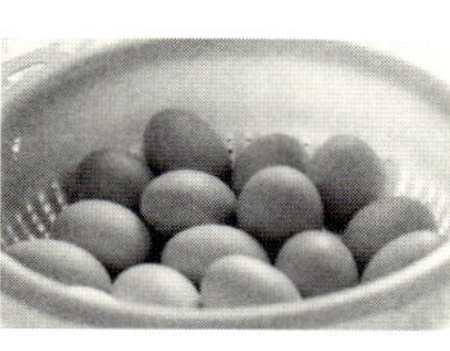

P 47 Eggs
Bona Fide Farm
Prince Edward Island
1970s

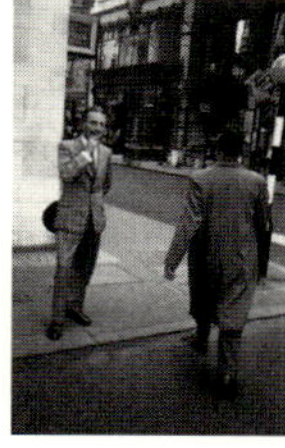

P 48 Smoker
London
1952

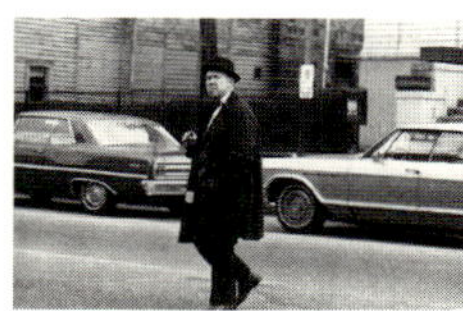

P 49 American Man
Peekskill NY
1970

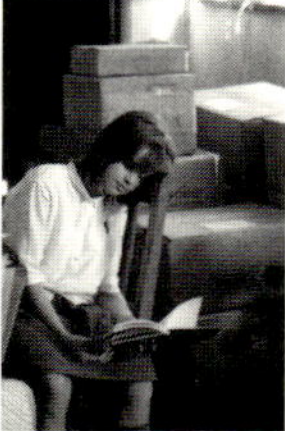

P 52 Girl among the Books
Middletown NY
1969

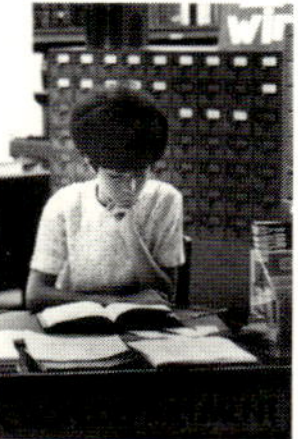

P 53 Fiction Department
Philadelphia Public Library
1968

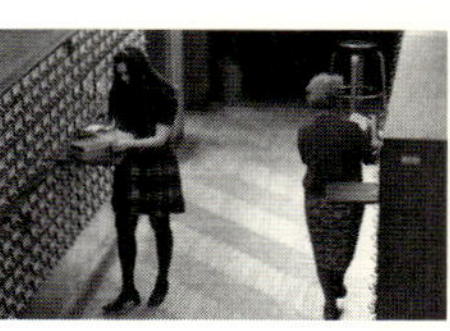

P 54 Two Librarians
Stephen's College Columbia MO
1964

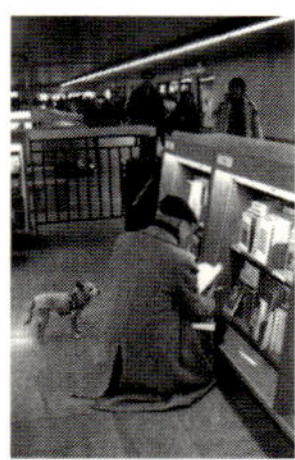

P 55 Man & Dog
Metro McGill Library Montreal
1986

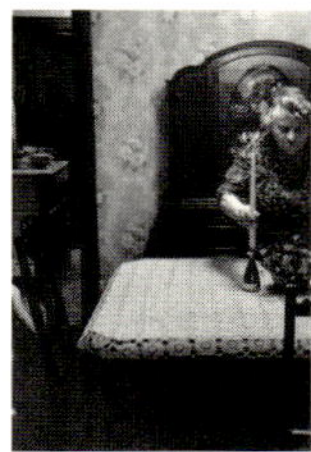

P 56 Libby & Little Ike
Milwaukee
1964

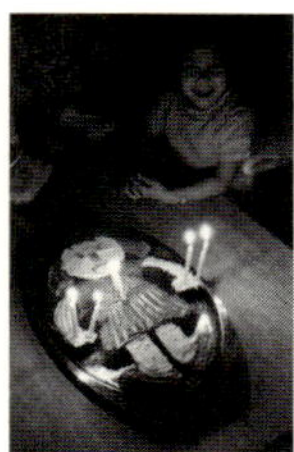

P 57 Jodi's Birthday
Peekskill NY
1967

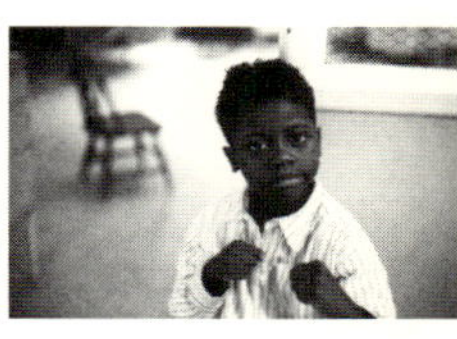

P 58 Little Joe Louis
Philadelphia
1953

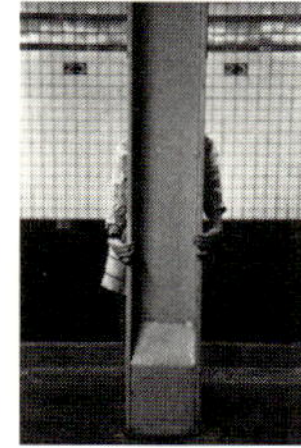

P 59 The Post
23rd St Subway Stop
NYC
1992

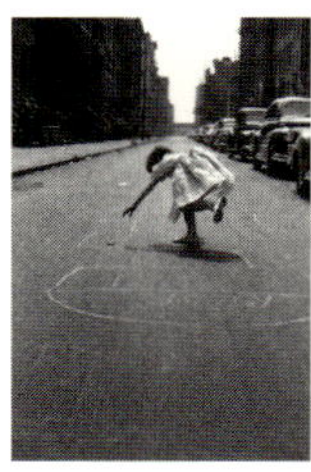

P 60 Hopscotch 93rd St
NYC
1950

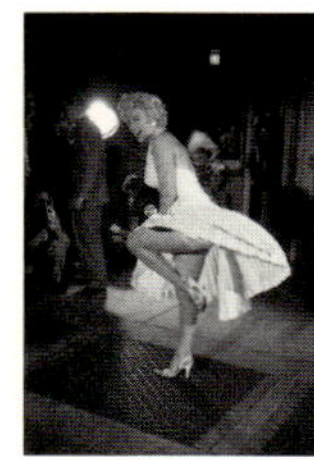

P 61 Marilyn Monroe Leg Up
NYC
1954

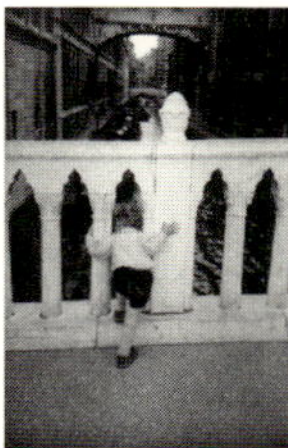

P 62 The Watcher
Venice Italy
1953

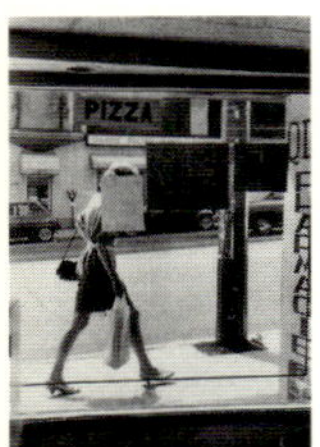

P 63 Pizza
Montreal
1987

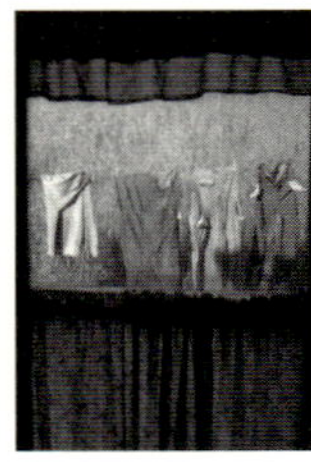

P 64 Laundry
Bona Fide Farm
Prince Edward Island
1976

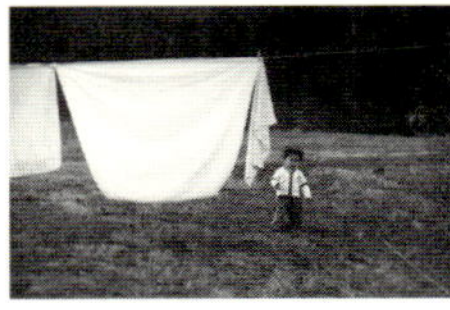

P 65 Jodi & the Sheets
Peekskill NY
1964

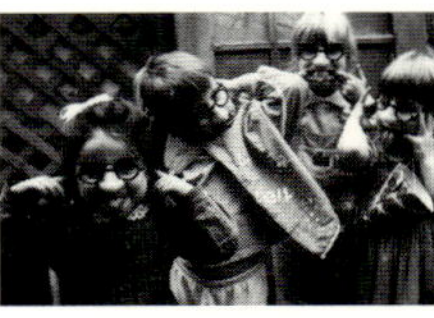

P 66 The Birthday Party
Montreal
1995

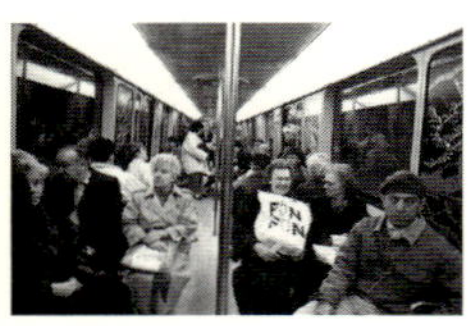

P 67 FunFun
Montreal
1986

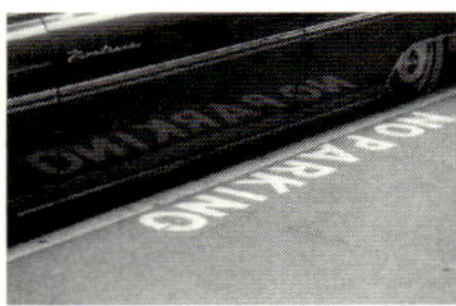

P 70 No Parking
NYC
1953

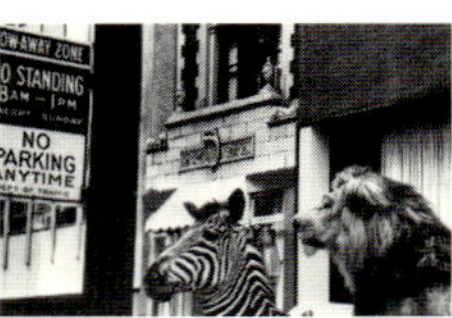

P 71 No Parking Anytime
NYC
1953

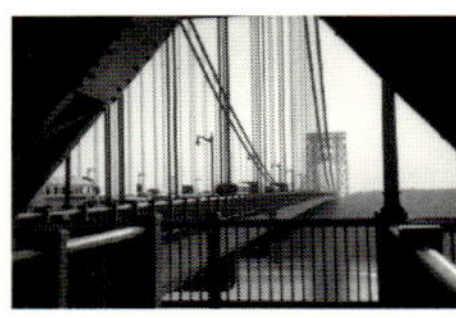

P 72 George Washington Bridge
NYC
1954

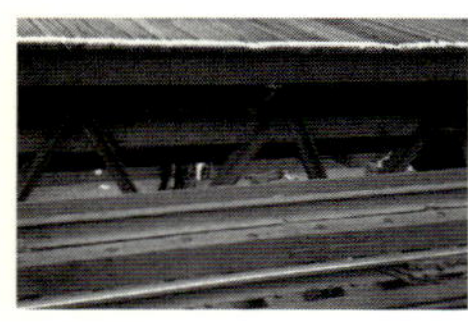

P 73 Dead Man under Third Ave El
NYC
1951

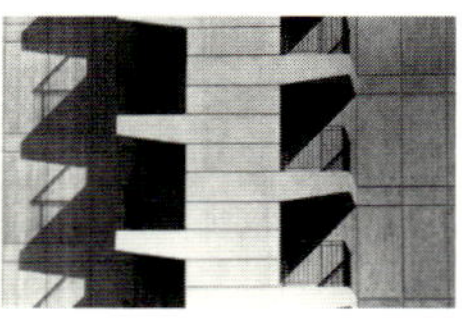

P 74 Horizon House
Englewood Cliffs NJ
1963

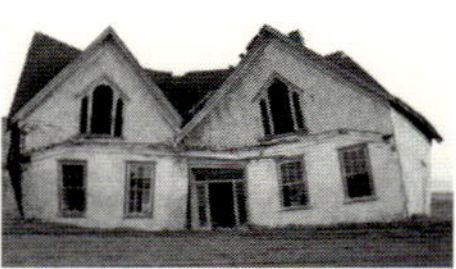

P 75 The Old Ferguson Place
Prince Edward Island
1980

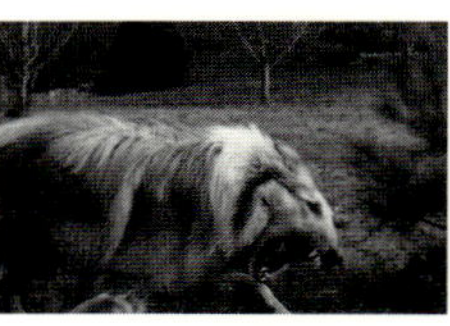

P 76 Snarling Dog
Peekskill NY
1960s

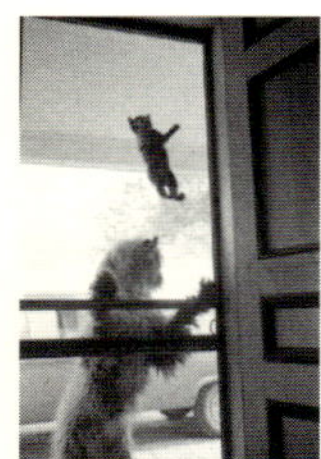

P 77 Dog & Kitten on Screen
Prince Edward Island
1976

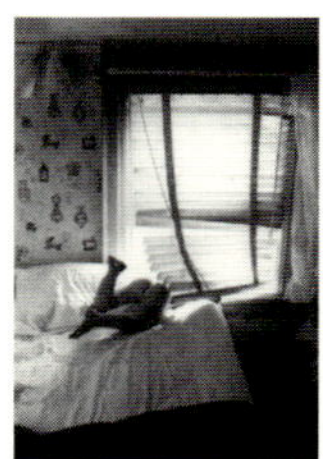

P 78 Matt Looks out Window
Peekskill NY
1959

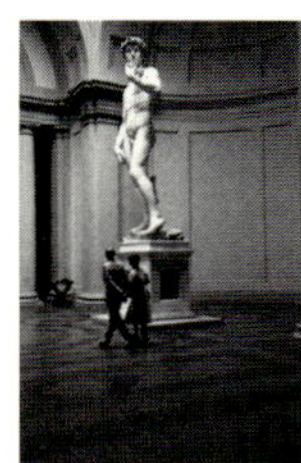

P 79 David
Florence Italy
1953

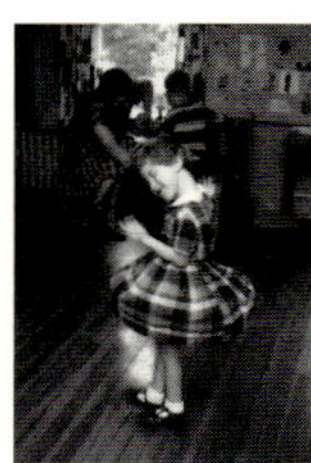

P 80 Girl Twirling
Talledega Ala
1956

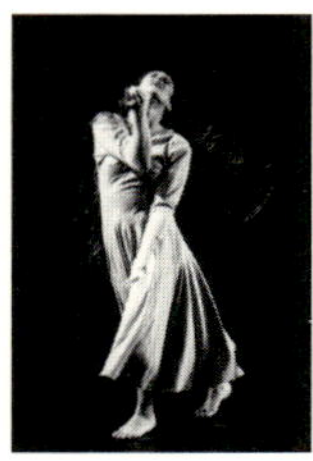

P 81 Margie Gillis
Montreal
1980s

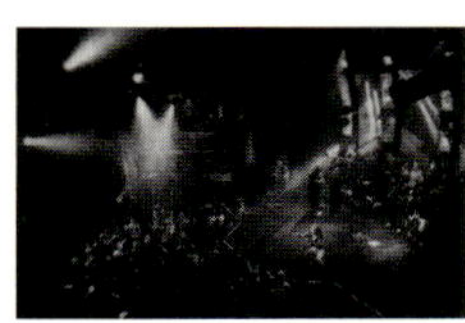

P 84 Amanda Marshall Rock Concert
Montreal
2002

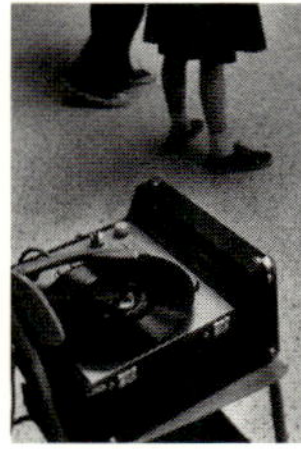

P 85 The Record Player
Peekskill NY
1960s

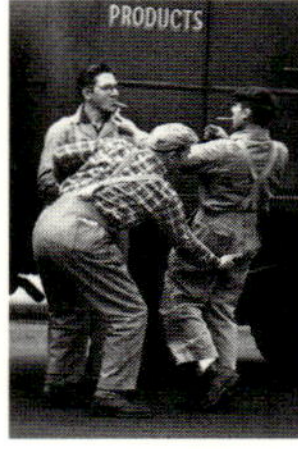

P 86 The Goose
Bronx NY
1958

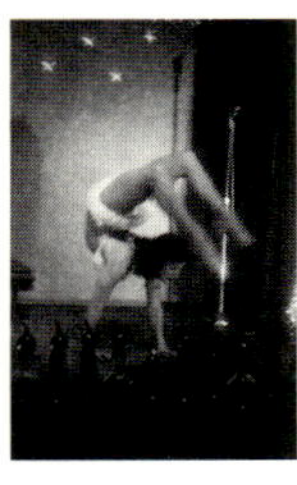

P 87 The Contortionist
New Orleans
1955

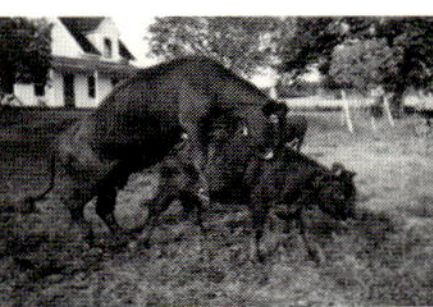

P 88 Two Cows
Bona Fide Farm
Prince Edward Island
1976

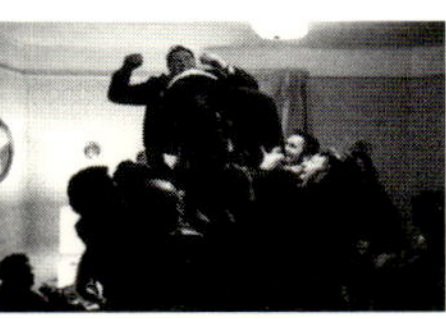

P 89 Bouncing Cecil Birthday Party
Prince Edward Island
1972

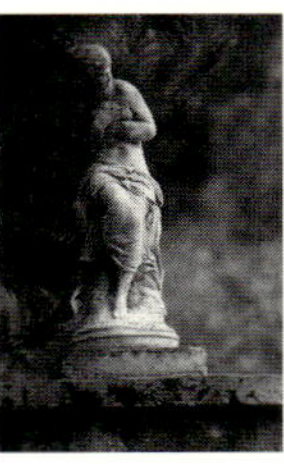

P 90 Somewhere in Quebec
2002

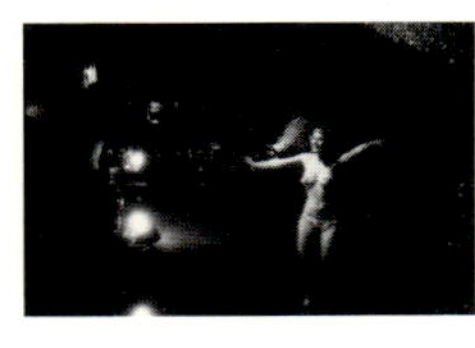

P 91 The Happy Stripper
New Orleans
1955

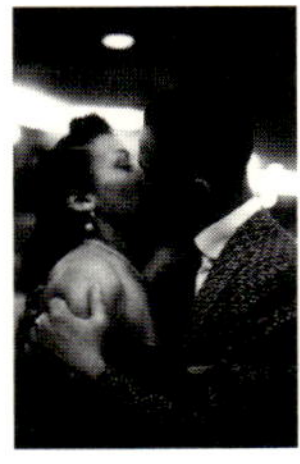

P 92 Late Night Kiss
Harlem NY
1951

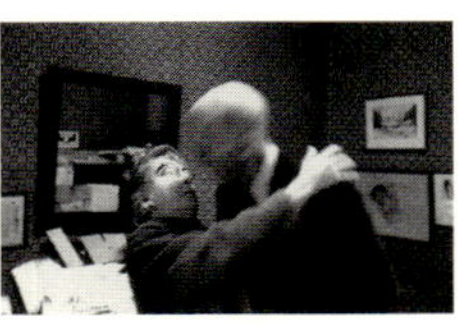

P 93 Latter Day Kiss
Queens NY
1969

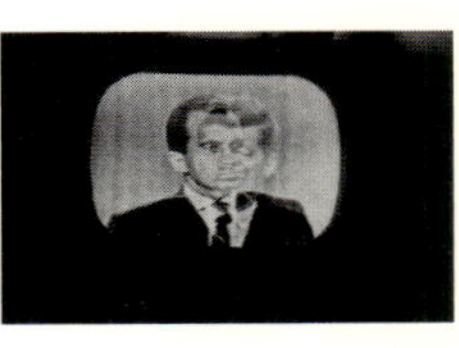

P 94 Nixon-Kennedy TV Debate
1960

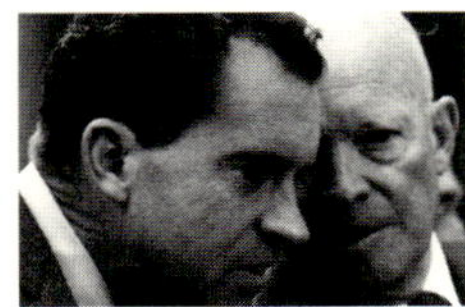

P 95 Eisenhower & Nixon
NYC
1960

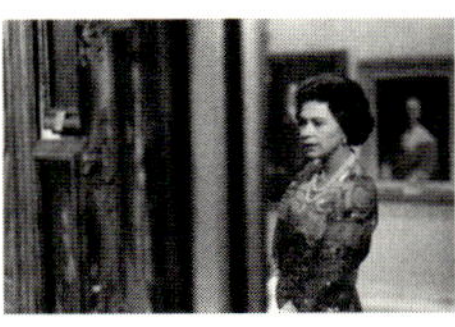

P 96 The Queen Regards Art
Prince Edward Island
1972

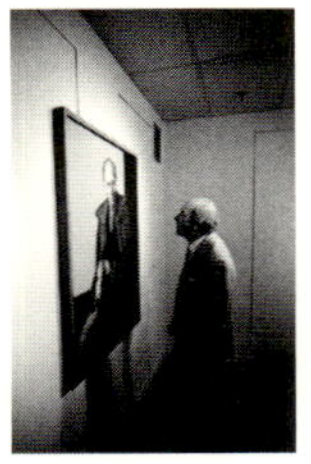

P 97 Trudeau Regards Trudeau
Montreal
1995

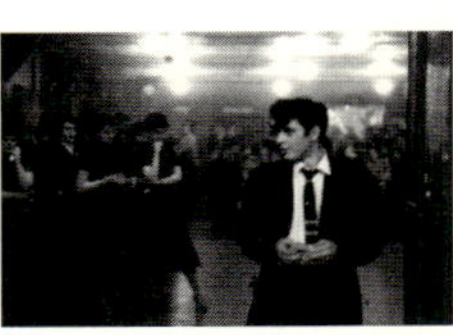

P 98 Irish Dancehall
The Bronx NY
1954

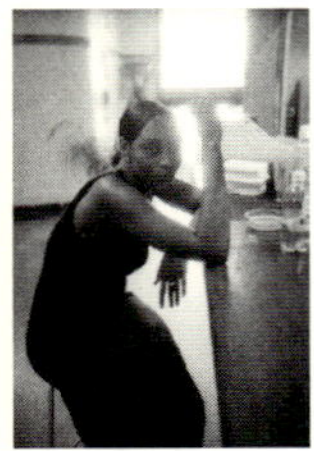

P 99 Woman at 10 Pine
Montreal
1997

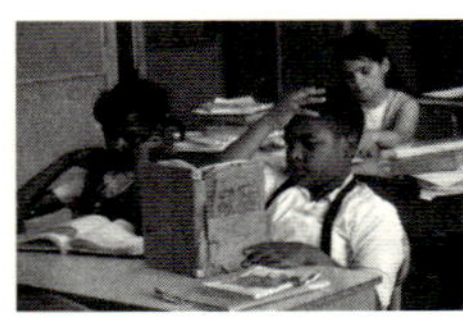

P 102 Flummoxed Reader
Bronx NY
1960s

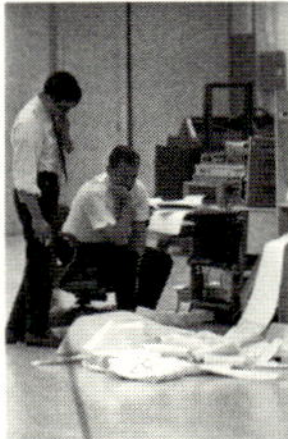

P 103 Flummoxed Programmers
Rochester NY
1962

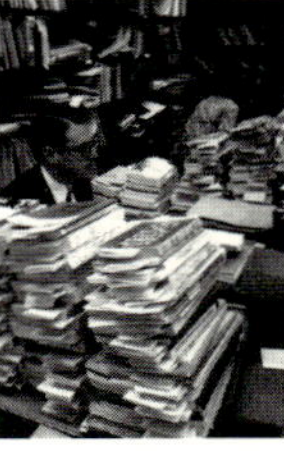

P 104 Immersed in Books
Yale Univ New Haven CT
1967

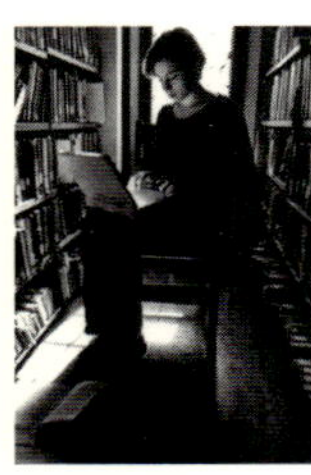

P 105 McGill Student in Library
with Computer
Montreal
1994

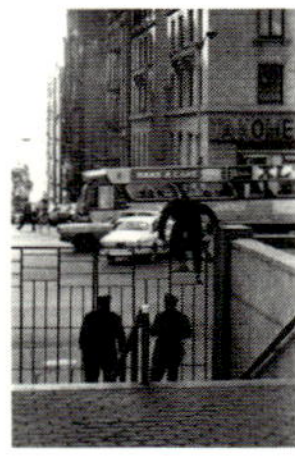

P 106 Bake a Cake
Columbia University NYC
1968

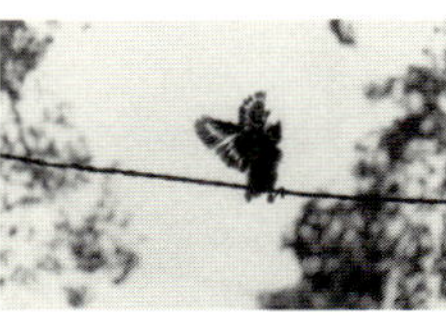

P 107 Bird on a Wire
Westchester County NY
1950s

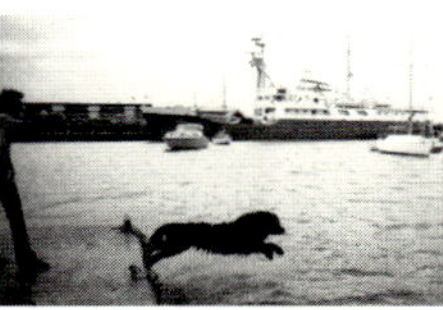

P 108 Dog Jumps
into Charlottetown Harbour
Prince Edward Island
1978

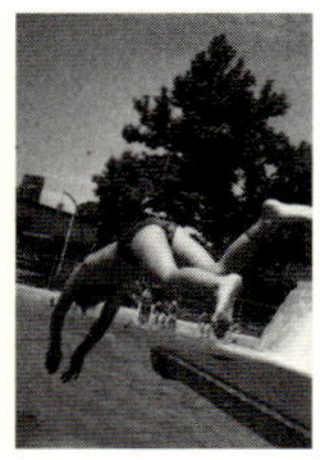

P 109 Boy Jumping into Pool
Teaneck NJ
1953

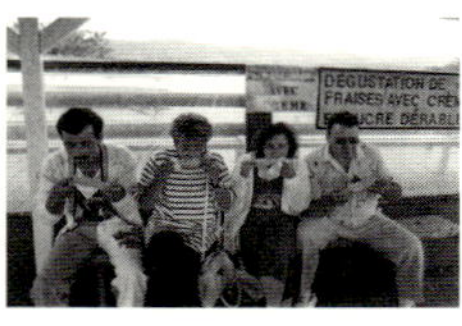

P 110 Corn Eaters Ile d'Orleans
Quebec
1990s

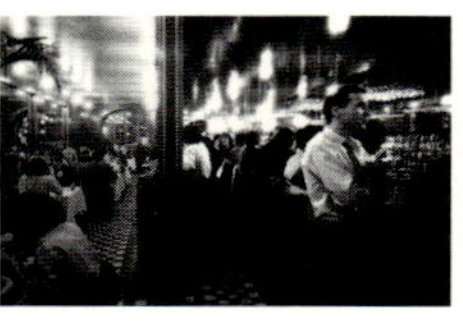

P 111 Restaurant L'Express
Montreal
1986

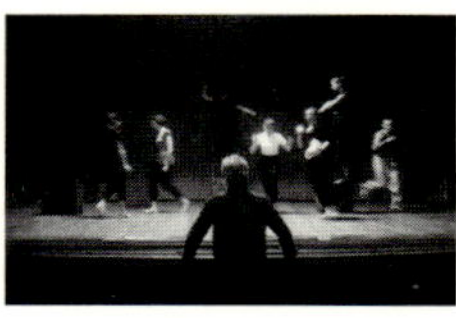

P 112 Henry Street Settlement
Dance Company
NYC
1951

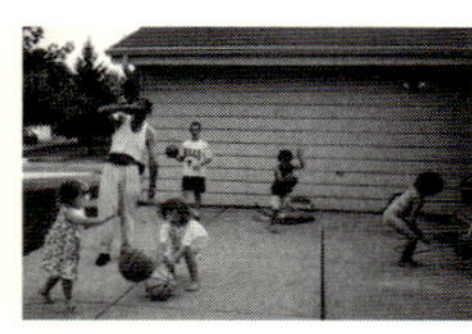

P 113 Balls
Hartland Wisconsin
1997

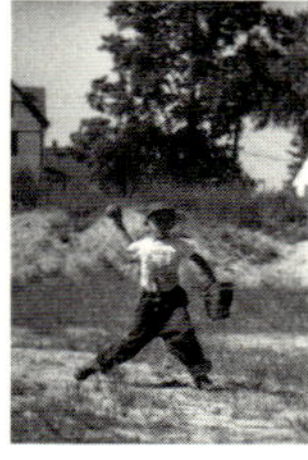

P 114 The Pitcher
Woburn MA
1955

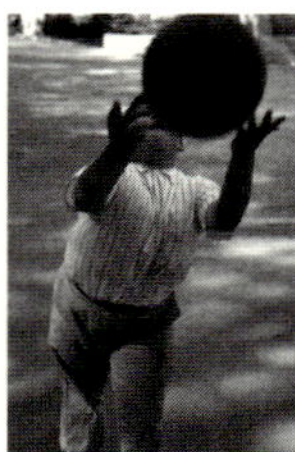

P 115 Boy with Ball
Milwaukee
1958

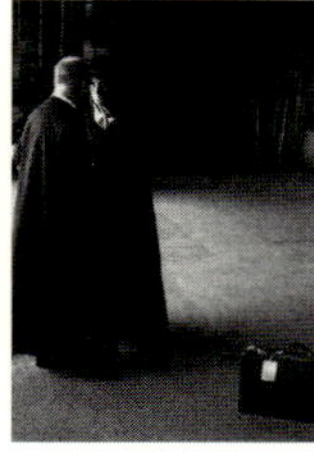

P 116 Priests
Stazione Termini Rome
1953

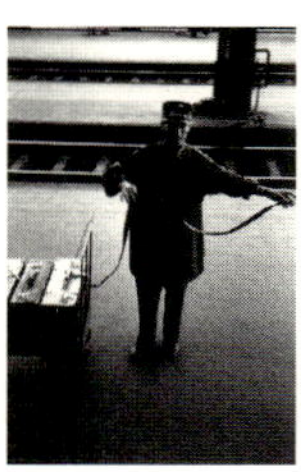

P 117 Porter
Stazione Termini
Rome
1953

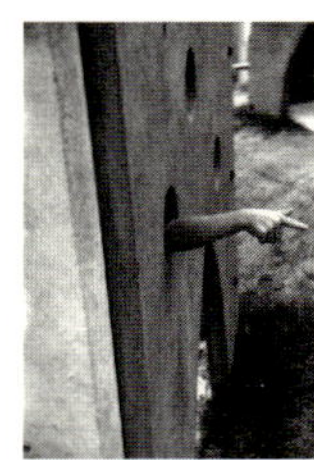

P 120 Pointing Finger
NJ
1953

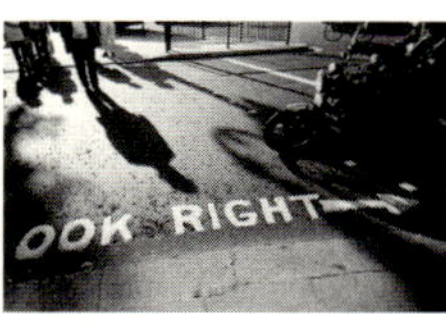

P 121 Look Right
London
1992

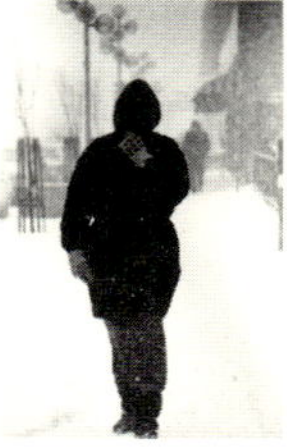

P 122 Mysterious Woman
Montreal
1986

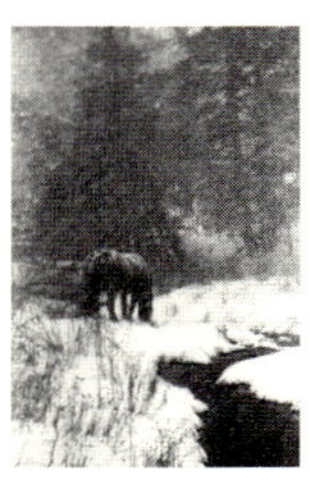

P 123 Dolly at the Stream
Prince Edward Island
1976

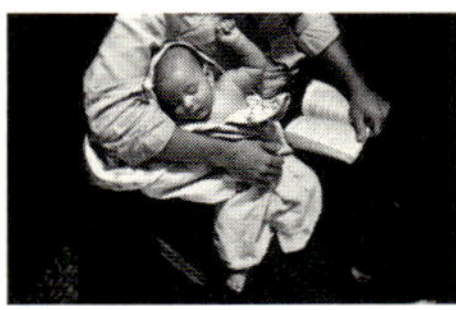

P 124 Matt & Oliver
Lac Mercier Quebec
1981

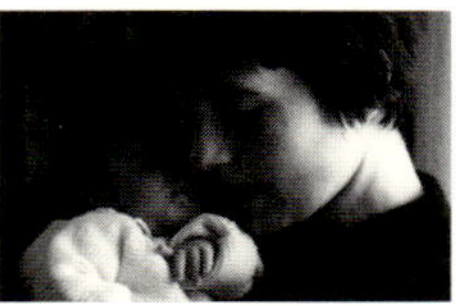

P 125 Annalies & Thom
New York
1964

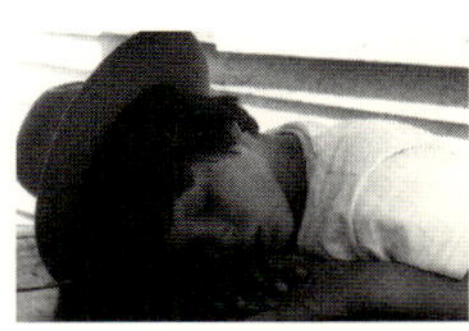

P 126 Andrew Sleeping
1969

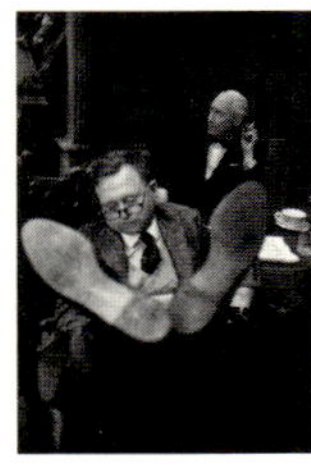

P 127 Mickey Rooney Sleeping
Queens NY
1957

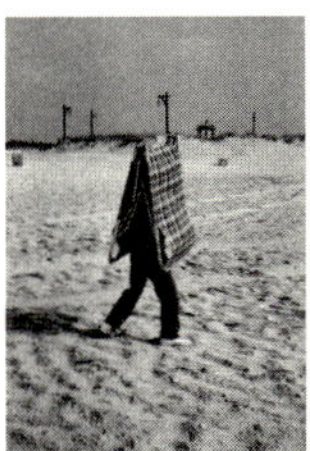

P 128 The Chair
Jones Beach New York
1959

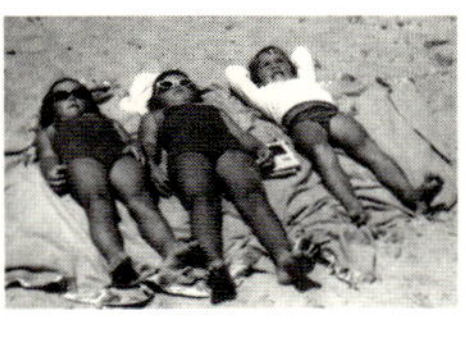

P 129 Space Babies
Jones Beach New York
1959

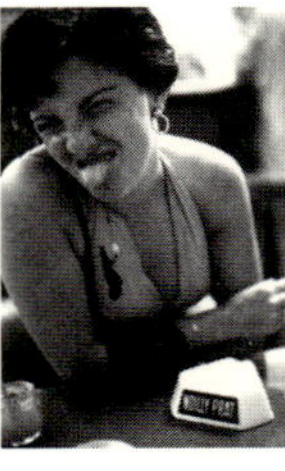

P 132 Woman with Tongue Out
Nice France
1953

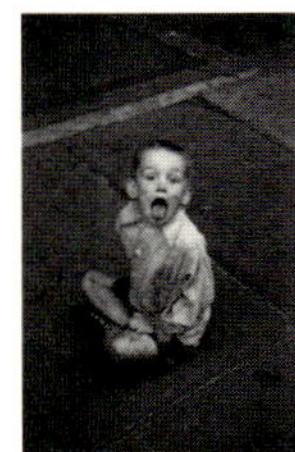

P 133 My Neighbour Jubjub
NYC
1955

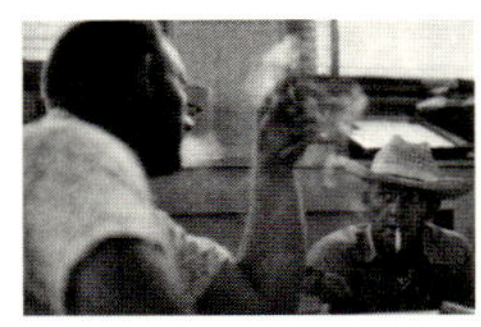

P 134 Rancher Smoking
Tishomingo Oklahoma
1957

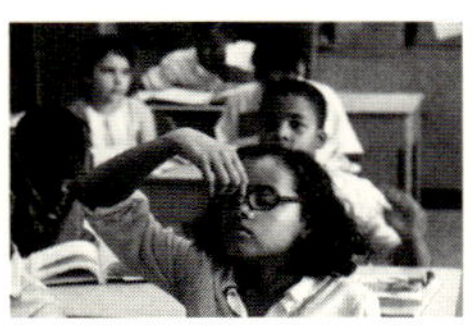

P 135 Reaction
Bronx NY
1960s

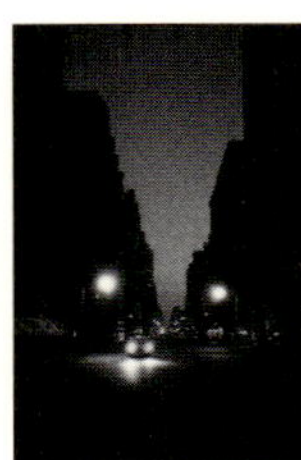

P 136 57th Street
Manhattan at Night
1951

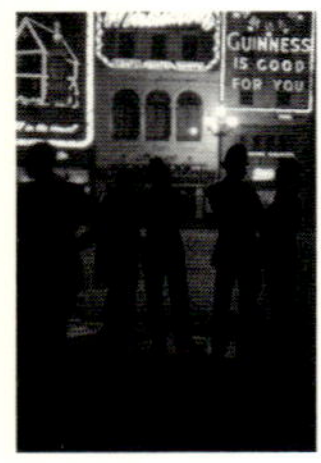

P 137 Piccadilly
London at Night
1952

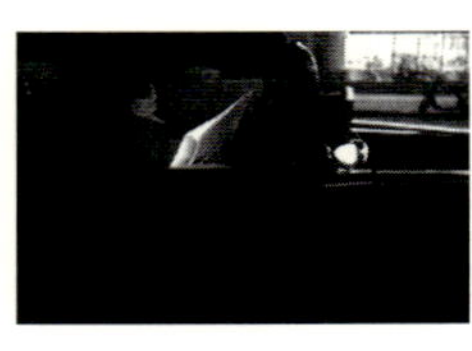

P 138 Taxi Driver Reading
Paris
1952

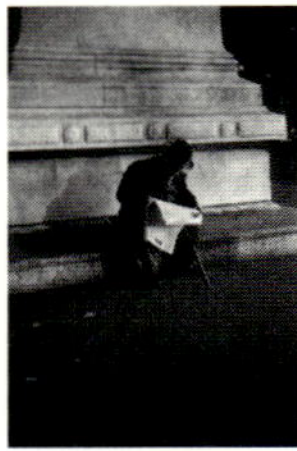

P 139 Reader at Night
Paris
1952

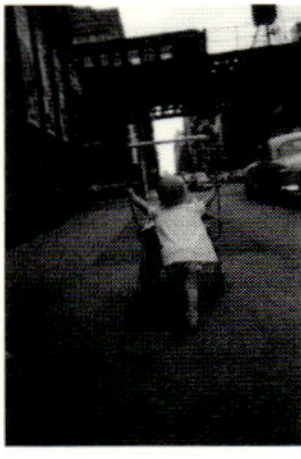

P 140 Woman's Liberation
NYC
1951

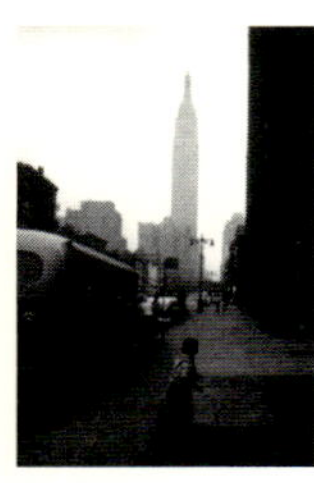

P 141 Boy & Empire State Building
NYC
1955

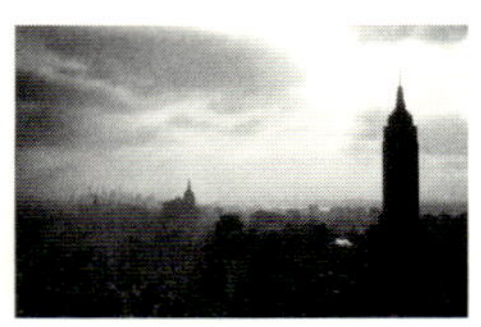

P 142 Manhattan Looking South
1954

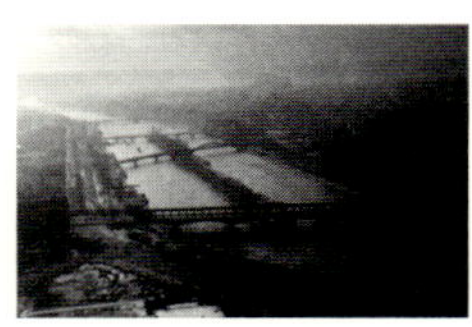

P 143 The Seine
Paris
1952

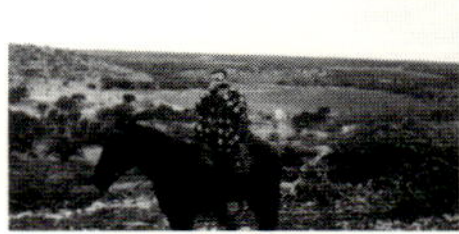

P 144 George on a Horse
Fredericksburg Texas
1955

ABOUT GEORGE S. ZIMBEL

He was born in Woburn, Massachusetts two weeks into the last half of 1929, the year of the stock market's Great Crash. While he spent his early years in the Great Depression of the 1930s, he seems not to have noticed, or, indeed he did notice and determined very early in his life to look the other way. His photographic career of more than 70 years has been marked by what critics and observers alike have called 'optimism' or 'humanism'. While he denies being 'a jolly person', he is said to have 'a jolly eye'.

His parents, Tillie and Morris Zimbel, born in Latvia and Lithuania respectively, were educated in the United States. His father, owner and—with the help of Tillie, mother of five and a very early multi-tasker—operator of Zimbel's Departmental Store on Main Street, was a faithful reader of the Sunday *New York Times*, along with his Boston newspapers. 'Georgie' was the one to fetch those papers for his dad from the paper store. That he would one day himself be a dedicated reader of the *Times* is no surprise, but it could not yet have been predicted that he would also be a photojournalist freelancing for the prestigious paper throughout most of his career.

That store on Main Street, by the way, was no Macy's, no precursor of Target or even J.C. Penny, yet for his Bar Mitzvah in 1942, George was given a movie camera that would soon, on a local fishing trip, accidentally end up in Hawn Pond (properly spelled "Horn"). George claims that he felt a fish bite on his line, jerked the line back causing the camera, safely enfolded in its case right beside him, to fly out of the case upwards into the air and before his very eyes, as if in slow motion, soar into the water.

It was not until 1944 that George persuaded his father to put up the money, which he would pay back, for a 4x5 inch Speed Graphic. He had managed to persuade the local newspaper he could freelance for them, and had persuaded the local camera store owner to vouch for him so that he could acquire the camera only available on a priority basis because it was wartime. Press use, aha! That worked for everyone.

Persuasions and passions, imagination and determination, this is the story of George's life in two countries, the United States and Canada. For specific details of this life as a freelance photojournalist, documentary photography, artist, proud family man, and in his words "failed farmer", and to view a catalogue of his photographs, please consult his website, **http://georgezimbel.com**. You will find there a long list of his solo and group exhibitions around the world, his honours and awards, his education, associations, many of the clients for whom he has photographed on assignment, and many of the self-assigned people and projects he has photographed as well.

George and his wife, Elaine Sernovitz, who married in 1955, have lived in Montreal, their chosen city, since late 1980. They had emigrated to their 100 acre farm in Prince Edward Island, Canada with their four young children, Matt, Andrew, Ike and Jodi in 1971.

George continues to produce new work and print previously unseen images from his archive. His activity reflects his feeling that creative people speed up as they get older because they have a backlog of ideas and projects eager for expression while at the same time the realisation dawns that time is fleeting. His grandchildren, Oliver, Luc, Rebecca, Noah, Samuel, Georgia, Hannah, Jonathan and Leah, some of whom are totally grown up and all of whom are taller than he is, remind him of that by their very welcome and loving presence in his life.

Elaine Sernovitz Zimbel
Montreal Quebec Canada, 2015

ACKNOWLEDGEMENTS

We say 'thank you' so many times during the course of a day I find it hard to use those words when I am so full of gratitude for the help I have received in making this book. Jean-François Gratton came to my rescue many times with his very special knowledge of things digital, and lent me two of his extremely gifted experts from Shoot Studio, Geneviève Demers and Audrée Desnoyers. The people at Typographie M&H Ltée took me a step further on that technical path, producing quality scans of my images, when the path was especially difficult.

I am grateful to the people whose comments appear in the heart of this book, Anne Tucker, Vicki Goldberg, Diane Charbonneau, Jean Bardaji, Josep Monzo, and Stephen Bulger, for making those comments in the documentary film, *Zimbelism—a Social Eye* created jointly by Jean-François Gratton and Matt Zimbel. Matt was right there for me throughout this whole endeavour. Andrew Zimbel had many good ideas and wasn't easily discouraged by my consistently stubborn resistance.

Robert Hebert was very helpful when I talked with him about my concept for this book. Larry and Boots Grossman, friends forever, have always been supportive and gracious hosts in New York whenever I needed to be there.

I am grateful to my immediate family, children and grandchildren, some of whose images pop up on these pages and all, every single one, whose love is reflected in the photographs in my heart or on the page.

Duncan McCorquodale of Black Dog Publishing in London, has been more patient than I have been, always in the service of producing a fine book. The book's designer, Sylvia Ugga, has been immensely creative and patient. I am grateful to the entire crew over there. And over here, it was a great pleasure working with Chantal Ringuet on the translations for the French version of *Momento*.

At home, in her office, on the phone, via email, everywhere, Elaine, who has from time to time lost patience, has been my editor, writer, communicator, my friend, my wife, my love.

George S. Zimbel
Montreal Quebec Canada, 2015

Black Dog Publishing Limited
10a Acton Street
London WC1X 9NG
United Kingdom

Tel +44 (0)20 7713 5097
Fax +44 (0)20 7713 8682
info@blackdogonline.com
www.blackdogonline.com

Cover Image:
Blond Girl & Black Dog
Queens NY
1962

Back Cover Image:
Out the Door
White Plains NY
1960s

Designed by Sylvia Ugga at Black Dog Publishing.

British Library Cataloguing-in-Publication Data. A CIP record for this book is available from the British Library.
ISBN 978 1 910433 42 3

Black Dog Publishing Limited, London, UK, is an environmentally responsible company. Momento is printed on sustainably sourced paper.

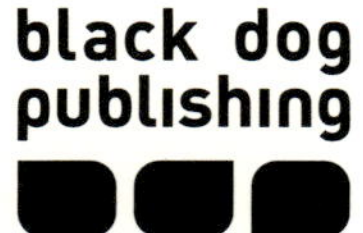

art design fashion
history photography
theory and things

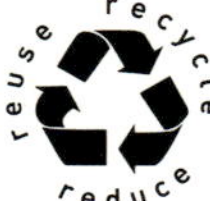

www.blackdogonline.com